MORGAN

First and Last of the Real Sports Cars

MORGAN

First and Last of the Real Sports Cars

Brian Laban

First published in Great Britain in 2000 by
Virgin Publishing Ltd
Thames Wharf Studios
Rainville Road
London W6 9HA

A catalogue record for the book is available from
the British Library.

ISBN 1 85227 899 4

Typeset by TW Typesetting, Plymouth, Devon

Printed and bound in Great Britain by CPD, Wales

Contents

Acknowledgements

A central theme of this book, beyond the cars and beyond the sporting history, is the personal story and the business philosophy of a unique company which has been steered through its first ninety years by a succession of remarkable people. Much of the flavour of the book comes from the huge amount of information that rests with the Morgan family, both as written record and as personal memories. This book would not have been possible without the exceptional support of the Morgan family proper, and the broader family of Morgan people in general. While finding time to launch a completely new car, the Aero 8, in the early months of the new millennium, and in Peter's case also fitting in two hip replacement operations, both Peter and Charles made time for many meetings and long conversations, and talked with all the enthusiasm that you might expect from the nature of the company and the product. They gave unlimited access to both the company's archives and their own memories, unearthing long unseen material which I hope gives a deeper than usual insight into the roots of the company philosophy, the reasons it has kept Morgan alive where others have failed, and most of all into the people who have made it work. There is a great deal of HG and HFS's first-person thinking from their own correspondence and personal records, and more of the same from both Charles and Peter, from their writings and in conversation. The majority of the illustrations are also from the Morgan archive, and again chosen to relate to people and the business rather than only to the nuts and bolts of the product. Many other people within the company contributed in one way or another, but I would offer special thanks to Matthew Parkin and to Chris Lawrence, for their viewpoints on the business and engineering sides respectively.

I'm grateful to other industry observers, including Professor Garel Rhys, Andrew English, Anthony Ffrench-Constant, Jeff Daniels, Phil Llewellin, Richard Feast and a number of others, for their outside perspectives and insights. And to previous writers on Morgan for a diverse background knowledge – including *Morgan Sweeps the Board, The Three-wheeler Story*, by Dr JD Alderson and DM Rushton (published by Gentry Books), and *Morgan Sports Cars, The Early Years*, by Dr Alderson and Chris Chapman (published by Sheffield Academic Press).

Thanks also to all the magazines and newspapers that ever published letters from HG, HFS, Peter and Charles, that ever visited the factory and that ever reviewed the cars – from the *Malvern Gazette* of the early 1900s to *The Cyclecar*, to *The Autocar* and *The Motor*, to *Car, Classic and Sports Car, Thoroughbred and Classic Cars* and *Evo* in the 1990s. Every one of them helped me, I hope, to understand a bit more of what Morgan is all about.

Brian Laban
August 2000

Foreword
by Charles Morgan

The Morgan Motor Company has started the new millennium in a fine state. A new chassis for the year 2000 gives the company the latest lightweight technology for low volume car production; recent research by Bath University and Imperial College London, sponsored by the European Community, has recognised that Morgan coachbuilding is an environmentally friendly way of building cars. The company has a workforce that combines experience and youth and it is training more young people than ever before. A new engine supplier – BMW – combined with lightweight chassis technology has given the company an opportunity to excel once again in sports car racing. The heritage of Morgan's contribution to the first one hundred years of the motor car is now firmly ingrained into the Morgan marque and into the history of the motor car itself.

Despite this, many observers still feel that Morgan's position is precarious at a time of globalisation and consolidation. Brian Laban's book states the case and restores the equilibrium; his writing provides lessons from history and insights gained from his experience of commentating on the car industry for more than twenty-five years and answers the question of what it is that makes Morgan a survivor where so many famous car makes have disappeared. Mr Honda, the eponymous owner and founder of the company, is once said to have made a prediction that, by the year 2000, there would only be five motor manufacturers; thankfully, he paused before adding 'and Morgan'.

Morgan sports cars continue to prove themselves popular in their thousands in many different foreign markets. It can be said that, over the last ninety years of car making – the lifetime of the company – Morgan has certainly withstood external disasters, yet the First World War, the Depression, another world war, and the boom and bust stories of the 1960s to the 1980s threatened but ultimately did not drastically affect the company. The company has also survived the loss of seemingly irreplaceable people. Among them, HFS Morgan was perhaps the initiator of all Morgan sports cars, and yet the cars and the company consistently evolve, like animals adapting successfully to their environment. Safety regulations and reductions in exhaust emissions proved a challenge to a small company with limited resources, but Morgan responded in style by proving that a coachbuilt car could, in certain circumstances, be even safer than the latest monocoque design. If recycling and environmental requirements pass Morgan by, it is partly because the cars are never scrapped. They are simply rebuilt by their new owners when they get tired. That is a part of the familiar, personal touch. Spare Morgan parts are available for models more than twenty-five years old from the factory and the Morgan car park continues to grow together with the goodwill and enthusiasm fostered by the marque.

The designs of the company also take a remarkably long time to date. When HFS Morgan's three-wheeler won the French Cyclecar Grand Prix in 1913, he could hardly have imagined that this same design would still be around and selling twenty-six years later. When the Morgan Plus 4 was dominant in 2-litre sports car racing in Europe and America, the design was just getting into its stride. This same chassis, with improvements, has been in continuous production from 1936 to the year 2000 – sixty-four years in all. The Morgan Plus 8, introduced in 1968, is still in production, thirty-two years later. These statistics must define the original designs as classics. To have such a long shelf-life, they had to be innovative in the first place, and the fact that HFS Morgan's three-wheeler continues to hold a fascination for modern car designers shows that they were.

Just as the original Morgan designs evolved and improved, so has the company. The actor Rowan Atkinson once suggested, after visiting Morgan, that this was because the company has 'a free-flowing, cooperative atmosphere in which company hierarchy is almost invisible to the outside observer ... You really get the sense that this is one homogeneous operation. What the company has to do now and how best to achieve it is manifest to all, because the organisation is so small and open-hearted.' Prescient words. It is clear that, during its history, the company has followed a novel but consistent strategy and that Morgan has always been proud of being a family business in the widest sense of the word. Like all good families, the company encourages learning and communication. This sense of family is extended to Morgan customers, who are encouraged to visit the factory to see what coachbuilding is all about. Collaboration with other companies in an extended family is also a strength and the company is not too proud to notice and take advantage where others lead. Morgan first used a Ford engine in 1936 and have continuously fitted Ford engines for the past sixty-four years.

Many interesting points are raised in this book, but perhaps one notable area of controversy has been the famous (or infamous) waiting list. I hope that I can contribute to a substantial reduction in this but I nonetheless continue to hope too that in the future all Morgans will continue to be built to a specific individual's order and, where possible, a future owner's wishes are complied with. My father Peter is fond of suggesting that the 1930s were the last time that most car manufacturers actually asked customers what they wanted and, as a result, the widest range of cars was available. Perhaps, ultimately, Morgan do hark back to that golden age. If so, I can honestly say that the company is not afraid to be old fashioned.

Charles Morgan
August 2000

Introduction

THE EARLY MONTHS OF 2000 saw chaos and confusion in the British motor industry. The very 'British' Rover Group was under threat of closure from the latest of its long string of recent owners, the German luxury car maker BMW, while American giant Ford was looking increasingly likely to close its huge British manufacturing plant at Dagenham in Essex. In the end, Rover was bought by Phoenix, a British business consortium, but the impending closure of Dagenham was confirmed. In the interim, Ford had bought one of the Rover Group's strongest badges, Land Rover, while others, including Mini and MG, were haggled over as potential profit-making jewels on a tarnished crown. (At the time of writing, MG remained with Phoenix, Mini with BMW.) The horse trading for Land Rover, Range Rover, Mini and MG showed the value still associated with strongly identifiable, cleverly targeted marques with genuine heritage. The other problems illustrated two major concerns of modern motor industry life – scale and capacity. Too little of the first is bad, too much of the second is worse. So small companies get snapped up by bigger ones, to form big, powerful, global conglomerates, and factories which are not paying their way, or are surplus to demand, can expect the bullet. There is no room for sentiment, independence or backward glances in the modern motor industry.

Or is there?

The Morgan Motor Company Ltd of Malvern Link is famous around the world for ploughing its own furrow, both with the cars it builds and the way it builds them. Morgan does not comply with the industry norms in almost any respect yet it survives where others perish. At the Geneva Motor Show at the end of February 2000, Morgan launched their first completely new car in more than thirty years – or, if you want to take design associations back to their ultimate conclusions, their first for more than sixty years. The new car was the Aero 8; it turned out to be an extremely impressive piece of modern engineering, even if its controversial styling unmistakably screamed traditional Morgan. Ironically, it is powered by an engine from the pariah of the moment in many British eyes – that scourge of Rover, the BMW Group – and coincidentally all the other cars in the current Morgan range are powered by engines from either Rover or Ford.

In theory, Morgan, a minnow by any conventional standards in the vast ocean of the modern motor industry, should have been alarmed by the turmoil directly involving such vital suppliers and more broadly suffusing the whole industry around it, but Morgan were typically upbeat. Aside from a few surface-skimming dissenters still screaming 'Luddites', the majority of observers recognised the Aero 8 for the major design leap that it is, and within weeks Morgan order books were filled to overflowing. They would have to find more production capacity, but, against the background of Ford dumping its Dagenham factory completely and Rover's new proprietors desperately trying to create work for idle facilities, how big a nightmare was that? Especially when the numbers of cars involved were in their hundreds, rather than hundreds of thousands, and when the customers were unlikely to worry about waiting?

Waiting lists have become another part of the Morgan legend, their impact sometimes overplayed but for most of the company's life a reality. At worst they are an embarrassment – but not as big an embarrassment as empty order books. Morgan developed the Aero 8 with what the mainstream industry would consider a minuscule budget, and did so without the intrinsic risk of huge borrowing. And they could increase production modestly, on the same basis, from their own resources, by their own methods and in their own time. Furthermore, Morgan was still steadfastly independent and entirely family-owned and controlled. BMW had been a development partner, but they had not become a lord or master and Morgan did not need them, any more than they had needed to succumb to previous suitors.

Morgan is unique in the modern motoring world. It is one of the world's oldest motor companies, and the oldest anywhere still to be entirely controlled by the family which created it. It is one of the world's most famous car makers, with a history of classic models and extraordinary competition successes. In its own terms, it is one of the most commercially successful companies in the history of the motor industry. In the financial year ending May 1999 its gross profits equated to more than 24 per cent of turnover; most companies would kill for a figure like that.

Almost certainly unique within an industry known for its volatility and uncertainty, Morgan has never had a strike of its own workers' making, never had big debts or borrowings, and for the vast majority of its existence has traded not only without losses but with steady profits – although deeper investigation reveals that it would be an over-simplification to think of the Morgan company only as a car maker, because for much of its life it has had investment interests way beyond that.

Through it all, that combination of manufacturing income and investment income has funded every stage of Morgan's expansion, every new model, every competition exploit, from its own reserves. Some years ago, the founder's son, Peter Morgan, described his pioneering father as having been 'not mean but careful', and suggested that his underlying philosophy was 'don't spend what you haven't got'. The first generation of the Morgan family planned carefully, sold skilfully and invested wisely. Later generations saw no reason to change that philosophy significantly. Through such thinking Morgan has remained proudly and fiercely independent.

Yet Morgan is also one of the most misunderstood of car makers. People who know nothing at all about Morgan will tell you that it has been making the same cars for nearly a century; that it has the longest waiting lists of any car maker in the universe, and that it goes out of its way to be old fashioned and anachronistic. Others more knowledgeable about Morgan know that, while there are elements of truth in all of the above, the real story is far more complex and subtly more progressive. For all the legend, Morgan is anything but frozen in time. Perhaps the only thing about Morgan that has not changed continuously over the years is the one thing that has not yet needed to – the underlying philosophy that makes it work.

In essence, that is easy to describe. Morgan makes a special kind of car for a special kind of customer, and makes cars in their own, traditional way, while using whatever benefits of modern technology, modern machinery and modern methods that they deem appropriate – but by no means all of them. From the beginning, the Morgan design philosophy was largely defined by local geography which put an emphasis on light weight and flexibility, and, while Morgans have spread far from the Malvern Hills, the philosophy has remained essentially unchanged: simplicity and lightness allow for a relatively simple build process, producing a car with excellent performance for its engine size and power.

Beyond that, is the philosophy of the market and the method. Strong performance (which has been proved and promoted through most of the company's history by motor sporting activity) sells sporting cars. A simple build process, founded on craftsmanship and low production volumes, rather than the machinery of mass production, allows Morgan to adapt to demand – without heavy capital investment. It is also a process that is capable of keeping up with the market, so long as the customer does not expect delivery by tomorrow, yet it avoids the risk of inevitable market downturns which leave expensive machinery expensively idle. Such a production process, again thanks to hand craftsmanship, also provides the flexibility to develop new products without hugely expensive retooling, and it allows Morgan to build the kind of bespoke car that its customers love. The company has been able to say in the past, and still can say, that it never built a car that it has not sold and never sold a car that it could not build. Put another way, Morgan's 'keep it simple and react gently' design and manufacturing philosphy would never have allowed the company to grow into an industry giant, but it has without doubt helped it avoid the kind of pitfalls now facing not only Rover and Ford in Britain but also many others around the world – massive investment chasing an unpredictable market in a volatile economic climate is as likely to fail as to succeed.

Through it all, Morgan's independence from both external shareholding and mainstream motor industry parentage has allowed them to make their own decisions, and to follow their own philosophy, even when others have questioned it; which they have, including, in the late 1980s, one particularly high-profile trial by television which highlighted the subtle difference in approach between the second and third generations of the Morgan family, Peter and Charles. That same independence has also allowed Morgan to shop wisely for the most suitable components, and especially for engines, finding the right tool for the job while avoiding the hazards of being drawn into other people's commercial problems. Peter Morgan refers to a time in the late 1930s when his father, HFS Morgan, considered following the path trodden by so many other manufacturers – to build his own engines rather than to buy them off the shelf. He rejected the idea, and Peter insists that resisting that commitment was a pivotal moment in Morgan history: 'Luckily he never made it, and I'm certain we would not be here if he had.' To date, Morgan has never built its own engines, while others that have gone down that road have been bankrupted by the luxury. It is fundamentally another illustration of Morgan's steadfast resistance to knee-jerk reactions to the market.

Continuity of styling themes, too, is part of the philosophy, but not simply out of perverseness. That continuity both capitalises on the Morgan heritage and satisfies the customer (who, experience in the early 1960s showed, can actually be put off by radical styling changes) while allowing changes under the skin that most people are blissfully unaware of but which allow Morgan to meet all modern legislative requirements.

This philosophy has now survived through more than ninety years and three family generations, virtually without hesitation or deviation, and this book is the story of how and why it has worked, apparently against all the odds. Alternatively, if looked at another way, it is the story of how others have ignored Morgan's logic and paid the price.

The Morgan factory, standing at the end of Pickersleigh Road, Malvern Link, is unashamedly a symbol of the Morgan enigma. On the fringes of the Malvern Hills, it is like no other car factory, at least like no other car factory of the twenty-first century. Instead of the frantic whirling of robot arms and the relentless roll of production lines, the place where Morgans are made has a comfortable scale, an appealing homeliness, and it has people: real people, with real skills, working only as fast as craftsmanship allows and almost exclusively by hand. Morgan has a soul, a house style, and the factory sums it up perfectly. People come from all over the world simply to look at it, to walk around and see cars being built, in much the same way as they have been built for the last ninety years.

Some customers will watch their own cars being built, perhaps time their visit for the day they will finally be able to drive their car away, sometimes after years of waiting. Others come just to look, because the Morgan factory is living, industrial history. The factory is not a part of some vast industrial sprawl; it is on a suburban road, with ordinary houses and small workshops on three sides and a recreation ground on the other. If you did not know its famous history, you could pass it without a second glance. To do so would be to miss a treat.

The factory is as traditional and as oddball as the cars it produces. From the road you see a long, single-storey brick building, with a pitched, flat-tiled roof. The low frontage abuts against the road. There is no front-of-house directors' car park, no glass façade, no token gardens or shrubbery, no vast name check. Just the pavement and then Pickersleigh Avenue – the road upon which the works stand, even though the address is given as Pickersleigh Road. That typically Morgan anachronism arose because, when the first parts of this old factory were built in the early years of the twentieth century, what became Pickersleigh Avenue was no more than a footpath through the surrounding fields, passing the end of the real Pickersleigh Road. Even today Pickersleigh Avenue is no more than an urban cut-through from West Malvern to Malvern Link, with a ribbon of houses and small shops on either side. An archetypal English setting for an archetypal English sports car.

The factory frontage is clean and tidy but darkened by age; it is quite plain, broken up by nothing more than simple brick pillars between the small, totally anonymous windows of what is actually the office block and parts stores. You would not know that the second and third generations of the Morgan family who still run the company are probably sitting with their backs to you in their adjacent offices behind the frosted windows in the middle. The only other feature is a single doorway near the right-hand end, under a small brick and slate porch, jutting out into the pavement. Over the entrance – just a narrow double wooden door under a semi-circular glass skylight – is the only adornment on the front of the building, a slightly ornate gable with a stone plaque bearing the initials MM – for Morgan Motors. Below it is a slightly more modern sign (perhaps 1960s: modern by Morgan standards) which simply says 'Morgan'. To the right-hand side of the building stands a small perimeter wall with a double wrought-iron gate opening to the rest of the works. Now-adays, that comprises seven main buildings, each similar in size and shape to the office and stores block, running parallel and snugly adjacent to one another down the gentle slope to the haphazard back lot and behind it the recreation ground.

By the ancient wooden sliding doors at the end of the roadside building, leading directly to the stores counter, there is an old fashioned petrol pump; it might have sprung fully formed, from the early 1920s. There are more buildings, big and small, to the right. The narrow, sloping yard between them all runs down to a small, cluttered car park, right at the bottom of the site. There are small lean-to storage sheds in the yard, and stores of bright new zinc-galvanised chassis and other components scattered here and there. Cars in various stages of assembly are usually being wheeled around, be-tween one part of the build process and the next; the feeling engendered is one of good-natured human bustle rather than industrial frenzy.

The cars have four wheels now, rather than three, but otherwise none of this has changed much over the decades that Morgans have been built there. Since 1913, in fact, when the Pickersleigh Road site was acquired to take some of the pressure off the original, already overstretched workshop, barely half a mile away at the other end of Pickersleigh Road, on the junction of Worcester Road and Howden Road. Nowadays, the factory is Morgan's face to the world; by the 1920s it was a clear sign of the company's growing success – expanding to cope with booming demand for the original Morgan three-wheelers, which within a few years of their introduction had become one of the cornerstones of the pre-First World War Boom for what came to be known as cyclecars.

Above all, it is impossible to separate Morgan the car from Morgan the family. The three-wheeler Morgan had been devised by Henry Frederick Stanley – 'HFS' – Morgan, a former railway apprentice turned garage proprietor, and an avid early motoring enthusiast. He was the son of a very supportive Herefordshire cleric, the Prebendary HG Morgan, the unconventional head of a fairly untypical Victorian family. Although to outward appearances a typical man of the Church and parish, the hard-working and popular HG was also a man with a spirit of adventure: much travelled, an accomplished amateur artist, a pioneer photographer of considerable talent, and an experimenter who gave the family home both electricity and hot water in days when neither was common. If not exactly an eccentric, HG was an extrovert by the standards of his calling. He was something of a financial wizard, too, dabbling very successfully in the stock market while managing what appear to have been quite considerable family resources, largely handed down through his wife's side of the close-knit family. And when it came to his son's education and choice of employment, HG Morgan was as supportive as any father could have been, both morally and financially.

It was that support, backed by HG's wife Florence, that saw HFS Morgan through often difficult schooldays, moving away from a prospective career in the Church to one in engineering, through his apprenticeship with the Great Western Railway and into the business of garage proprietor in rural Malvern. All of this, it is worth remembering, as a supposedly conventional vicar's son at a time when the motor car was still mistrusted and disdained by a highly conservative and genteel local community.

The garage was only the beginning. Now HG was ready to back his son's ultimate fall from grace in the eyes of their Malvern neighbours, as a car manufacturer. In 1909 HFS built a single-seater, twin-cylinder prototype – and in 1910 he put it into production, as the Morgan Runabout. It was the simplest, lightest design possible, somewhere between motor cycle and light car, and – importantly – it took advantage of prevailing tax concessions for cars of its kind. After a slow start, HFS added to its practicality and popularity by producing a two-seater, and through speed and reliability trials (and much favourable exposure in the motoring press) it became a great success.

In April 1912, with the practical and financial support of his father, and working capital including deposits from Morgan's first agency, Harrods of Knightsbridge, HFS Morgan, aged thirty-one, formed the Morgan Motor Company. Then as now, all its shares were held by the Morgan family. It began to grow, around a very distinctive product.

Although he designed and built a four-wheel prototype in 1914, the success of HFS's business was entirely built on the three-wheeler design. It flourished after contemporaries from the cyclecar years had long disappeared and survived to the beginning of the 1950s. By then, Morgan, demonstrating a much underestimated ability to adapt and evolve, was building four-wheelers, introduced in 1936 for a changed market, and the next generation of Morgan family was also emerging.

Peter Morgan was born in 1919, in the house next door to the original workshop. In 1947, after military service, he joined the company as development engineer and draughtsman, and contributed greatly to the success of the four-wheel Morgans, while absorbing the family philosophy at his father's side. For one brief interlude, however, it seemed that Morgan might not become his inheritance. But in this period after the war, when the three-wheeler market was collapsing and the need to export was paramount, HFS Morgan made one of the most important decisions in the company's history. In 1950, in the face of a serious take over bid from Morgan's major engine supplier, the Standard Motor Company, run by an old friend, Sir John Black, he decided that Morgan should remain independent. It has remained steadfastly independent ever since.

In 1959, following the death of his father and fifty years after HFS had built his first Runabout, Peter Morgan became chairman of the Morgan Motor Co., in addition to the role of managing director which he had held since the previous year. With his four sisters he inherited a company which superficially seemed to be quite straightforward but whose business affairs were far more complicated than they appeared, and which had some very dangerous structural problems.

Not long before, HFS Morgan had feared it would not survive at all, and even his will referred to the possibility of it being sold off or wound up. Peter was determined to keep it alive, however difficult the odds. When he took over, there were major problems with the Inland Revenue over the company's liabilities following HFS's death; furthermore, it was a fact that Peter's sisters did not share his enthusiasm for running a car company. So the family, led by Peter, initiated a total restructuring of the company and at the same time entered into a long dispute with the tax authorities. That dragged on for more than a decade and was only ultimately resolved (in the company's favour) on appeal to the High Court. And what is more, while the company was being restructured there was a prolonged period when it was being run personally by Peter Morgan without limited liability status, exposing him to enormous risk at a time when the industry overall was experiencing volatile times. But, while fulfilling his sisters' wishes, Peter was not prepared to give up his heritage.

Like his father, Peter competed regularly in Morgans to maintain one tradition, and by way of maintaining another he insisted that Morgan would remain an independent, family-owned company. On the commercial side as well as on the legal side, however, he did not inherit an easy task. The market for sports cars in the late 1950s was extremely competitive; it was heavily populated by models from the mainstream manufacturers – notably MG, Austin-Healey, Triumph and Jaguar – even without looking beyond the major British marques. Morgan's style of car, with traditional flowing wings and running boards, once the essence of the British sports car, was starting to look like a throwback, particularly when compared with new generation cars with smooth, all-enveloping bodies like the MGA, the big Healey 3000s, the Triumph TRs and Jaguar XKs.

By the early 1960s, those rivals would have moved on again, to the even more modern genes of the unit-construction MGB and the stunning and remarkably inexpensive Jaguar E-type. Peter Morgan saw them, and for one moment in 1963 tried to emulate them, with the Morgan Plus 4 Plus, a two-seater coupé with all-enveloping glass fibre body and a Triumph TR engine. Only twenty-six were made; it was more or less a complete flop. Morgan owners had, in effect, told Morgan that if they wanted another type of car they had plenty of other choices; what they really wanted was still a traditional Morgan. It was one of Peter Morgan's very few mistakes.

He would admit later that he had been convinced that Morgan's style should change, and that he was wrong. The fact is that he had to try something; going into the 1960s the company was at one of its lowest points. For some years the European market had been shrinking while the American one grew, and now America itself was entering a recession and sales were down to a trickle. Nor did the restructured company have quite the same safety net from outside investments as it had through the year's his father and grandfather had held the reins.

Peter Morgan's response – one which saved the company – was to rebuild Morgan's market in Europe, expanding the sales effort, increasing production to meet new demand, and simultaneously reducing manufacturing and marketing costs wherever possible. Perversely, perhaps, the failure of the Plus 4 Plus actually helped in the longer term, refocusing Morgan's mind on what they were best at, and on what the customers wanted. They responded with new but traditionally styled models and the European market responded positively, helped immeasurably by another piece of Morgan serendipity well worthy of HFS's day – an unexpected but thoroughly deserved class win at Le Mans in 1962.

Unquestionably, all this once again saved the life of the company; within a few years new safety and emissions regulations meant that Morgan not only had a severely diminished market in the USA, but it had no way of selling its cars there at all. So Morgan survived, on the strength of revitalised European sales, because of one of Peter Morgan's initiatives; a few years later it went back to America, and back into the public eye everywhere, with a major bang, because of another initiative – the Plus 8.

The Plus 8 was unveiled in 1968, the same year that earlier, four-cylinder Morgans were effectively outlawed from the USA by new emissions regulations, and just before the company was finally reorganised into a new limited company as part of the redistribution of capital shares among members of the family. The new car comprised a comprehensively uprated Plus 4-type chassis powered by a version of Rover's much admired all-aluminium 3.5-litre V8 engine, and odd as it might sound, that was just a modern version of the original Morgan philosophy – lots of power in not too much weight. The Plus 8 was obviously very quick and, alongside the continuing four-cylinder models, proved to be very success-ful, launching a new era for Morgan with a car that might have resembled all the other Morgans but whose straight line performance would challenge anything on the road, and for a very reasonable price.

For a while, it even took Morgans back into the American market, but within a few years they were outlawed again, because Rover themselves, makers of the V8 engine and therefore the people who certified it, withdrew from the American market. While a handful of American dealers found ways around the problem and continued to import tiny numbers of cars, Peter Morgan pursued his own crusade of expanding the market in Europe. His efforts were successful enough for the factory to be expanded again in the early 1970s, with the aforementioned buildings to the right of the yard; and in true Morgan style the biggest investment the company had made in more than thirty years came entirely out of reserves, with no borrowing involved.

And so the story has continued. In the times when the market has been slow, production has been kept to a steady minimum, with no overtime but with no redundancies or lay offs either. In the boom times the waiting lists have grown, sometimes embarrassingly, but the factory, determinedly, has not. That is not to say that it never will and it certainly doesn't mean that it hasn't become more efficient. Peter Morgan celebrated his eightieth birthday in November 1999, and he is still a regular visitor to his cluttered and homely office (once his father's) and to the factory floor. But the real boss now is his son Charles, HFS's grandson.

Charles was born in 1951, worked in television and had his own video production business then gave it up to join the company in 1985, having studied business management. Following the fundamental Morgan philosophy, he has always had a passion for motor racing, and he is a firm believer in the on-going ideals of independence, craftsmanship and high power with low weight. There are areas where he is determined to move on from his father's methods, just as Peter moved on from his own father's. Under Charles, Morgan will build more cars, and will build them in a subtly more modern way, albeit without losing the character that continues to make Morgan unique in an increasingly ordinary motoring world. There will be new technology, too. It was Charles Morgan who presided over the production and launch of the Aero 8, that first, big, new project for thirty years, in association with BMW. Another phase was beginning.

1 Making Morgans

A T THE HEART OF what makes Morgan unique is the cars Morgan build and the way they build them: classic designs built by traditional, coachbuilding methods, a regime that is heavy on craftsman skills and very light on automated processes but which brings with it a car of a particular character, and the advantage of almost total production flexibility. That character has always sold the cars, and the flexibility has helped Morgan to survive as a very small scale manufacturer with extraordinarily long-lived designs, in an industry almost exclusively dominated by huge volumes and ever shorter product cycles. Contrary to popular myth, that flexibility has also meant that the product is not quite as unchanging as the outside world imagines it to be, and nor is the production process. Building Morgans, however, has always been a family affair and it still is.

Charles Morgan, the son of Peter Morgan and the grandson of the company's founder HFS Morgan, is the third generation of the Morgan family to head the company, and he is rarely far away from the traditional old buildings where Morgans have been made for more than eighty years. In the last weeks of the twentieth century, he walks from one of the seven adjacent workshops to the next, climbing a short flight of open stairs to a wooden door with an old-fashioned catch, in a corner of the shop. As he reaches the top step, his hand goes to the door handle and, quite subconsciously, one foot gives a firm, precisely aimed kick at a well-worn spot on the bottom edge of the door, at exactly the same moment he slips the catch and pushes the door open in one fluid movement.

This is a man who knows every inch of his working environment.

That is one side of Morgan, the one most people think they know, Morgan the throwback; but there is another side to Morgan for which fewer people give full credit: a willingness to change. Not change for change's sake, but change with full commitment when it is genuinely necessary, and prudent. Fifty yards away from the door Charles (and several generations before him) kicked, there is a small workshop, hidden among the newer buildings which were incorporated into the site in the early 1970s, across the yard through which part-built Morgans are still wheeled from shop to shop. In this workshop, half a dozen Morgan craftsmen have spent many months through the end of 1999 and the beginning of 2000 putting the finishing touches to a very different kind of car, a new generation of Morgan.

Allowing for the evolution of Plus 8 from Plus 4 and beyond, it is the first radically different Morgan since the first production four-wheeler, the 4-4, was introduced in the mid-1930s. From 4-4 to Plus 8, every Morgan model for more than sixty years has had essentially the same layout of fairly flexible pressed-steel frame and super-stiff suspension, with sliding pillars at the front and cart springs at the back. But in place of the familiar ladder chassis with its Z-section side members, the new car has a super-stiff but very lightweight all-aluminium-alloy chassis. It is constructed from new-tech panels and extruded sections, neatly fabricated into something that will take the motoring world by surprise. Instead of the old sliding-pillar front suspension, which has survived in principle since HFS built his first prototype in 1909, there are race-developed double wishbones and coil springs. At the back, there is no old-fashioned rigid live axle but more coils and wishbones, for all-independent suspension. In the front, there is a BMW V8, and not a cast off but the very latest generation.

The chassis carefully hidden from outside view in the workshops at the birth of the new millennium is a show chassis, built with cotton gloves and plenty of swank for the car's launch, due in just a few weeks' time. This particular example does not have a body, and it won't have one when it is unveiled either. It will be shown alongside the first complete car, unclothed – to show off the impressive new chassis technology. And bang up to the minute as the engineering is, even without the shell you can see from the shape of the chassis members that this will be instantly recognisable as a Morgan.

Nor will this be just a cosmetic launch. Even three months before its show debut, while the car for the unveiling is still being built, fully engineered prototypes have already been running for quite some time, and opening a few eyes. On BMW's test track in the south of France, running on road tyres, the new Morgan has recorded better than 1g cornering forces, which is in genuinely modern sports car territory. The engineers from BMW, Morgan's engine partner for this car, have been involved with the project from the outset, and are impressed. The new car has already passed its statutory impact tests quite easily. On 29 February 2000 it will be unveiled to the press at the Geneva Motor Show. Charles Morgan knows exactly how important the launch is and he is determined that it will be a real unveiling: apart from a handful of engineers, nobody will know the details of this car before the big day.

Fast forward to the end of February 2000. The Geneva Salon is always the first big European motor show of the year and traditionally a venue for important and exciting launches. Over the past few years those have included any number of show-stopping Ferraris, Porsches, Lamborghinis, Mercedes, BMWs, Jaguars et al. The launch of the new Morgan is as important as any of them, and it grabs its own headlines.

The car is due to be unveiled at 3 p.m. GMT, and pictures from the launch will be relayed live to Morgan's website, for Morgan enthusiasts (and potential customers) who cannot be there. This is a Morgan launch of a car with cutting-edge technology, flashed around the world by modern communications. But there is room for a touch of Morgan family pride. Peter Morgan, who ran the company for so long and who, even in semi-retirement, had a real influence on the new car, cannot attend the launch, but it will still be a family affair. Almost at the last minute, a British journalist suggests to

Charles Morgan that it would be a nice touch for the covers to be pulled from the car by his daughters; for, if history is anything to go by, one day they are likely to be involved with running the company. Charles makes the speeches and Kate and Harriet, aged six and eight, draw back the covers in front of an apprehensive crowd. The new Morgan and its naked chassis become the slightly unlikely stars of the show. Within an hour of the unveiling, the Morgan website, too, has had more than 30,000 visitors.

The new car is an extraordinary combination of Morgan tradition, race-bred design and the most modern technology. It is badged the Aero 8, for its eight cylinders, and revives a name used on some of the fastest Morgan three-wheelers in the early days. The styling is controversial, but that is hardly a surprise. It could not be anything but a Morgan, but it has an odd mix of aggressive angularity and smooth curves, at least partly based on the racing Morgans of recent years. Not everybody likes the faired-in headlamps between the front wings and the radiator cowl, or the flat slab of tail that immediately brings to mind both Morgans of old and the original Triumph TR2. But as Charles Morgan remembers with a smile, back in his office at Pickersleigh Road a few days later, 'they kept coming back and looking at it, just walking round and looking'.

Thus the Aero 8 began the next chapter in Morgan's production history, an entirely new and in many respects mould-breaking Morgan, but one to be built with many aspects of the traditional Morgan method that has survived for ninety years. It would also, however, introduce some vital changes in production philosophy, and if all went according to plan would be at the heart of a significant Morgan expansion.

It would be built by the same craftsmen who are already building the Plus 8, the Plus 4 and the 4/4, in the same works, with essentially the same programme, brought up to date more by what is assembled than by how it is assembled. But there will still not be a production line, nor any significant degree of mechanisation, and there will still be the scope to match every car to its customer. Just as it has always been.

Morgan is one of the very few survivors from the earliest days of the British motor industry, and the only one to retain its full independence. Such other British marques as there are of anything close to Morgan's age are nowadays no more than badges of the big corporations, and hundreds of others are long ago dead and buried. Yet Morgan has survived in spite of (or, arguably, because of) bending all the accepted rules.

The Morgan way is to stay small and lean, to be flexible and above all independent. That approach was commonplace when Morgan was founded in the early years of the twentieth century but it is no longer how the world works for the rest of the mainstream industry. Nor is it even how life is for the majority of today's lower volume specialists.

The conventional position today is that the viability of building motor cars is rooted in volume sales, and supplying volume sales necessitates modern production technologies, which in turn require substantial and on-going investment. Nor is that a new philosophy. It was already the norm in manufacturing industries far beyond the building of motor cars long before Morgan joined the market. And it was already common in other areas of the motor industry by the time Morgan arrived on the scene. In the early days, HFS Morgan himself even flirted with going the whole hog and becoming a mass manufacturer, with the help of bigger partners. But that did not work out, and once Morgan had settled back into a more modest regime, they stayed there.

For those motor companies which followed the conventional route, developing mass manufacturing processes involved adopting and adapting existing production methods and technologies and inventing new ones specific to the product, but in the early days there was always a degree of flexibility according to scale. In the early 1910s when Morgan was founded, the industry was already dominated by larger manufacturers, but there were also hundreds of smaller, entrepreneurial ones in the Morgan mould. There was room for them to grow, as Morgan did, by pursuing niche markets. To a degree there still is today, but the number of niches not covered by the big manufacturers is far smaller than it was in the early 1900s, and even to break into those niches demands considerable resources. Likewise, the sheer complexity of the motor vehicle of today, much of it the result of safety legislation and pollution controls, the rest the corollary of vastly greater customer expectations, is something HFS Morgan could never have dreamed of. Today, Morgan may be the odd one out, but before the First World War, HFS Morgan's way was not wildly out of line with the ways of many other smaller manufacturers. To an extent he was even a moderniser.

When HFS Morgan set up the Morgan Motor Company Ltd in 1912, with the help of his father HG Morgan, he set up a limited liability company with a nominal share capital of £100,000 and only two shareholders, himself and his father. HFS's investment was essentially in modest workshop buildings, a small inventory of machine tools, on buying in components from outside suppliers and in a small but skilled workforce. In that respect, in his day, he followed the conventional way of starting small-scale production and, among the ranks of the smaller scale manufacturers, of which there were dozens, it was only his products rather than his methods that were notably out of the ordinary.

In the early days of the three-wheeler Runabout, HFS, like many of his contemporaries, did not manufacture cars from zero so much as assemble them from bought-in components, which meant that the investment in machinery and the size of the works could both be relatively modest. In the beginning, the Morgan factory was simply an extension of the former Morgan Garage in Worcester Road, Malvern Link, and its first function was to put together the tubular chassis, which were brazed together with the bought-in transmission bevel boxes in the chassis shop, with the vee-twin motorcycle-type engines, mainly made by JAP. The chassis erection shop also added the sliding-pillar front suspension, quarter elliptic rear suspension, rear brake, chain drive and the three-wire-spoked wheels (which were also built up in-house until the mid-1930s), to create a complete rolling chassis.

Those could then be kept in store in comfortable numbers until they were matched up with their bodies – in the early days very simple affairs of metal panels over wooden frames with only minimal trim. Those bodies, too, were built completely independently of the chassis, which actually made for a very efficient production process. The wooden body frames were not made in-house in the early days but were built by a local coachbuilder, William Clare's (also in Worcester Road), then clothed in sheet metal made on Morgan's behalf by another local firm, Langley's, whose premises backed on to the Morgan works, in Redland Road. For a while, Langley's shaped the panels for the bodies and also made fuel tanks and radiators, but by the end of the war Morgan (who employed around seventy people before war broke out, making about fifteen cars a week, to be sold through a network of more than fifty distributors) had already set up their own sheet metal shop, and their own carpenter's shop, in the Worcester Road works.

In addition, at the very beginning of the war Morgan added the first of the workshops on the new site at Pickersleigh Road, which would eventually grow into the current factory, as described in detail in later chapters. The initial plan for Pickersleigh Road was to finish, trim and paint the bodies which had originated in Worcester Road and to fit them onto the chassis which had also been assembled there and were pushed by manpower along the short lane from Worcester Road to Pickersleigh Road. The complete cars were then sent back to Worcester Road for despatch to the dealers. Nowadays they are only wheeled backwards and forwards across one factory yard.

But for the outbreak of the war, Pickersleigh Road should have seen the workforce increase almost immediately to about a hundred, and production capacity potentially to double, to as many as thirty cars a week. But the war meant those plans were modified, and when it was over the changes in the market also caused Morgan to think again, with Pickersleigh Road taking over chassis manufacture and starting its expansion to become first the main production facility and eventually the only one.

Aside, however, from bringing more of the body-building process in-house, moving the premises and adjusting the numbers to suit demand, the process for building the original type three-wheeler would not change significantly for the rest of its production life, because it did not need to. The process was already as simple as it could be.

That was fundamentally why HFS Morgan set up his new works the way he did, without production lines, even though they were already becoming an intrinsic part of the mainstream, volume-producing industry – led in Britain, as in America, by Ford.

In 1911, the year in which Morgan became a serious car builder following the introduction of his two-seater Runabout, the shape of the British motor industry had been changed significantly when Ford established their first British manufacturing operation, at Trafford Park in Manchester, to build the Model T, the car that was changing the face of the industry worldwide. Two years after the British factory was opened it was already Britain's biggest motor manufacturer, with an output that year of some 8,000 Model Ts, compared to Morgan's production of fewer than seven hundred and fifty Runabouts.

And while Morgan continued to build enough Runabouts to satisfy their market, Ford did everything they could to build enough Ts, at a low enough price, to dominate theirs. In 1913 Henry Ford began the process leading to assembly-line mass production, by introducing the principle of a moving conveyor belt for assembling one component, the magneto. In 1914 he introduced full assembly-line production, which cut the time taken to build a Model T from twelve and a half to only one and a half hours. Rapid production enabled Ford to sell the Model T at what before the manufacturing revolution had been unimaginably low prices for a real car. And Ford also offered the Model T in just about every variation, from doctor's coupé to farmer's truck.

At the same time, Ford developed another strand that would become familiar to most of the motor industry's big producers, but which again would have been completely alien to Morgan's way of thinking. In the early years, Ford, like American rivals Buick, began a new process of buying out many of its major components suppliers, not only stabilising his supply base but also bringing their profits in-house. In the 1920s Morris extended that strategy to the British industry, while Morgan remained supplier-dependent, but more importantly for them at least, still financially independent.

While Morgan continued with their craftsman-based production, other Europen manufacturers gradually adopted the methods pioneered by Ford and already eagerly taken up by many of his American rivals. The first European company properly to adopt production-line mass production was Citroën, with the Model A in 1919. The rest of the industry gradually followed, although, extraordinarily, not until 1934 did Morris finally instal their first moving production line in their Cowley, Oxford, factory.

Ford's methods, and the low costs that they allowed for what was actually a large and very capable car, gave them a comprehensive sales advantage. By 1920 half of all the motor vehicles in the world were Model Ts, but Ford, like everyone else, was about to experience the other side of the business as America's post-war boom in vehicle sales collapsed and the American industry faced a slump which threatened even the biggest manufacturers. Ford responded by cutting prices, a ploy soon repeated by many others, but not always as successfully as in Ford's case – largely because few others had the buffer of Ford's massive resources. The same strategy worked for Morris in Britain, and was also applied by Morgan in the face of the threat to cyclecar sales from Britain's homegrown alternative to the Model T, the Austin Seven. Between 1923, when production was near an all-time high with some 2,300 three-wheelers built, to 1935, when only two hundred and eighty-six were made, Morgan saw its three-wheeler market collapse, and from there it continued in freefall, albeit supplemented by the newly-launched four-wheeler. Yet Morgan – having stuck firmly to their philosophy of not expanding in the good years beyond what was sustainable even if things should slow down – survived.

Today, much else has changed, but that philosophy has not. Into the twenty-first century, Morgan's way is still to build a smaller number of cars with guaranteed sales and to build them with low capital investment, high 'craft' content, and maximum flexibility.

The manufacturing process remains at the centre of the Morgan creed, and the major changes to that came in the 1930s with the introduction of the four-cylinder, pressed-steel frame three-wheelers, but even that did not change the Morgan method completely. The biggest change it did bring was something that was already familiar to the rest of the industry, and in some ways only an extension of what was already a vital part of building Morgans – that of buying in a major component. They had always done it with engines and a number of other components; with the Ford-engined F-type three-wheeler they began to buy in the largest remaining single component, the pressed-steel chassis. That now came from Rubery Owen, in Darlaston, Staffordshire, who would continue to supply similar chassis for both three- and four-wheelers until the late 1970s when the contract was moved on, and Morgan became more than ever an assembly operation. It was an assembly operation, however, which still kept enough of its own operations in the building of bodies, the machining of smaller parts and the skilled assembly of cars, to justify its character as a builder of bespoke sports cars, not simply 'kit-cars'.

That change of chassis brought a change of build process, but still no change of underlying philosophy: Morgans would still be built by hand, and there would be no moving production lines. Now, the rolling chassis, complete with engine, was assembled in the chassis erecting shop as normal, but instead of a virtually complete body simply being dropped onto the chassis, it was now built onto it. It was built on in two stages – first the wooden frame, in the body shop, then the metal skin, in the sheet metal shop. After that the virtually completed car went to the paint shop, the upholstery shop, then for its final trim. That process changed very little with the arrival of the four-wheelers (which were essentially the three-wheeler F-type with a rear axle and additional rear wheel) in 1935. It also remained recognisably similar right through into the 1990s, with the biggest changes in the Pickersleigh Road works being the disappearance of the three-wheeler chassis building and machining shops rather than the appearance of anything radically different or unconventional.

Touring the factory towards the end of 1967, the man from *Motoring News* wrote, 'Visiting the Morgan Motor Company Ltd in Malvern Link, Worcestershire, directly after touring BMC's Abingdon works, reminds me forcibly of the Peter Sellers comedy film, *The Mouse That Roared*, in which a tiny state takes on the might of the East and West blocs. Here a small workforce totalling ninety-five people, including the office staff, turn out eight cars a week, maybe nine if all goes very well. The production rate could be higher if more craftsmen could be found, but any thought of expansion somehow goes against the grain; it might lead to conveyor belts, production lines that move under their own power, and goodness knows what might happen then . . .'

The chassis still came from Rubery Owen in batches of eight or nine which represented a week's output. On Monday morning they were set up on trestles in the works and the build process for that particular batch of cars began. Moss gearboxes and Salisbury rear axles were bought in, like the chassis, but virtually everything else was made on site. The ash for the body frames came from Normandy, and it was not unknown for the craftsman shaping the pieces to find a piece of shrapnel from one or other world war embedded deep in what had recently been a living tree. The man with responsibility for that area at the time was Sid Powell, who had been in charge, barring a brief return to the railways as a coachbuilder, since 1932. The spares and service manager, Cecil Jay, and the chief tester, Charlie Curtis, by 1967 had ninety-five years service between them. They had shared the winning Morgan in the 1929 Cycle Car Grand Prix at Brooklands, averaging 64.7 mph. Charlie Curtis, who joined the firm in 1917, had driven virtually every Morgan built since he began testing them in the early 1920s.

And so it continued. In 1975, *Thoroughbred & Classic Cars* magazine took a look at the build process as it then stood, in an article appropriately titled, 'The Morgan Wasn't Built in a Day'. At the time of writing, the process, almost unbelievably, took ninety days. Output was eight cars a week and the waiting list, in spite of these being relatively hard times, was around two years, in the worst cases more than three. Peter Morgan said at about the same time that he would like it to be between nine and eighteen months, but anything much less and he would be worried. The waiting list has always been something of a Morgan legend. Peter never did get it down to nine months, but demand in the late 1980s and early 1990s did get it up to more like nine years.

In 1975, Day 1 of the process began with the chassis being put up on trestles, to start its transformation into a rolling chassis. By Day 7, with axles and wheels fitted, among other things, it was ready to be wheeled down the shop to where the ash frames were assembled. Twelve days later the ash frame has been made up and fitted to the chassis, via a 'damp-proof course' between wood and metal, the individually shaped wooden door frames hung, the wooden shield under the fuel tank and the wooden floorboards all fitted. Day 23, and some of the most complex woodwork was being added, with the laminated ash rear inner wheelarches being made up and fitted.

On Day 33 the steadily developing car was wheeled out into the open, across the yard to the sheet metal shop, to be panelled in either steel or aluminium, to customer choice. The body started as flat sheet metal, cut out manually with shears, individually beaten to shape and mostly fastened to the ash frame with wood screws and tin tacks. It took around two days to make the panels for each car, and that did not include the complicated parts, the front wings, the front cowl and the bonnet.

The wings and cowl were the only double-curvature panels, but all, like the rest at this time, were hand-formed. And finally, another man made each individually fitted bonnet, the only way to ensure a perfect fit on individual cars which inevitably had minor variations. On the bonnets with louvres, each louvre was hand-cut, using a fly-press which had been in the works since the end of the First World War. That whole sequence of panel-beating and fitting took the process through from Day 35 to Day 47, when the car was wheeled on its way again, this time to be prepared for the paint shop.

That preparation involved spray priming, then filling all the minor blemishes, in the joints and the welds and so on, with body putty which was then smoothed down – by hand, because 'the man who does the job is convinced that any kind of sanding machine would have a disastrous effect at this stage'. The car was then given two or three coats of surface primer, rubbed down again, by hand, before the undercoat was applied – and finally sprayed with anything between two and six coats depending on finish colour.

It is now, almost unbelievably, Day 61, almost nine weeks since the chassis first sat on its trestles. Next to go in and on were the wiring and lights, followed by the carpets and trim to cover all the innards. All of it, the leatherwork over the transmission tunnel, all the upholstery, the tonneau cover and hood, was cut out individually and stitched individually, to fit each car. Almost another two weeks on, Day 73, and it was starting to look like a nearly complete car, but it was not there just yet.

The windscreens were fitted, the rest of the wiring done (and occasionally redone if someone had put a tin-tack through something live and important) and on Day 90 the nearly complete car went into the finishing shop, for all those nice odds and ends like bumpers, badges and side screens. The car was then ready to go on its first drive, the road test which every new Morgan was given, of approximately ten miles around the demanding and fault-revealing country roads around Malvern. In 1975, that was still done by Charlie Curtis, after almost sixty years with the company, and many thousands of cars tested. He would request fine-tuning here and there, then repeat the test drive as necessary; when he was happy he would sign the car off, after which it would wait in the despatch bay for delivery or (often) collection by its owner. And save for the details, none of this, of course, had significantly changed since 1935.

Even now it was not so much that Morgan were being perverse as being cautious, and selective. Nothing better illustrated that than the infamous trial by television, on *Troubleshooter* in 1990, and the way Morgan changed after it – but only as they saw fit to change, not necessarily as outside pressure had suggested they change. The full story of the *Troubleshooter* episode and its aftermath is told in Chapter 7, but the gist of Sir John Harvey-Jones's advice was that Morgan had to build many more cars, build them much more efficiently and sell them at much higher prices with a hugely reduced waiting list.

Troubleshooter was broadcast at the time of the Thatcherite yuppie boom, a period when classic cars were seen as investment opportunities commanding massively inflated prices, and when anything new, sporty, exotic and in short supply – including Morgans – was ordered in its hundreds purely for the paper investment value of the order in process. Harvey-Jones saw an opportunity not to be missed; Morgan, with their more measured approach, saw a short-term phenomenon to be treated with caution. They saw a better, safer way ahead in a few more cars, a little bit more efficiency, modestly increased prices, and a slightly shortened waiting list. When the market collapsed, not too long after the programme was made, their approach was vindicated. They had changed what they thought prudent, and had actually made improvements, but they had not made knee-jerk investments that would now have been unsustainable. Prices did increase slightly, the waiting list was brought down by a few years (as much by the more rational market as by Morgan's own actions) and production was increased, as Morgan refined, rather than changed, its production methods. Some of John Harvey-Jones's messages were taken to heart. For example, instead of cutting out sheet metal blanks by hand with tin snips, they were now bought in, laser cut, in batches, and used from stock. But even that was not an automatic decision, as Morgan's sales and marketing manger Matthew Parkin explained in June 2000. 'In 1997 we introduced the superformed aluminium wings and I had one person, just one, cancel their order because they were no longer hand-beaten wings. If we built a car now by mistake with the old type wings on, nobody would buy it. We understand now that people like the shape, they like the tradition, they like people assembling it by hand, with care and attention and the specific materials that we use. But they do not mind that we use modern processes where they're appropriate . . .

'That was one of the things that Harvey-Jones probably did get right. If there are easier ways of doing something that are not just easier but also better, then they are appropriate. You'll see it with things like the laser-cut blanks; they're actually better. They're more accurate, they're better material (they're made out of stainless steel) and it's not actually cheaper for us to do – in fact it's more expensive – but the end product is just millions of times better, and that's good for the customer. There are still enough men with hammers to make this a craftsman-built car and the thing is that people were saying "laser-cut components? The next thing you know they'll be laying people off", but it just is not like that. What we actually want is not fewer people, it's more cars.'

The Superform wings, which started with the Plus 8 generation and will continue, alongside many other 'super-formed' panels into the Aero 8, are the best possible example of a component made by modern methods not automatically being at odds with a car made by traditional craftsmanship. Instead of being hand-shaped at the factory, the wings were now made by an outside supplier, Superform. They use a new process called superplastic aluminium forming, which allows the complex shapes to be manufactured as one-piece form-ings, rather than being welded up from several separate pieces. That gives better corrosion resistance, a more consist-ent shape, and greater production efficiency, although the finishing of the wing edges and the fitting of the headlamp pods is still done by hand at Pickersleigh Road.

The introduction of Superform wings and all that it involved was significant, one of the rare occasions when Morgan chose to invest in a major piece of production tooling, as opposed to handcraftsmanship and traditional technology. Using computer-aided design tools, the new wing shape was digitised from a composite of three separate hand-formed wings, with the final line subtly modified by Charles Morgan. The forming tool, manufactured for Morgan by Survirn Engineering of Birmingham, was the largest Superform had ever used, the main tool weighing some 4 tons and the whole assembly more than 6 tons. It was a major investment for Morgan, but it improved both efficiency and quality.

In these post-*Troubleshooter* days, Morgan was making real efforts to increase production without losing track of its fundamental principles, and this was part of that process. At the same time as the switch to superforming wings, the factory layout was improved, and the assembly operation was (in Morgan's own word) 'streamlined'.

The main change in that late 1990s reshuffle was to reduce the amount of 'work in progress', by changing the way the cars passed through the assembly process. Basically, the system now changed from working in batches to working in a continuous flow. The chassis shop, crucially, instead of supplying ten rolling chassis at the end of each week, began to supply two on each of the five working days. In another key change, Morgan set up a new 'assembly shop'. With the new system, instead of chassis being taken to the body shop to be fitted with ash frames, then to the tin shop for the fitting of panels, the ash frames are panelled in the tin shop and fitted as complete units in the assembly shop. Wing fitting and bonnet making were also moved into the assembly shop, freeing up useful space in the tin shop for more efficient working.

Chassis could now move through the assembly shop at the rate of two a day, an improvement of a car a week, which might not sound much in mass-production terms but to Morgan it represented a production increase of more than 10 per cent. In the new assembly shop, panelled bodies are fitted first, then the superformed wings (after finishing in-house in the sheet metal shop), then the bonnets shaped, the louvres cut and the whole assembly fitted to the car, before final quality checks are made. Instead of holes for minor components being drilled piecemeal as the car moves through trim and fitting stages, there is now a pre-drilling station in the assembly shop, which drills all the necessary holes in the assembled bodies at one time, before the car is painted, saving time in other departments and leading to a better quality finished product.

From assembly, the car then goes to the new paint shop, installed in January 1997 and working with ICI water-based paints and the most modern equipment to produce high-quality finishes while complying with modern environmental legislation. The painted cars then go to the trim shop, for installation first of the wiring loom, then the interior trim to each future owner's individual specification. The completed car is then taken to the despatch area, either to be collected or shipped.

This has further reduced the time the cars spend in the production process. What used to take more than ninety days as recently as the mid-1970s now takes only about twenty – and no matter that the modern mass-market manufacturers can build a car in fewer than that number of hours; to Morgan this represents massive progress.

Today, with better production control systems in place, with a firmer understanding of the ordering system, and with more sensible use of the available factory space (including adding mezzanine floor space in some shops to free ground-level production space while creating 'lineside' component storage space), the whole build programme is more efficient. For the older generation cars, Day 1 sees the rolling chassis completed, with engine, transmission and suspension fitted. At this point they do not have a wiring loom in place, but at this stage the Aero 8 will also have that fitted. Fitting the body, the wings, the bonnet, and drilling all the holes (for everything) all take one day each. The new storage space allows up to a dozen bodies to be in buffer storage waiting for their rolling chassis, and when the Aero 8s reach production these will be painted bodies, not bare ones. For now, the paint shop is still the bottleneck, and each car spends five days in there, before moving on to up to ten days in final fittings and trim – for everything from the distinctive beading in the wing joints (one day) to wiring, pipework, exhausts (another day), and finally seats, soft trim, the rest of the interior, hoods, and all the myriad details that make every Morgan an individual car, to individual customer order.

Matthew Parkin, who came to Morgan from the mainstream industry, where he worked latterly for Volvo, has also overseen changes to the way the ordering system is managed, and the way the cars are sold. 'When I arrived, in 1997, I inherited a completely passive sales process, a situation where we had this massive comfort zone of the famous order bank, but very little idea of what it actually meant. People say it's all a fable but it is not, we really do have this enormous order book. In August 1997 we were delivering cars that had been ordered in 1989 or early 1990 – so a seven-year wait – and that was only to contacting the customer to confirm the order. Really it was a seven and a half year wait for the car. And even that was not as bad as it had been; I think it had been out to eleven years at one stage, which was absolutely hopeless.

'What we never knew then, and we do now, was what effect the length of the waiting list had on the numbers of customers. People say, "you've got seven years' worth of orders, or eleven years or whatever, but I bet you've got a lot of people dropping off, so it's not really seven years, is it?" And we do have a lot of people dropping off, but the reality is that it still is seven years even allowing for the drop outs. In fact it's just as well that they do drop out, because without that the wait would be about fourteen years. That was based on ten cars a week, which we'd gone up to as a regular figure on the basis of the changes we'd made in 1997, building cars in small batches so that every car was in effect being worked on all the time.

'Before that the production rate had actually been steady for a long time. If you go back to the Harvey-Jones days, we were looking at nine and a half cars a week, over forty-seven working weeks a year – about four hundred and fifty cars a year. With the new factory layout, we created a lot more space, with fewer bottlenecks, where people in the chassis department, for instance, did not just have to do repetitive jobs, as they'd being doing for such a long time, but now had all the skills and knowledge to build up a complete rolling chassis. Once we passed the settling down period it soon became apparent that we had quite a lot of excess capacity, because people's lives were so much easier. So from around March 1998 we went to eleven cars a week, which again is a big percentage increase.'

But as Matthew Parkin readily admits, the system as it stood, even with the recent improvements, was reaching saturation point. 'What puts the ceiling on the numbers at the moment, is the paint shop capacity. That's the biggest bottleneck, but that's how it works: you clear one bottleneck to increase production and you find another bottleneck somewhere else. The bottlenecks are never really in the nuts and bolts. The mechanical assembly is easy enough to control just by getting more people in to do it; the real problem has always been either with paint or trim. Then on 5 June 2000 we went to twelve cars a week – and that's based really on slightly better organisation again, and helped by some new foremen who we've appointed recently.'

He knows that the changes of the late 1990s were the key to everything that has followed, and which will follow. 'The big change has been working on individual cars rather than working in big batches, so in effect we work on small batches and that was the fundamental change that has led to this increase in production.'

Once again the process had benefitted from the underlying philosophy – the philosophy laid down almost ninety years before by the man who created Morgan.

2 In the Beginning

IN THE EARLY YEARS of the motor industry it was not unusual to find individuals who were synonymous with their companies' names. From Henry Ford to Herbert Austin, from WO Bentley to Ettore Bugatti, from the brothers Renault to Mr Rolls and Mr Royce, real people gave their names to what became famous companies producing equally famous cars. Even more gave their names to companies which disappeared without trace almost as quickly as they had been created, but a few of the pioneer family names survive among today's industry giants. Almost none of them, however, still has direct family links. Of those that do (most notably Ford) the links are increasingly remote – shareholdings, perhaps, but rarely any executive control.

One company in particular has bucked the trend: the Morgan Motor Company, founded as a limited company in 1912 by HFS Morgan and his father HG Morgan, in the heart of rural England. Today it may not be on the same scale as some of those other famous names, but against all reasonable odds it still exists, and in one way the Morgan Motor Company is unique amongst the industry's long-term survivors. For almost ninety years the Morgan Motor Company has been run by Morgans. The company is still entirely owned and controlled by family interests. As well as still being independent it is still successful, and able to look to the future with confidence. For its entire life it has been controlled by just four generations of the family. Charles Morgan, grandson of HFS Morgan, is steering the company into the twenty-first century; his father Peter, HFS's son, has been there since the late 1940s; and HFS founded the company with his own father – one providing the engineering creativity, the other the business organisation.

They were true pioneers. When Henry Frederick Stanley Morgan, the man who created the Morgan three-wheeler Runabout, was born on 11 August 1881, the motor car did not exist. In 1881 the only alternatives to the horse were walking, cycling or the railway. There were a few steam carriages on the roads but no motor cars.

The gasoline-fuelled, internal combustion-engined automobile as we came to know it was no more than a dream. But, after years of experimenting, it was a dream that was coming close to reality. When it finally made the leap, 'Harry' Morgan, or HFS as he would be known in later life, was in his early school years. That was in 1886, when Karl Benz made his first runs in what became known as his Patent Motorwagen – Harry Morgan was five at the time.

In a suitable preface to Morgan's later preferences, Benz's pioneering machine was a three-wheeler. If not exactly the sort of three-wheeler that HFS Morgan would design, it proved that three wheels could be just as acceptable as four even in the early days of motoring. It was still a long way from being a reliable means of everyday transport, and further still from marking the beginnings of what was to become one of the world's biggest industries, but it showed what was possible. The Benz car also marked the transition from decades of tinkering to a new age of development. That was the age in which HFS Morgan grew up, a period in Britain when the Empire was strong and prosperous, when Victoria was queen and invention was king.

HFS Morgan was born a long way from any direct contact with the new motor car, at Moreton Jeffries Court, the manor house of Moreton Jeffries, a village between Hereford, a few miles to the south west, and Great Malvern and Worcester, a few miles further away to the north east, all straddling the Malvern Hills. The popular image is of HFS as the son of a country churchman, but that is not the whole picture. Looking back through the earliest family archives it is clear that the Morgan family's background, long before there were any ideas of going into the new motor car business, was financially a very comfortable one. Far back, HFS's forebears on his mother's side, the Williams family, and before them the Joneses, had been London merchants, while on his father's side his immediate ancestors had served God rather than Mammon. Far from being impecunious parsons, however, they were conspicuously well-heeled. It is apparent that most of the family's wealth before the turn of the century – which ultimately steered HFS Morgan through his early years at school, college and his apprenticeship before helping him to set up first his garage business, then his motor manufacturing enterprise – came initially from the complicated relationships on his mother's side.

HFS himself recorded that he could not remember meeting his maternal grandmother, Sarah Williams, but he did remember that his father, the Prebendary Henry George Morgan, and his mother, Florence, were staying in a hotel in Tunbridge Wells when his grandmother Sarah died of diptheria. HFS's mother had told him that when she was young her family had been quite poor and had lived in France for some time, largely as a result, it seems, of diputes over the terms of the will of another Williams' forebear. When that will was settled, the Williams family came back to England, in rather more comfortable circumstances. In later life, Sarah Williams lived at Shirley Hall in Surrey and, having finally become main beneficiary of the disputed inheritance, her assets, giving her an income of £10,000 a year, would have made her a wealthy woman for the middle of the nineteenth century. She died having apparently learnt little from earlier experiences, for she left no will of her own.

Money from other areas of the extended Williams family and its in-laws also filtered through to HFS's mother and then to her own children, HFS included, as he described in some detail. 'When I was a boy,' he wrote, 'a Mr Williams lived at Boons Park. He was a bachelor and I think he had something to do with the law suit [over the earlier will]. His money eventually came to Sydney Williams [HFS's cousin]. I remember a Mr James, who painted pictures and lived in Folkestone, and when he died his money came to my mother, so I suppose he was also a near relation. I also remember an old lady we always called Cousin Nelly, who was another James and lived at Sevenoaks.'

In a footnote, HFS records that his maternal great grand-parents (the Joneses) had four children – Henry, Helen (who became Helen Peele), his grandmother Sarah, and great aunt Amelia, who became Amelia Rollins – but he suggests they may have had other children, including a daughter who married a James – hence the connection.

Of the relations he actually knew, HFS continued, 'Uncle Henry [really HFS's great uncle] and Mrs Henry I remember well, as my father had a house in Ramsgate near theirs for some years. Uncle Henry died in Ramsgate when I was a boy and Mrs Henry also died there in about 1904. She was a peculiar person and for some years she never left the house, but when she died what money was left came to my mother, and I think to Aunt Edie.' [Aunt Edie was another daughter of Sarah Williams, and sister to HFS's mother Florence, along with their brothers Stanley and Frederick. As such they were among the many nephews and nieces of Henry Jones, but maybe favourites. Edie, or Edith, married Fred Boscawen, who was master of hounds at Shirley Hall. Uncle Stanley, HFS remembered, lived at Ivy House, near Edenbridge, and 'he married while at Cambridge but kept it a secret until after his mother's death.']

'Aunt Amelia,' says HFS, 'lived and died at "Theobalds" in Hawkhurst. She was very well off and she left a very complicated will [problems with wills must have been a family speciality], with most of her money eventually coming to my sisters and the Williams girls – but she did not leave anything to any male member of the family.

'I was a trustee for the amount that came to my sisters on the death of Ada Peele [one of the daughters of HFS's great aunt Helen Peele]. Helen Peele had three daughters and I think two sons – Walter, who was unfortunately an alcoholic, and Harry who was a curate at Lowestoft. He left his money to give Padstow a steam lifeboat, called the *Helen Peele* in memory of his mother . . . none of the Peeles was married.' The three daughters and Walter, according to HFS, lived together at Childrun Hall – another apparently grand house in that side of the family's background.

On HFS's father's side, the family history is slightly less complicated, and firmly tied to the Church. His great grandfather was the vicar of Trethern, and of his two sons, George, who remained a bachelor, was rector of Stoke St Milborough, while Henry, born in January 1798, was at one time rector of St Mary Magdalen, Blackheath, before becoming chaplain to Nunhead cemetery. That is now absorbed in the sprawl of south-east London, but in 1850 when Henry Morgan moved there from Blackheath, the massive cemetry was only recently opened, and Nunhead was one of the group of hamlets including Peckham and Dulwich in the genteel fringes between the city and the Kent countryside. Henry married twice, the first time to Lady Jane Morgan (who, HFS noted, is commem-orated on a plaque in Gloucester Cathedral) and the second time to Mary Ann, who was twenty-seven years younger than Henry, who was now in his mid-fifties. They lived in a large house (destroyed by bombs during the Second World War) in Linden Grove, near the cemetry and Peckham Rye. Henry George Morgan (Henry and Mary Ann Morgan's only son, and HFS Morgan's father) was born there on 27 May 1852, not long after his father had moved to Nunhead.

The young Henry George went to nearby Dulwich College public school as a day boy, but in July 1871 his father initiated the move which took the Morgan family to live in the Malvern area, where it would become famous in a very different business. That was when seventy-three-year-old Henry Morgan purchased the living of Stoke Lacy, a village in the Diocese of Hereford, very close to Moreton Jeffries and a few miles from Malvern.

The purchase of the 'perpetual right of patronage and presentation of in and to the rectory and parish church' with the imposing house, extensive gardens, stables, coach houses, barns, yards, outbuildings and some nineteen acres, cost Henry Morgan £3,900, and with it HFS Morgan's grandfather became the rector of Stoke Lacy; given his age at the time of the purchase it is fairly obvious that he saw the move more as a legacy to his family. By the time he died, on 3 November 1886 at the age of eighty-eight, he had been succeeded in the Church by his son, HFS's father, the Prebendary Henry George – 'HG' – Morgan. HG had become curate working alongside his father in the late 1870s, and shortly after his father's death he became rector in his turn. HG's mother,

Mary Ann, died exactly a year and a day after her husband, and is buried with him in the family plot in Stoke Lacy churchyard.

HG had met Florence Williams when they were near-neighbours in south London before the move to Stoke Lacy, and they were married in 1875 from Florence's mother's home, Shirley Hall. Born in the same year, they were both twenty-three when they married. Six years later HFS was born. He was their first child, but what isn't generally known is that he wasn't the Morgans' only son. In November 1884, when HFS was only three, Florence gave birth to another boy, christened Charles George, but he died on 4 November 1887, sixteen days short of reaching his third birthday. He is buried in the family plot at Stoke Lacy, and although infant mortality was a familiar feature of family life in Victorian England, both Peter and Charles Morgan have no doubts that Charles George's death would have affected the family very deeply. They are equally sure that HG's faith and practicality would have helped them through the loss, and that it would have strengthened HG's relationship with young Harry, as the surviving son. HFS was brought up against a religious, rural background, with his three younger sisters, Freida, Ethel and Dorothy (youngest of the family and born in April 1891). It seems they lived a relatively well-heeled existence in the sprawling rectory, in beautiful surroundings: a family photograph from the early 1890s shows HFS, aged about ten, mounted on his pony outside the rectory, his mother beside him in a carriage with a liveried driver.

From his infant schooling at home in 1891 at the age of ten, HFS went to prep school at Stone House in Broadstairs on the Kent coast, where the fees were £52 10s plus £3 10s 6d expenses per term, and here his life began to change dramatically, as is clear from numerous letters home. Many years later he recounted, 'I arrived at Victoria accompanied by a friend of my father, as owing to illness my people could not see me off. I was introduced to a master, Mr Hussey, and was soon on my way in a saloon coach attached to the 3.35 "Granville Express". I knew none of the boys on the train and as far as I can remember I was the only new boy on the train. I felt extremely lonely and homesick. The other boys had plenty to talk about, but I was left severely alone, as was the custom. We arrived at Broadstairs station at 5.20 and drove to the school in large wagonettes. On arrival we were met by Mr Stone who in my eyes looked very severe and imposing. He certainly was a fine looking old man, although how old I do not know. He had curly grey hair, was dressed in clerical clothes and used large spectacles. I soon found he was a very kindly man and although strict was always fair. He was wrapped up in classics – I think he thought in Latin and Greek. I shall always remember the kind talk he had with me when I left the school, and he gave me a book of his poems, *Dorica*, inscribed "with Mr Stone's love and best wishes".'

HFS was at Stone House for three years, had a very mixed academic record, was frequently quite ill and was always considered a frail boy. But he found new interests, all as revealed by his letters home.

Most of them were short and always hurriedly written, the spidery writing and hit and miss spelling suggesting that HFS was not a particularly careful pupil. He usually wrote about struggles with his work, and his regular promotions and demotions in class.

'The system of working,' he wrote later, 'was as follows: so many good marks made an alpha, and a certain number of alphas [which could be lost for bad conduct] put you in the "honour class". All honour class boys got a slab of chocolate given them on Sunday evenings. Our punishments were working overtime or writing lines. I wrote many lines, mostly in Latin, and I made a pen to write three lines at once . . .'

Making things became one of HFS's great interests, along with drawing, and what he drew showed the direction in which his attention was moving. Almost every letter home from the ten-year-old (he wrote at least three times a week) contained a drawing of either a sailing boat or a train, often both, and occasionally a bicycle. These interests were also reflected in his regard for one of the masters. 'Mr Wallis, who taught the fifth,' he wrote later, 'was my favourite as he was fond of ships, railway engines and all mechanical things. He was reputed to be very rich, I think chiefly because he owned a small yacht which he kept at Whitstable. I was very delighted when he took us for trips to Shellness etc. He also went abroad for his holidays, taking photographs which he turned into lantern slides, showing them with a lecture to the school. He was a bit of an inventor and as I remember it he made a special kind of blow lamp which made a great noise and looked very dangerous.' Mr Wallis was clearly an influence on the boy.

HFS played football, cricket, hockey and golf, the latter on a nearby six-hole course of which he drew maps in his letters home. He told his sisters his nickname at Broadstairs was 'Barrel Organ' which he thought quite funny. He liked roller skating and riding, and seemed to be active in spite of his frequent illnesses: whooping cough, earache, bronchitis and measles all kept him in bed for long periods and prompted several letters between Mr Stone and HFS's father. One of HFS's own letters home said, 'the doctor saw me yesterday and has ordered me some wine to have at dinner. It is so nice, it is called Clarert [sic].' His health problems had a bad effect on his learning, and he moved up and down between the slow lane and the 'honours' class like a yo-yo. Adorning them with drawings of stationary engines, steam engines, 'slide valves', windmills, bridges and the inevitable boats and trains, he wrote letters to say when his classics were bad or his arithmetic good, and once to say, 'I am going to be put in the bottom class again. I am so sorry but I cannot help it.'

Academically, he turned out to be best at mathematics and drawing and most interested in engineering. He made cabinets in woodworking classes, and in 1893 wrote to say, 'I have made a little steam boat in the carpenters' shop'. He also sent a drawing home of a complicated machine he had designed for turning zero marks into alphas.

But for all his worries at Stone House and Broadstairs, these appear to have been the happiest years of his school life, which was about to move on again. When he went to Stone House, as he explained later, it was supposedly in preparation for Eton before following his father into the Church, but two things intervened. First, his academic standards were not sufficient to get him into Eton; and secondly he was starting to think of a career outside the Church, in engineering – 'into which occupation,' he wrote, many years later, 'my father gave me every assistance'.

Before he made that move, there was more schooling to come, and in 1894 HFS was sent to Marlborough College in Wiltshire. Marlborough, once the second largest public school in England, and second in size only to Eton, had more ecclesiastical connections. Originally founded as a school principally for the sons of clergymen, by HFS's time such sons of the Church were still prominent among its pupils. Many had their futures mapped out by their pasts; HFS, however, while suitably God-fearing, continued his move away from the family tradition of serving the Church, and from here on his main interests were in mechanical things, and in experimenting with them.

Marlborough was a short and far from happy experience. HFS's report for June 1894, soon after he had arrived, showed him as twentieth in a class of twenty-one. His form master commented '. . . very feeble. The quality of his work is thoroughly bad and he is rather listless.' His headmaster was more succinct, writing just one word – 'poor'. His general conduct was described as good, but his relationship with the authorities was not. Before he had been in the school for long, HFS was taken before the headmaster and told, 'It is all very well for you to have inventive genius but it is an intolerable nuisance at school.' Marlborough itself was just as intolerable to the young Morgan, who further undermined his reputation when he was delegated by fellow pupils to complain about the school's appalling food, said to be at best insufficient to keep the pupils properly fed, and at worst frequently maggot-ridden. For his impertinence, HFS was again severely reprimanded, and soon afterwards his concerned parents took him out of the school altogether.

The Morgans were a considerate family who wanted HFS to have a say in his own future. To help him recover from the miserable experience of Marlborough (not least the malnutrition) they took him to Italy, a trip which his father, a keen amateur artist, thought might stimulate an interest in art in his son, too. Both travelling and visual arts played a big part in the life of the Morgan family, and of HG Morgan in particular. The flow of letters shows that that they spent quite a lot of time touring Europe, and indulging another of the Prebendary Morgan's great passions. His paintings were one hobby (as well as his originals Peter Morgan remembers he was particularly keen on copying the works of John Constable), but photography, at a time when amateur photography was quite an innovation, was another. His early scrapbooks are full of extremely accomplished photographs, many of them featuring home life and the children (especially HFS's photogenic sister Ethel as a young girl). There are photographs of family holidays in Devon in 1894 when the family visited towns like Ilfracombe, Bideford, Woolacombe and Lynmouth; photographs from the Matterhorn in 1893, and of a grand tour which apparently also took in Villefranche on the Côte d'Azur, Pisa, San Remo, Florence and Venice. One of that series, titled 'Bettineralp', won HG a bronze medal from *Amateur Photographer* magazine, and there are many other pictures with awards listed.

It was already apparent, however, that HFS Morgan was developing far more interest in mechanical sciences than in the arts. That took him, immediately after his post-Marlborough Italian recuperation, to start his further education at Crystal Palace Engineering College, in one of the two landmark towers of Thomas Paxton's great glass exhibition centre, recently moved from its original site in Hyde Park to the outskirts of south-east London which took its name. Crystal Palace was no distance from Peckham Rye and Nunhead where his family had lived only twenty-five years before, and to turn-of-the-century Londoners and thousands of visitors the Palace was another towering example of Victorian England's obsession with engineering. An enticing place, too, for someone as keen as young HFS Morgan on novelty and invention.

Starting his courses in the college's School of Practical Engineering in September 1899, HFS studied engineering and design, and became proficient in technical drawing. He completed his studies, including the Mechanical Course and the Civil Engineering Division, in August 1901, and passed all his examinations. He started to build things, too, including his first vehicle – a bicycle of his own design, which he used to good effect in student races, showing competitive as well as engineering instincts, and setting a new college cycling speed record. In one letter home from his lodgings at Palace

Road, beside the Crystal Palace park, which also had a famous cycle track, HFS wrote, 'My Dear Father, the Cycle Show begins next Friday and the bicycles are arriving. Some of the bicycle men are in this house. Mr Turner who invented the Bicarrier is here. He has got a lot of samples with him. There is a motor car on the cycle track, which is going to try to do 1,000 miles without stopping. It is going to start tomorrow, this is not very good weather for such a trial . . .' It was probably the first time that HFS mentioned a motor car in any of his correspondence, but it would not be the last.

Very early on, the Prebendary HG Morgan had made the first of several important paternal moves in shaping HFS's future, not by steering him in the obvious direction, but by allowing him to make his own decisions.

HG was a remarkable character. A curate and a rector for sixty years or so of his long life, he was nonetheless not the archetypal Victorian country churchman. Aside from his interests in drawing and painting (nothing unusual in that), he also took, less conventionally, an interest in the stock market – making considerable sums from investing in gold shares, and further enhancing the Morgan family's already comfortable standard of living. It also foreshadowed something that would become a fact of life for the Morgan Motor Company – that far beyond being a motor car manufacturer it was a company making large sums of money from outside investments, in areas way beyond manufacturing. Significantly, that helped the company to survive even when times were hard, and it was almost certainly a philosophy laid down by HG from the very beginning.

He was a clever and worldly man, with a talent for figures, and once the Morgan Motor Company had been set up (with his help), he organised its finances for many years. He was also something of an extrovert, in later life a tall, elegant figure, often frock-coated, with white hair and a large white moustache. Many photographs seem to show him smiling to himself, and for his day he was clearly something of a modernist. He was responsible for giving both the rectory and the church electricity and hot water, the former very successfully, the latter less so, as it tended to be either very hot or very cold.

He made no great effort to push his son into the Church but instead became an enthusiastic supporter of the course that HFS had now definitely chosen in its place, engineering. By 1900, HFS's father had arranged an apprenticeship for him with the Great Western Railway (known appropriately enough to many people by the affectionate nickname 'God's Wonderful Railway'). HFS went to work first with William Dean and later with GJ Churchward, Locomotive Superintendents in their turn at the GWR's famous engineering headquarters in Swindon, Wiltshire, not far from Marlborough.

HFS was much happier in Swindon. He worked his apprenticeship as a draughtsman, in the office in which Isambard Kingdom Brunel had once been in charge. He stayed with the GWR until 1905 and it was during that period, when he would often travel from Swindon to his home in Herefordshire, that he began to take an interest in the motoring movement that was beginning to gather pace in Britain. His scrapbooks from the turn of the century are full of cuttings of motor cars, and while working for the GWR HFS Morgan became a motorist himself.

His first hands-on experience of the motoring world was around the turn of the century, when he hired various machines from a Mr Marriot, whose motor business was based in Hereford, in the county town, and who HFS later described as 'the first motor trader in Hereford'. The first vehicle HFS hired from Mr Marriot was a Minerva motor cycle, and the first car he hired, in 1899, was a 3½hp Benz; he had his first accident in this car, when the brakes failed to cope with the steep, 1-in-6 descent on the road into Hereford. That resulted in a substantial bill for repairs, £28 according to HFS, paid for by his remarkably tolerant and supportive father. In 1901, still with parental approval but now with his own money, HFS bought his first motor vehicle, an Eagle Tandem. It was an interesting choice – a tricar, which was an early cross between car and motor cycle, and significant in the Morgan context both as a three-wheeler and as an example of the British motor industry's evolution from the bicycle industry.

These were very early days for the motor car in Britain, and even earlier days for a domestic manufacturing industry, while motoring of any kind was normally only associated with considerable wealth. In 1885, Ralph Jackson, of Altrincham, Cheshire, started to build Ralpho bicycles and fourteen years later he built a two-seater, three-wheeler powered by a 2¼hp engine, which he sold as the Century Tandem. In 1901, the company moved to Willesden in north-west London, and two years later, under new management, expanded its range by building Century cars alongside the Tandems, until it stopped production in 1906. In the meantime, Ralph Jackson had returned to Altrincham and, with new partners, set up the Eagle Engineering & Motor Co. Ltd, to build a thinly disguised copy of the Century Tandem which he called the Eagle Tandem, the type with which HFS Morgan began his motor-owning life.

At that time such enterprises could be set up relatively inexpensively. The Eagle Company had been founded with a nominal capital of £6,000, of which just £4,000 was taken up. In 1903 it followed the same path as Century, by adding larger Eagle cars, and both those and the Eagle Tandem were well regarded. As with many rivals, however, that was not enough to guarantee commercial success, and in February 1905 Eagle went into voluntary liquidation, before being wound up by the receiver in January 1907. With new associates, Jackson started again, building what he called the New Eagle. These were sold through another new company, the St George's Motor Car Co. of Leeds, which was founded on a capital of only £1,500, and lasted just another couple of years. Jackson moved on again, and in 1913 launched one more vehicle, a cyclecar, in direct competition with the ones that former Eagle owner HFS Morgan had by then started to build. As well as the Eagle Tandem being Morgan's first car, the convoluted story of the company that built it is an illustration of how things often worked in the early days of the motor industry, and how it was possible to begin from almost nothing. It was an observation perhaps not wasted either on young HFS Morgan or on his father.

In 1904 Eagle built a powerful single-seater version of the Tandem called the Eagle Racer, with a 16hp engine and capable of some 80mph. That was fast enough to earn the company a certain amount of publicity at the time, and that

again would not have escaped HFS's notice. His own Eagle
Tandem was less exciting, an 8hp De Dion-powered model
with the single wheel at the rear, the passenger seat between
the front wheels, and the driver perched high up ahead of the
rear wheel, in a bucket seat on what otherwise looked like the
rear half of a motor cycle frame, behind a steering wheel and
fuel tank. Still, HFS's example was quick enough to earn him
his first summons, for exceeding the 12mph speed limit
which was in force up to the beginning of 1904. As HFS said
fifty years later, 'It was fast but not too reliable, and it gave
me considerable experience during the eighteen months that
I owned it.'

After the Eagle, HFS moved on to a 'real' car, a Star, built
by another company which had evolved from the bicycle
industry. That concern had gone into the car-building business in Wolverhampton in 1898 as the Star Motor Co. Ltd,
alongside the Star Cycle Co. Like plenty of others, in moving
on from bicycles to automobiles it started by building Benz
copies, and later progressed to Panhard-type designs. As the
Star Engineering Co., from 1902 it made increasingly sporty
cars, even racing cars, not dissimilar to contemporaneous
Mercedes models. As with his Eagle, HFS's version was a bit
more modest than the racing versions. Bought as a twenty-
first birthday present in 1902 and financed by a £200 legacy
from his godfather, HFS's Star was a twin-cylinder, 7hp
chain-driven four-wheeler, and, as with the Tandem, he used
it for visits home from the railway shops in Swindon. As he
wrote later, he also used it in the early days of his business,
and 'with modifications it gave good service for many years'.

It would do around 30mph and its only problems were
with the friction-drive water pump cooling, which HFS,
already an inveterate tinkerer, replaced with a cruder but
obviously more reliable thermo-syphon system. He eventually sold the Star, and writing in 1915, noted that it was still
being used quite regularly by a local clergyman.

When he left Swindon and the GWR for good early in 1905,
aged twenty-three, HFS headed for home, and towards a
future which involved machinery, and in particular the motor
car. In 1905, intending to settle in the area where he had
spent his childhood, he bought a house on Worcester Road,

Malvern Link, on the northern outskirts of Malvern itself, on the edge of the Malvern Hills. It was (and is) a genteel part of the world, and at the turn of the century when HFS returned to it, it was still enjoying considerable popularity as a spa town. It was home to a number of famous residents, among them the singer Jenny Lind, 'the Swedish Nightingale', who lived at Wynd's Point while HFS was a small boy, and, most famous of all, the composer Edward Elgar, who lived at Craeg Lea in Malvern Wells from 1899 to 1904. Elgar used to ride around the district on a Sunbeam bicycle which he later gave to his friend August Jaeger the 'Nimrod' of the *Enigma Variations*.

Adjacent to HFS's quite spacious new house, called Chestnut Villa, was a plot of land with some small buildings. In March 1905 Morgan applied for planning permission to build a larger, more useful building on the site, literally next door to his new home. In April permission was speedily granted and building work began immediately.

When the structure was completed, also in a matter of weeks, it was revealed as a substantial workshop, built in brick and comprising a single storey with a high-ridged roof and a quite elaborate façade on Worcester Road which stood somewhat higher than Chestnut Villa next door. Conveniently close to Malvern Link Station, the whole building measured some 72 feet from front to rear and almost 40 feet wide, giving a floor area of close to 2,800 square feet. It was split into two by a low crosswise partition with a central gap, with a wide door opening onto a yard at the rear.

The Worcester Road frontage had another wide, part-glazed doorway, offset to the left between the second and third of four brick pillars, between the other pairs of which were tall, elegant double windows, topped by scalloped skylights. Those were echoed in the tops of three more panelled windows in the wide brick gable which topped the impressive façade. Aside from the distinctively shaped front windows, there was just enough decoration to make the new building slightly more than a simple shed – two carved stone cappings to the outer pillars, stone copings on top of the front wall, and a wrought-iron bracket over the centre window to carry a hanging sign.

This was a considerable undertaking and obviously the basis for a well-thought-out business plan. Running the full width of the frontage, above the lower windows and between the carved embellishments, was a smartly lettered, gold-painted sign on a deep red background. It read Morgan & Co. Garage and Motor Works. HFS had planned and built it in partnership with his long-time friend Leslie Bacon, with moral and financial support, amounting initially to some £3,000, from his father. And Prebendary Morgan was among those present for the official opening, on Saturday 20 May 1905.

The occasion was heralded by a single-column advertisement under the Trade Notices section of the local newspaper, the *Malvern Gazette*. The advertisement announced that the new garage had an inspection pit fitted with electric light, that it sold petrol, recharged accumulators, vulcanised tyres and undertook 'All kinds of repairs, executed by competent workmen and first-class machinery'. Morgan & Co. advertised themselves as sole agents for Darracq, Wolseley and Siddeley cars, and dealers in cars of all makes. They had Dunlop and Continental tyres in stock, and on opening day they could offer at least two cars for immediate delivery: a 12hp Darracq and a 6hp Wolseley. For 'early delivery' they could promise a 15hp Darracq and a 12hp Wolseley. In addition they advertised for sale 'several first-class second-hand cars'.

Morgan & Co. also offered 'Cars Let on Hire'. Terms (including driver) were three guineas (£3 3s) per day, 15 guineas (£15 15s) per five-day week. They were available by distance, at 1s per mile, plus 6d per mile for return, or for circular runs at 9d per mile, all with a minimum charge of 3s. Morgan offered 'Cars to rent to any distance' and promised 'mechanics sent to all parts immediately on receipt of wire'. The Garage was said to be 'one of the largest and best equipped in the west of England', with accommodation for forty cars. It was an impressive start.

There was the promise of another element to come – Morgan & Co.'s 'First Public Service Car'. A public coach service, in fact, running the five-mile route from Malvern Link through Great Malvern, south to Malvern Wells via Worcester Road, the Belle Vue Hotel and Wells Road, advertised as being due to commence running 'on or about' 29 May'. It duly started, using a 22hp Daimler coach, and later it seems he added a fifteen-seater 10hp Wolseley and ran services to Wells and between Malvern and Gloucester. Strangely, the service was not welcomed by all in this traditional and quite up-market rural community, for the familiar reasons that the motor vehicle was noisy, smoky, smelly, and it frightened the horses. HFS's reaction to the local critics was to display their letters of protest in a prominent position in his garage windows.

That was a typically unorthodox Morgan approach, but the criticism itself was hardly unusual and this was the prevailing atmosphere into which HFS Morgan and Leslie Bacon launched their garage venture. The new Motor Car Act had become law little more than a year earlier, on 1 January 1904, but although it created some concessions, the British motorist was still severely restricted by rules. The Motor Car Act had raised the speed limit outside towns to 20mph but it had also introduced the numbering of cars, and, for the first time, driving licences, which made it considerably easier for the authorities to control the motorist; and control them they did.

But there were supporters, too. In 1905, just as Morgan was setting up shop, the Automobile Association had been founded, to look after the interests of the motorist. One of its policies was to combat the police's favourite sport of 'trapping' drivers, for alleged offences against the draconian speed limits of the day – the ones HFS Morgan himself had fallen foul of with his Eagle Tandem. In 1905, an English policeman, Sergeant Jarrett of Chertsey, had arrested so many motorists on charges of breaking the speed limit that he was promoted within the year to the rank of inspector.

Enthusiasms like those of the young HFS Morgan, therefore, were hardly the sort of thing expected from a son of the Church, let alone to be openly supported by a clerical father. And in the broader picture, HFS's move into the motor trade would have been seen as a pioneering move in the Britain of 1905, whatever his background.

By the time HFS had decided on his future course, the motor car was not only still a novelty in rural England, it was an object of suspicion and disapproval. Any kind of beginnings for a car-building culture in Britain had lagged far behind those of its European neighbours, although it would be fair to say that the motoring message had initially been quite slow to spread anywhere. Even in Germany, where the automobile had been invented, it created surprisingly little interest in its early days, and it says a lot about its early limitations that Karl Benz and his pioneering rival Gottlieb Daimler lived and worked within barely a hundred kilometres of each other in the middle of Germany, and clearly shared a common passion, but never actually met.

Daimler himself did not exactly throw his life into the new invention. He built his first motor car (in effect a four-seater horse carriage with the shafts removed and an engine and transmission fitted below the rear seats) and tested it at almost the same time as Benz's first experimental runs in 1886. After that, he did not build another car for three years, preferring to continue his earlier work with engines, putting them into boats, tramcars, fire pumping engines, electric generating plants, dirigible balloons – anything except cars. Benz, meanwhile, began to make a modest number of machines with commercial ambitions, and the first went on 'general' sale in 1888 – with remarkably little public interest. Ultimately, the industry would take root in France – all during HFS Morgan's childhood and adolescence.

It is hard to imagine that the news would have had any great impact in Stoke Lacy at the time, but HFS was six in 1887 when Karl Benz made his very first sale of a car (in fact the world's first sale of a petrol-engined car) – to Emile Roger, a bicycle maker from Paris who was the agent for Benz's stationary engines in France and who commissioned the vehicle while visiting Benz on business. In theory, from 1887 Benz would have sold anyone a copy, a further developed, wooden-wheeled version of the three-wheel Patent Motorwagen, but it seems that Roger was not only his first but also his only customer that year. Late in 1888, however, Benz drove one of his machines the two hundred miles or so from Mannheim to Munich and showed it at the International Exhibition, where, finally, it created a modicum of public interest. He began to sell a few more, and in 1892 he introduced a new model, his first four-wheeler, which he called the Viktoria, to sell alongside the original. By 1893 he had sold sixty-nine cars, but in 1894 he launched a third design which started to change the face of the business.

That was the Velo, and, quite importantly so far as Morgan's later design philosophy was concerned, it represented a new approach. What made the wire-wheeled, two-seater, four-wheel Benz Velo more popular than any of its predecessors was that it was smaller and lighter, as a consequence of which it had more performance and was easier to handle. It was also much less expensive, at 2,000 marks on its introduction in 1894, compared with 4,000 marks for the more stately four-wheeled Viktoria. That year, Benz sold sixty-seven cars, just two fewer than he had sold in the previous six years altogether, and the majority of them were Velos. Now, thanks largely to a lightweight car with improved performance, the experiment began to turn into a business.

In 1895, Benz sold one hundred and thirty-five cars, and the following year one hundred and eighty-one. In 1896 that was more than the combined output of every other car maker in the world. To add to Benz's influence, many of those other pioneer makes based their earliest models on the trend setting, lightweight Velo. Gottlieb Daimler, meanwhile, with partner and chief designer Wilhelm Maybach, had returned to the motoring arena in 1889 with a car reflecting, in its own way, the lighter, more manageable and more affordable direction of Benz's Velo. Called the Stahlradwagen, it took its name from its steel-spoked wheels, like the rest of the vehicle a more modern and elegant, lightweight construction than Daimler's original, horseless carriage – also substituting a steel frame for the old wooden carriage platform. Independently, both Benz and Daimler had recognised, as Morgan would shortly recognise himself, that unnecessary weight was an enemy of efficiency. It might not be totally irrelevant that the first car HFS drove in 1899 was that 3½hp Benz.

This, however, was still very much a period of experiment and innovation, of trial and (frequently) error. In the beginning, there was no fixed pattern for the automobile, and virtually every designer had his own preference. Hence three-wheelers with two wheels in front and one at the back, three-wheelers with the opposite configurations, four-wheelers, cars with engines in the front, engines in the middle, engines in the back, driven by chains, belts, gears, steered by wheels or tillers – all were perfectly acceptable. Through the late 1880s and into the 1890s nothing was yet regarded as conventional, so nothing, strictly speaking, was unconventional either. But in 1891 one convention was arrived at which would be something for HFS Morgan subtly to bend, but for the majority of the motor industry to follow for at least another seventy years, and in plenty of instances even through to today – the Système Panhard.

The layout itself was invented by Emile Levassor, who, with his close friend René Panhard, had built his first car in 1890. Still experimenting, they looked at most of the things other designers had tried, including putting the engine at the back, before they attempted something no one had consider-ed before. In 1891 they put their vee-twin engine at the front, under a box-like *capot*, or bonnet. Where other designers mounted their engines sideways to keep the driveline simple, Levassor set his with its crankshaft running front to rear, which meant he had to incorporate a bevel gear arrangement to turn the drive through 90 degrees to turn the wheels, but it also gave him the option of using bigger, more powerful engines without too many changes. Behind the engine he installed a friction clutch, controlled by a foot pedal, and in place of the smooth and simple but generally unreliable sliding belts he put a three-speed sliding-pinion gearbox, with changes controlled by a lever. The gears were not actually in a box, but once that had been added the whole layout was recognisably 'modern', except that final drive, as with most cars of the day, was by chains to the rear wheels.

Levassor said of his arrangement, notably the noisy but effective sliding-pinion gears, *'c'est brutale, mais ça marche'* – 'it's crude, but it works' – and it worked well enough for virtually all rear drive cars to follow the layout even up to today. And aside from having only three wheels and, in the early days, no sliding-pinion gearbox, even HFS Morgan's designs would broadly follow the Système Panhard.

By the time that convention was established, Karl Benz's Parisian agent and first car customer had become the world's biggest car importer, and in 1897 he sold nearly three hundred and fifty Benzs in France, which made France the company's biggest export market. By 1898, Britain had bought a total of around two hundred Benzs, making it the second largest market – but it had recently produced, for the first time, a competitor of its own.

For the first decade of the motor age, Britain had been content to rely almost exclusively on imported machines such as the Benz; not until a new British Daimler company was set up by entrepreneur HJ Lawson in 1896 were the first cars built commercially in Britain, a full decade after Benz's pioneering run and years after automobiles were in commercial production in Germany, France, and even America. Only thirteen years later, HFS Morgan would be a car builder himself, but in the year the British industry was officially born, he was only fifteen and still at school.

He would not have seen much of it first hand, either around home, at Marlborough, in Crystal Palace or in Swindon. When the motor industry did start to evolve in Britain, it had strong connections with the cycle industry, so the new motor makers largely located themselves like the cycle makers, in the industrial Midlands of England, particularly around Coventry. Britain's bicycle boom of the mid-1890s funded some of the earliest moves into motor car manufacture, before that boom was ended by the import of cheaper, mass-produced bicycles from the USA. Daimler founder HJ Lawson was among those who made his fortune from bicycles. He was also one of those who foundered early in the motor industry's history, losing that fortune and with it control of the Daimler company early on – by around 1897 – as the bicycle bubble burst.

At the turn of the century, France was the world's biggest car producer, building some 4,800 cars in 1900, while Germany, in second place, built barely eight hundred. Britain was way behind and in the same year built only about one hundred and fifty cars, which is an indicator of the point to which the domestic industry had evolved by the time the young railway apprentice HFS Morgan began to take notice of its products, even to drive them.

In the few years immediately before Morgan and Leslie Bacon set up their business, Britain's biggest car builder had been Wolseley, a make which became one of Morgan's first agencies when the Garage opened for business in 1905. As a car maker, Wolseley itself was less than five years old at the time, and it too had come via the bicycle trail, if only indirectly. Wolseley's original business had been making sheep-shearing equipment, first in Australia in the late 1870s and by the start of the 1880s in England. By 1895 it was established in the heart of British engineering country, Birmingham, and was also, almost inevitably, making bicycle parts and some complete bicycles.

Its general manager was Herbert Austin, who, like Morgan and another famous motoring patriarch, WO Bentley, should have been apprenticed to the railways – in the case of both Austin and Bentley, with the Great Northern Railway, in Doncaster. Unlike Bentley and Morgan, however, Austin never took up his place with the railways. The son of a Buckinghamshire farm worker who had moved to Yorkshire as farm bailiff for Earl Fitzwilliam, Herbert was sidetracked, aged eighteen (and fifteen years Morgan's senior), to Australia with his uncle. There, the ex-Rotherham grammar school and Bampton Commercial College student worked in an engineering workshop in Melbourne and later for a company making the sheep-shearing equipment designed by Frederick Wolseley.

When he returned to England, Austin went to Wolseley's Birmingham factory as works manager and in 1896 developed two cars, an experimental two-cylinder model for himself, and another with which, in the same year, he persuaded Wolseley to start plans for car manufacture. Both Austin's designs were three-wheelers, the first Morgan-like with twin front wheels, the second with twin rear wheels. Just one example of the two-seater Wolseley Autocar Number 1 was made before Austin designed a four-wheeler replacement in 1899, and with it laid the foundations for Wolseley's success, from 1901 under the ownership of Vickers. Austin himself, however, fell out with the management and in 1905 he walked out, to found the Austin Motor Co. It was the same year in which HFS Morgan opened his Malvern Link Garage. Within twenty years Austin would have a major, life-threatening influence on Morgan's products.

By the time HFS left the railway, the motor industry was spreading around the world, but in Britain, much of the establishment did not like the new invention at all and had not made its early life easy. Before 1896 and the introduction of the 12mph speed limit which HFS broke with his Eagle Tandem, pioneer British motorists had been subject to the notorious Red Flag Act of 1865, which was originally meant for 'road locomotives' but was still in force when the automobile was born. It restricted maximum speeds to 4mph, and originally required any self-propelled road vehicle to be preceded by an attendant carrying a red flag, or at night a red lantern. The part of the Act specifically requiring a flag or a light was actually repealed in 1878, but the bit about the walking attendant was not, and nor was the absurd speed limit. Furthermore, the police, diligently upholding the prejudices of the horse-owning establishment, left the motorist in no doubt that the law would be enforced – holding the automobile back in Britain, both literally and metaphorically, at a crucial time.

Fortunately, approaching the turn of the century there was also evidence that the attitude of the establishment to the motoring movement might at last be softening, and that the motor car was beginning to find some powerful allies. In 1895 Britain's first motoring magazine, *The Autocar*, was launched, to promote the cause of motoring and to lobby for motorists' rights. In 1896, in the biggest concession yet to the British motorist, a new Locomotives on Highways Act came into effect, raising the speed limit for vehicles under 1½ tons to 12mph and dropping the ludicrous requirement for a walking attendant. On 14 November 1896, the day that the old Act was repealed the newly formed Motor Car Club celebrated with an 'Emancipation Day' run from London to Brighton; it is still commemorated every year.

In January 1904 the next Act, raising the speed limit to 20mph, came into effect, and early in 1905, just a few weeks before HFS Morgan applied for planning permission for what became his Garage, the Motor Show had brought large crowds to London's Olympia exhibition centre. This was Britain's biggest automobile exhibition so far, and it was opened on 11 February by the Prime Minister, Arthur Balfour, with the

Foreign Secretary Lord Lansdowne also in attendance. Even their presence was overshadowed, however, by that of the Prince and Princess of Wales, who arrived early for a preview of the exhibits, and added to the feeling that the British upper class's prejudice against the motorist might at last be starting to wane.

Over the next couple of years in Malvern, HFS Morgan would meet with plenty of criticism but he would also sell a respectable number of cars. The bus service would prove to be rather short-lived, but in spite of the early objectors, Morgan & Co. Garage and Motor Works proved overall to be a successful business, and its success allowed HFS Morgan to embark on the next stage of his career, as a motor manufacturer.

3 The HFS Years

S OME YEARS AGO, Soichiro Honda, the late founder of the Honda Motor Company, reviewed the way the motor industry was restructuring itself, with smaller marques being swallowed up to become part of ever bigger conglomerates, usually to become niche badges in a global business increasingly dominated by mergers and economies of scale. Mr Honda, another of that increasingly rare breed with his own name over the door, observed – accurately as it would turn out – that eventually there would only be half a dozen major car makers in the world. Then after a pause he added, 'and Morgan'.

What Mr Honda had recognised in Morgan was not so much the idiosyncracy that many outsiders see, but rather its core values. And he recognised them as core values that the industry in general, in its own quite different way, was actually striving for – a strong marque identity serving an enthusiastic niche market, flexible development and production methods with low capital investment levels, and an order book which, with very rare past exceptions, comfortably supported available production volumes.

A large part of the reason why Morgan is still in business today is that those basic principles, established by HFS Morgan and his father HG at the outset of the twentieth century, on the one hand for building cars and on the other for running a company, have survived virtually intact through Morgan's ninety-year history as a car maker. But HFS's early path from garage proprietor to car manufacturer, supported by his father's wealth and business brain, had more to do with his love for designing and building things for his own use than it did with any commercial ideas. In the first instance he claims he never intended to build his three-wheeler Runabout commercially; in the beginning he was not even thinking of three wheels, only two.

At about the same time as he had set up the Garage, HFS acquired a 7hp vee-twin Peugeot engine, with the idea of building a motor cycle, even though he claimed forty years later that he never cared for motor cycles. Gradually the idea evolved of creating something a little more elaborate, in effect a vehicle somewhere between the exposed simplicity of a motor cycle and the heavier complexity of a motor car. Although he did not know it at the time, HFS was planning what the motoring fraternity of the day was soon to know as the 'cyclecar'.

Across Europe, several similar ideas were beginning to take shape at much the same time as HFS Morgan was building his first experimental car, which was ready for testing in 1909. Its design was an indication of the direction one branch of motoring had been moving in even in the few years since Morgan and Leslie Bacon had opened their Garage. In the early days, rooted in Europe and European social structures, motor cars had been expensive and exclusive, playthings and status symbols for the very rich. They were the only ones who could afford not only to buy an automobile but to keep it supplied with fuel, oil and notoriously short-lived tyres; the only ones wealthy enough to employ the skilled help to keep it working, and not least to hire someone to drive it – something few gentlemen and even fewer ladies would dream of doing themselves.

Even when the Morgan Garage opened in 1905, that was still largely the status quo, but the motor car would never have survived if that had been maintained. Its real future depended on a social – led by a manufacturing – revolution.

The melting pot was America, where no class system existed to stifle novelty as it did in Europe, and where the automobile was soon recognised for its potential as a hardworking servant rather than as a mere fashion accessory. It was America that really democratised the motor car. In America by the turn of the century, with the likes of the

Curved Dash Oldsmobile, the automobile was approaching true mass production, leading to very low prices, whereas in Europe it was still assembled by old-fashioned methods and still expensive enough to be mainly for the upper classes. The notion of a car for the ordinary man would eventually be championed principally by one man, Henry Ford, but before Ford created the big, powerful but incredibly cheap Model T, low-priced motoring for the masses went through several earlier phases.

In Britain, the wheels ground very slowly. The first petrol-engined vehicle built in England, and the only one built during the 1880s, was a single-seater, three-wheeler, but not one like Morgan's would eventually be. Edward Butler's extraordinary looking Petrol Cycle, built in Greenwich in 1888, was of much heavier construction; the driver was perched between the two front wheels, with the single rear wheel tucked up close behind, and driven directly by a two-cylinder engine which virtually filled the space between. Its name, the Petrol Cycle, marked the first time the word 'petrol' was used, several years before it was taken up as a trade name. The Petrol Cycle also had some design features well ahead of its time, including a spray carburettor, mechanically operated inlet valves, and Ackerman steering geometry for the first time ever on a petrol-engined vehicle.

It had some crude features, too, like the lack of a clutch, which meant the only way to start it was to lift the rear wheel on rollers and the only way to stop it completely was to stop the engine. And clever as the steering geometry was, the mechanism was operated not even by a tiller but by two levers. Yet Butler's Petrol Cycle worked quite well, and it might have gone into commercial production but for the restrictions placed on it by both the notorious Red Flag legislation and public antagonism.

What it did do was pre-date the first type of lower priced vehicle to become popular in the early days, the kind of thing represented by HFS Morgan's Eagle Tandem, and known generically as tricars. The tricar was similar to a motor cycle with two wheels at the front and room for one, occasionally two, passengers between them – or as several people observed, 'nearest the accident'. The driver sat behind, on a motor cycle-type saddle, steering either by handlebars, tiller or occasionally (as with the Eagle) a wheel. They began their brief flurry of popularity around the time HFS bought his Tandem in 1902, and there were several English makes including some, such as Humber, Lagonda and Riley, which would go on to greater things.

The main problems with tricars were that they were too heavy, in many cases too complicated, offered none of the weather (or accident) protection of a small car, and were not particularly cheap. By about 1907 tricars were being over-taken by the next big thing – light cars. These were 'proper' cars, including Riley and Humber, from manufacturers who had grown out of the tricar business.

Humber was another from the ranks of the bicycle manufacturers turned car makers, and after their tricar (or forecar) in 1903 they introduced the first of the really popular British light cars, the 5hp, single-cylinder, front-engined, four-wheel Humberette. Although it only had a brief produc-tion life, its success laid the foundations for a major expan-sion of Humber's car making operations. And then came 1910, 'the year of the Cyclecar', marking the birth of a new kind of ultra-light, ultra-cheap and popular vehicle – heralded by the press as 'The New Motoring'.

The cyclecar could be described as the missing link between the motor cycle and sidecar and the light car. It was more car than motor cycle, more motor cycle than light car, and combined the best elements of both. It was light and simple, inexpensive to buy and run, and it was also reason-ably comfortable and at least partly protected against the elements. The quality of the designs varied as much as the quality of the manufacturers, from the most fanciful and fragile to some very clever thinking, and HFS emerged among the cleverest of the clever thinkers.

His first self-built motor vehicle would be a three-wheeler, and he started work on it in 1908, putting himself at the start of the cyclecar movement. Perversely for someone schooled in the heavy engineering of the railways, HFS's idea was to build the lightest, simplest vehicle possible. By giving an unusually good power-to-weight ratio, he would gain maxi-mum performance and economy from modest power – a useful balance for a vehicle which he expected to use mostly around his home base, where the roads were narrow and the hills steep. And from another angle, reducing the number of components to an absolute minimum would make the vehicle simple to build, while minimising costs.

Those were the guidelines to which HFS would adhere throughout his working life, and which his son Peter and grandson Charles carry through to the present day; the roots, in fact, of the entire Morgan design and manufacturing philosophy.

The first three-wheeler was HFS Morgan's own concept, but he had collaborators in completing the design and turning it into a functioning prototype. Malvern and Malvern Link, being in a rural location with precious little engineering activity, offered no easy access to the machining or metal-working facilities HFS now needed, but he saw a way around that. For some time he had been friendly with the Stephenson-Peach brothers, both of whom shared his interest in building mechanical things; their father, William Stephenson-Peach, was the engineering master at nearby Malvern College. Stephenson-Peach, who was also the grandson of the railway pioneer George Stephenson, not only worked with HFS Morgan on the design of his first prototype but allowed HFS spare-time access to the engineering facilities at both Malvern College and Repton School, near Derby, where Mr Stephenson-Peach had also taught before moving to Malvern. Those facilities were sufficient to help HFS build his first car.

He built it with William Stephenson-Peach over a period of about twelve months during 1908 and 1909, as an after-hours project outside his business commitments. In the first instance, as HFS later admitted, he built it for his own personal transport and enjoyment rather than with any thoughts of future commercial production.

HFS began testing the three-wheeler as soon as it was complete; it was registered for the road in June 1910, with the local registration number CJ 743. Many years later, its creator wrote about its beginnings in *The Light Car* magazine: 'I drove the machine, which I called the Morgan Runabout, in 1909. It was most successful, due to its rigid frame, independent front-wheel suspension and light weight; the power-to-weight ratio was about 90hp per ton, and it was, therefore, more than capable of holding its own with any car on the road at that time.

'Although I had made the Runabout for my own use, and had no intention in the first place of marketing it, the car caused such favourable comment wherever it was seen that I decided to make a few, and with the enthusiastic support of my father [the Rev. Prebendary HG Morgan] who risked some capital in the venture, I bought a few machine tools, enlarged the garage and started to manufacture.

'I obtained my first patent for the design in 1910, my patent agents being Stanley, Popplewell and Co., of Chancery Lane [London]. It is interesting to recall, that the patent drawings were produced by a bright youth [then articled to Mr Stanley] who is now the famous Sir John Black, of Standards.' Remember that name.

In November 1910, HFS took space at the Motor Cycle Show in Olympia, London. He showed two three-wheeler Runabouts on the Morgan stand, both tiller-steered, single-seaters, both powered by air-cooled JAP motor cycle-type engines – a 4hp single-cylinder and an 8hp vee-twin. They created considerable interest and favourable comment in the motor cycle and motor car press, if less from potential customers. *The Motor Cycle* reported, 'A three-wheeled runabout which should on no account be missed by visitors to the show is the Morgan in the annexe. It is very lightly constructed throughout, and some very clever notions have been adopted in its design. It is low and rakish looking; so low, in fact, that it might with its present sized wheels prove unsuitable for use in districts where the roads are very rough . . .' The Morgan's subsequent record in trials soon disproved that particular theory.

The Car, meanwhile, said, 'As our report of last week demonstrated, quite a number of the motor-cycle exhibits have a strong flavour of the car about them. One conspicuous example of this was the Morgan Runabout; in fact, this machine is a motor-car for one person, and he is not invited to balance himself on two wheels either . . .'

A contemporary cartoon showed a front view of the single-cylinder show car with a bowler-hatted gentleman at the tiller and several people peering into the car, with the caption, 'The Morgan Runabout has a fascination for every kind of road user'.

HFS must have enjoyed the publicity. In that same *Light Car* story in the late 1940s, although mistakenly quoting the year as 1911, he noted, 'they created quite a stir!'. He went on, however, to put his finger on the first Runabout's biggest problem, when he added, 'They were too novel to attract many orders [about thirty materialized], but I found there would be a very much larger demand for a two-seater model.'

Other sources suggest different levels of interest for the Runabout in 1910, one quoting as few as four orders taken directly at the show, but all ultimately agreeing that the total number was around thirty. So while still running the Garage in partnership with Leslie Bacon, but agreeing to drop the controversial bus service, HFS created space to start a small assembly area, and with his father's help bought the tools to build a series of cars. It seems the capital HG Morgan risked in the venture, including the original Garage building and the first changes to it, amounted to about £3,000, which paid mainly, as HFS said, for more space, tools and some new machinery, plus a stationary engine to power it. That left a little working capital, which was supplemented by the early deposits. Although the first moves towards becoming a motor manufacturer were not particularly auspicious, by the end of 1910 it was certainly HFS's intention to offer cars for sale. Both he and Leslie Bacon had been disappointed with the original response, but one brighter part of the episode was that, soon after the 1910 show, HFS was contacted by Richard Burbridge, managing director of Harrods in London (itself quite a new venture at the time), and he wanted to take an agency – the first – for Morgan's Runabouts. The first car ever shown in Harrods' windows was a Morgan three-wheeler.

It is likely, therefore, that whatever the balance of orders between the show and the quoted thirty orders in total, many of them may have come from the top people's store. It also seems that Burbridge, possibly by way of further deposits, injected capital into the venture, and this association as much as anything else prompted HFS to carry on. Sadly, he would be carrying on alone, because Leslie Bacon now decided the risk was too great and the two parted company.

Crucially at this time, Morgan decided first to build the cars that had been ordered and then to pursue his theory that a two-seater would be more saleable.

He also put into practice another theory, that competition success could earn favourable publicity, and that such publicity would surely sell more cars. On Boxing Day 1910, only a month after the Morgan had made its first public appearance at the show, HFS entered the first running of the London–Exter Trial with his tiller-steered, 8hp JAP vee-twin powered single-seater, and, in spite of wet weather and generally abysmal roads, he won a gold medal for a penalty-free performance. It was the start of the remarkable Morgan competition history outlined in Chapter 4, and of much increased public interest in the cars. It played one major part in kick-starting Morgan's success as a car maker. The other was that option of two seats.

That came at the next Olympia Motor Cycle Show, in November 1911, and the turnaround in Morgan fortunes from just a year earlier was extraordinary. The two-seater had been available for some months before the show, and sales were already starting to improve, but that was nothing compared to what happened after the 1911 show. Two months earlier, in September 1911, *Motor Cycling* magazine had run a full test of one of the earliest two-seaters under the headline 'Speed & Sport on a Morgan Runabout'. Morgan could not have asked for a better advertisement.

It began with a dig at those who were still not convinced by three-wheelers in general, then went on to praise the Morgan to the skies. 'Critics may criticise from lack of experience, and croakers may croak in sheer ignorance as to the decadence of the three-wheeler, but let them take one of the latest patterns of these machines for a lengthy test on the road, and they will quickly alter their opinions. After a trial of the 8hp twin Morgan Runabout, both as a single- and double-seater, extending over 300 miles, I must admit that it is one of the sportiest and speediest little vehicles that I have ever driven. Indeed, barring a TT motor-bicycle and a 75hp Bianchi car, I have never been on anything that gave me more pleasure on the road.'

It continued, 'Let us consider this little three-wheel marvel, which only weighs 3cwt and yet goes like a 40hp car. This is the proposition we have to face. The outfit costs something like £90, and when compared with a two-speed motor-bicycle, possesses the following advantages. It is weatherproof; by which I mean that one does not have to wear grotesque looking overalls in which to drive it. It is comfortable, for one does not sit perched up on a saddle, but instead there is a comfortable seat with a back for one to lean against. Then there is more room for luggage than there is on the motor-bicycle. It is quite a simple matter to take a really big suit case on the Morgan instead of sending it by train, as I should have been obliged to do had I travelled on the motor-bicycle. These are just a few of the points on which the three-wheeler scores.'

And then a very important comment in relation to Morgan's future plans: 'Regarding the machine as a two-seater, there can be no two opinions. Let anyone try the Morgan, and I'll warrant that he will foresake the unmechanical side-car for ever. Though the seating accommodation is rather cramped ... the positions of the driver and his passenger are comfortable and sociable. Both are protected from the weather, whilst the no-trouble shaft and chain transmission system and wheel steering are other points to win favour with the erstwhile side-carist. One thing more and I will progress with the tale of my adventures on the road. I found that the machine ran more sweetly with two up than when driven solo. The back wheel held the road better, the vibration was less at speed, and the whole affair appeared to run more steadily. The weight of the passenger seemed to bring with it a sobering effect on this festive little car.'

After several days and several hundreds of miles, the adventure, as reported by 'Platinum', reached its climax not far from where the Morgan was built. 'From Worcester we travelled to Malvern, intending to deliver up the machine to its rightful owners, but as we still had an hour or so to spare we resolved to attempt a bold thing. We planned to climb to the very summit of the Worcestershire Beacon, which rears its head to a height of nearly 1,400 feet above sea level. We decided to make the ascent via Red Lion bank, which ascends suddenly and steeply from the centre of Malvern, the average gradient for the first 300 yards being something like 1-in-5.

Before taking the sharp right-angled bend I dropped into low gear – clutch out and gear in in half a second – and then the long climb began.

'Remember that we had never stopped the engine all the way from Ludlow, and realize the severity of the task before the Morgan. Pumping up pressure and oiling the engine occupied us during the first stretch of the climb as we wound our way up past the donkey sheds, up and up, being met here and there by astonished spectators, who looked on at the little three-wheeled marvel with gaping eyes. Up and up, round a hair-pin bend, now up the other flank of the hill we ground our way. Higher and higher, with the view below us ever widening to our gaze. Now on one side a sheer drop for hundreds of feet and on the other the grassy slope of the mountain still stretching upwards. The road sadly degenerated, and we travelled on a narrow grass track round and round to the summit. Narrower and more rocky became the track until at last the Beacon itself came into sight a hundred feet above us. We pumped up pressure, and in a few moments were at the summit, the feat accomplished non-stop with two passengers and a hot engine; a magnificent tribute to the three-wheeled Morgan.'

In 1911 such an achievement was the motoring equivalent of a 200mph supercar test today. Hillclimbing was still one of the greatest challenges in motoring, for big and small cars, and what 'Platinum' had achieved with the Morgan was spectacular.

But it was only one of a growing list of famous climbs for the little car – including first ascents of such famous challenges as Arkengarthdale Hill and Wass Bank in North Yorkshire, Bwlch-y-Groes in Pembrokeshire, South Wales, the Honister Pass in Devon, Edge Hill and Mow Cop in Staffordshire, and most famous of them all, the notorious Porlock Hill in Somerset – all these pioneering climbs glowingly reported in the press of the day, and all, with the competition successes, adding to Morgan's fast-growing reputation as an affordable and attractive little giant killer.

This time, when the two-seater Runabouts were exhibited at the Motor Cycle Show, Morgan were overwhelmed with orders, to the extent that HFS did not think he could cope: 'I showed several two-seaters at Olympia. They attracted a good deal of attention and with trade support, I obtained far more orders than I thought I could meet. I approached several large manufacturers and [luckily] they turned the proposition down, so, partly with the aid of deposits on orders, I bought machine tools, built some new workshops and, giving up my garage business, did my best to satisfy the demand.' Morgan was no longer a dabbler but a full-time car maker.

Efforts to find a production partner at this time perhaps showed that HFS was still thinking flexibly about Morgan's long-term future, but the unwillingness of another manufacturer to take him on was the first of several pivotal moments in the company's history. It gave HFS time to make the business work on his own terms, without having to wait for the agreement of another partner. Thereafter, he guarded that independence forcefully. Failure to find any bigger manufacturer to take on production did, however, present him with the immediate problem of fulfilling orders, so he began to look for smaller outside contractors to supply certain parts and processes. The design of the Runabout and its simplicity meant that it was possible to build mechanically complete rolling chassis and add the minimal bodywork and trim later. Bodies were initially bought in, but the Worcester Road garage still did the chassis building and the final assembly and trim, so it needed to get bigger.

Some of the pressure was coming from an area which had helped Morgan bring his business even this far – Harrods. In 1911 Harrods circulated a letter informing potential customers that they had been able 'to arrange for a slightly increased output from the Works and have the following machines to offer', going on to list the availability of seven Morgans of various kinds per month, with premiums payable over the purchase price depending on how soon delivery was needed, a foretaste, perhaps, of later waiting lists. The cars were to be sold on a first-come, first-served basis against a deposit of £30, and the circular went on, 'This letter is being sent by the same post to four hundred and twenty-six persons who have addressed enquiries to Messrs Morgan and Co or ourselves. We may add that we are the sole concessionaires and contract the whole output of Messrs Morgan and Co.'

By 1912, the problem was getting worse, and Harrods were becoming concerned about deliveries. In January 1912 they wrote to Morgan confirming 'a second order of fifty Runabouts' and enclosing a deposit of £520, while saying that future orders would be considered as and when. The letter was signed by Richard Burbridge (very much a Morgan supporter), but shortly afterwards he wrote to say that he was worried that Morgan were unable to meet some orders in time, which was not good either for his own store's reputation or for Morgan's.

So with more competition success and more favourable press reports bringing even more orders, HFS Morgan had little option but to commit himself further, which he did by taking two big steps. In April that year Harry Martin's Morgan won the first International Cyclecar Race at Brooklands, and more than a hundred orders were placed virtually on the spot. On 1 April 1912 the Morgan Motor Company was registered, with HFS Morgan as managing director and his father as chairman. It had a nominal capital of £100,000, divided into 500 A preference shares, 49,500 B preference shares and 50,000 ordinary shares, all of £1 each. The same nominal share structure would apply for the next fifty-three years, until the company was restructured in the mid-1960s following HFS Morgan's death. On formation, none of the taken up shares went outside the immediate family and HG set out to manage the company while HFS built the cars.

In July 1912 they applied for plannning permission to extend the Garage, which had now become the Morgan factory. As soon as permission was granted, new workshops were added on the land behind Chestnut Villa and the original Garage building, as well as some less permanent sheds in what used to be the Garage yard, for final assembly and painting, all of which was done by hand. Also behind Chestnut Villa and next to the factory site, in Redland Road, was the recently opened sheet-metal workshop of Edmund Langley, who was now contracted to produce fuel tanks and make the panels to fit onto wooden body frames. Those were supplied by another local craftsman, William Clare, whose works were also nearby, in Worcester Road.

Almost fifty years later 'Platinum' remembered visiting the Morgan factory: '. . . there was a door in the house that led direct into a sort of garage, "the works", wherein Morgans in various stages of assembly were strewn about the floor. True there were machine tools, but most of the parts were made out in Birmingham. A scraggy figure by the name of [Alfie] Hales, in a bowler hat and with a prominent nose, was the works manager. Works managers always wore bowler hats in those days. Though his appearance belied it he was very good at his job of making things work and converting HFS's ideas into practical form, for I never discovered a drawing office, nor indeed a drawing and from what Peter Morgan, the son, told me recently, the drill was to invent and make the part first and then do the drawings. His father was apparently a genius in being able to make a thing cheaply and simply and also ensure that it did the job efficiently at the same time. A mere handful of locals constituted the works force and the output was only a few machines weekly, but as time went on it rose to fifty.'

By some standards it was a small undertaking, but in a way the Morgan Motor Company in its earliest days was a microcosm of the mainstream motor industry in the Midlands, a central operation surrounded by its own specialist suppliers. The big differences were that Morgan was independent, adaptable and compact.

1912 saw three further landmarks in Morgan history: one commercial, one personal, one sporting. In 1907, at a dance in the Grand Hotel in Malvern, HFS Morgan had met Hilda Ruth Day, younger daughter of another local clergyman, the Reverend Archibald Day, vicar of St Matthias Church, Malvern Link, and twenty years old in 1907, about six years HFS's junior. In June 1912 Ruth Day and HFS were married and the report in the local newspaper was headed 'A Cycle-Car Wedding'.

The accompanying photograph shows Ruth and HFS in a white two-seater, with the same registration as the prototype – CJ 743. Both bride and groom are wearing all-white motoring clothes, Ruth with a huge white hat held down by a white scarf and the two of them with a rug over their knees as they prepared to leave for a honeymoon in Wales, before coming back to Malvern Link and setting up home in Chestnut Villa. In years to come, they would share many thousands of miles in the three-wheeler Morgans, as Ruth became HFS's regular companion in trials and even races, although she never competed alone. She was also an enthusiastic driver of other makes of car, and over the years her transport included a Fiat, an Alvis 12/50, an Alvis Speed 20 and a Hillman Minx.

Standing behind them in the wedding day picture is Ruth's father, waistcoated and bowler-hatted, and with him is Geoffrey Day, her brother. Geoffrey, a tutor and Fellow of Emmanuel College, Cambridge, became a regular competitor in Morgans, including passengering HFS in the famous 1913 French Cyclecar Grand Prix, and he became a director of the company. He might have become an even closer part of the family had circumstances been different. Another picture, taken outside the rectory at Stoke Lacy, shows most of the Morgan family, all in cars. HG and his wife Florence are in the front of their large tourer, HG at the wheel, with HFS's sisters Dorothy and Freida, and Freida's future husband George Hinings in the back. They tower above two two-seater Runabouts. In the middle car are HFS's other sister Ethel, by this time Ethel Cowpland, and her husband William. In the Runabout in the foreground, again with the famous registration CJ 743 (but now in dark paint with a huge acetylene-powered searchlight on its bonnet, for the winter trials of December 1912) are HFS and Ruth.

The second major landmark of 1912 was the launch of a new magazine, *The Cyclecar*, aimed specifically at owners and would-be owners of what was now becoming a major motoring phenomenon, and of which the Morgan was acknowledged as one of the finest. The magazine was edited by W Gordon McMinnies, an Oxford graduate, a successful motor cycle racer and formerly a journalist with *Motor Cycling* magazine, where he wrote under the pen name 'Platinum' – the same 'Platinum' who had been so enthusiastic about the two-seater Morgan in that September 1911 road test.

In 1910, echoing the earliest Morgans, a new breed of car was appearing, with similar credentials (not always as well executed as Morgan's) of light weight and simplicity. Falling somewhere between a motor cycle and a light car, they were dubbed cyclecars, and the Morgan was counted among them. In 1910, before the Morgan appeared at the Olympia Show,

McMinnies saw the pioneering French Bédélia in Paris and suggested to his publisher, Arthur Armstrong of the Temple Press, that there was a market for a magazine to cover this new type of car. Armstrong needed some persuading, but when the first issue of *The Cyclecar* appeared, priced 1d, in November 1912 to coincide with that year's Motor Cycle Show it took off like a rocket, selling more than 100,000 copies. Its first one hundred and forty-eight-page issue described more than thirty vehicles recognised as cyclecars and a few that were really light cars. They included three-wheelers and four-wheelers, the cheapest of them being the Rollo Monocar at 70 guineas, while Morgan prices started at 85 guineas, a price that would be prominent and unchanging in Morgan advertising until the First World War.

In Britain there were other advantages to cyclecar motoring beyond a low initial price, and, in the case of cars like the Morgan, surprising performance. There were tax advantages in an era when tax was assessed on a complicated and largely meaningless 'horsepower rating' based mainly on piston area and devised by the RAC. The scale was introduced in 1910, and as well as being (not entirely coincidentally) one reason behind the sudden rush of small cars and cyclecars, it also explained why so many engines of the day had such a long piston stroke – to create capacity without paying taxes for it, even though it made for some very underachieving designs.

The system survived until 1920, when the Motor Car Act taxed cars in Britain at £1 per RAC horsepower. Ironically, that penalised the cheap but large capacity Ford Model T and damaged its sales quite badly, while helping cars that were not nearly as good. It was also complicated by the provisos that any car built before 1914 paid only half the horsepower rate, and (with typically British middle-class thinking) cars used solely for taking servants to church or voters to the polling station paid no tax at all. On the other hand, it paved the way for the next generation of small British cars, led by the Austin Seven and leading to £100 cars from Morris, Ford and several others, which would present Morgan with a life-threatening challenge in the mid-1920s.

Still, low taxes were a large part of what made the cyclecar attractive, and for Morgan there was a further advantage, because three-wheelers, of whatever capacity, paid a much reduced annual road tax of only £4, rather than the sliding scale for four wheels, which went up again in 1938 to £1 5s per horsepower; this was not abolished until 1948, when a flat rate tax, initially of £10, was introduced.

The £4 three-wheeler tax was a big Morgan selling point, one frequently emphasised in the company's advertising, and it was an advantage which lasted for most of the three-wheeler's life, even beyond the Second World War – although in the end losing it also became one of the final nails in the three-wheeler's coffin.

The £4 tax of the golden days is probably the reason why HFS Morgan abandoned his early experiments with a four-wheeler car. He had just started to look at the possibility of a four-wheeler in 1913. Drawings were submitted to the Patent Office in September 1914 and a patent was granted in May 1915. The drawings show a chassis layout identical to the three-wheeler's in almost every respect but for a crossmember ahead of the bevel box carrying swinging arms and quarter elliptic springs at its outer ends. Those in turn carry a simple rear axle, driven by the usual twin-speed, twin-chain arrangement, with two conventionally spaced wheels but no differential. It was narrower than the three-wheeler's wide front end, because HFS reasoned that four wheels would make it more stable even with narrower tracks. A twin-cylinder prototype car was built and by 1914 was running. Geoffrey Day was photographed in it, in front of a mixed group of half a dozen cars of which only one other was a Morgan (Dorothy's three-wheeler), at Stoke Lacy early in that year. A suggestion in *The Cyclecar* that it would appear in a Cycle Car Club hillclimb at the end of June was, however, wide of the mark.

Something that HFS wrote in 1911 suggests that his early thoughts on the possibility of a four-wheeler were influenced not only by a fondness for three wheels but by the tax situation, the cost of development, and not least the potential for competition. 'As one who has had a good deal of practical experience with light cars, from an Eagle Tandem in 1901 to the Morgan Runabout in 1911, may I venture to offer a suggestion? It is very easy to plan such vehicles on paper, but somehow what satisfies even an expert on paper often proves dismally disappointing on the road. In completing the little Runabout which bears my name, and with which I had the good fortune to secure a gold medal in the London-to-Exeter trial, I have had again and again to discard ideas which, when put into concrete form, proved unsatisfactory. A good sized scrapheap is a painful reminder of past mistakes! To complete a light vehicle which will stand the road test (not merely a trial run) is an expensive amusement, and anyone who attempts it must be prepared for disappointments. For the same reasons a wise purchaser will not give much attention to any car until it has proved itself equal to a severe road test. I share your regret that quadricycles (I have almost completed one myself) are barred from some trials, but there is, no doubt, considerable difficulty in drawing a dividing line between such vehicles and light cars. Other tests, however, such as the London and Exeter run, are open to them. The designers of quadricycles have a more serious grievance in the fact that these cheap machines are taxed equally with more expensive cars, and the taxation is borne by those who can ill afford it. Strong representations in regard to the injustice of the taxation, and its possible effect upon a growing industry, should be made to the Chancellor of the Exchequer.'

Whether such representations and a successful outcome might have led Morgan to build a production four-wheeler even before the First World War is a fascinating question, but in the end, while he tried a four-cylinder, 1-litre Dorman engine in another four-wheeler prototype, HFS decided, for now, to stay with the configuration he knew best.

At this point there was really no reason for him to do anything else. As part of its launch promotions, *The Cyclecar* had offered a valuable and prestigious silver cup, the Cyclecar Trophy, for the person holding the one-hour distance record for a cyclecar by the end of the year. The record changed hands several times, until at Brooklands late in November, HFS Morgan, with Ruth and his father offering support, fell just 640 yards short of putting sixty miles into the hour. HFS's achievement won him the Trophy and brought a flood of orders for the Runabout. That and the earlier achievements led to a third Morgan landmark in 1912: the first year that the enterprise was registered as the Morgan Motor Company was also the first year that HFS Morgan's car-building operation made a profit – of £1,314 – on three-wheelers alone.

That was followed up by profits of £4,797 in 1913 – the year in which McMinnies won the French Cycle Car Grand Prix at Amiens and gave the Morgan even greater fame – and by further profits of £10,450 in 1914. With one blip in 1919 for the extraordinary circumstances at the end of the war, the company would make manufacturing profits every year until 1931, when a string of eight out of ten losing years marked the final decline of the three-wheeler and one of the most difficult periods in the company's history as a car maker, although, as ever, those later trading losses would be more than offset by the company's substantial investment earnings.

In spite of the approaching war, 1914 had been easily Morgan's best year to date, and they had sold almost 1,000 cars, including exports to France, where the Grand Prix win had done untold good, to Russia, India and both North and South America. As well as the sporting successes and favourable press reports, clever advertising had played its part in the sales boom, and Morgan's early advertising, encouraged by HG, was primarily about the Runabout's performances in trials, racing and record breaking.

In January 1912 the headline read THE MORGAN RUNABOUT. NOT AN EXPERIMENT BUT A WELL-TRIED MACHINE, and it listed 'Some Successes to Date' – a gold medal in HFS's first-ever venture, the London to Exeter (and back) Trial of Christmas 1910, certificates of various kinds in the ACU's winter, spring and autumn Quarterly Trials of 1911, non-stop awards and a gold medal in Inter-Club Runs and the Inter-Club Championship, and a special gold medal in the MCC's London to Edinburgh (and back) Trial of 1911. Early in 1912, under the headline THE PICK OF THE BUNCH, Morgan trumpeted 'The First Cycle Car Race held, and run off at Brooklands, 27 March, resulted in a great triumph for the MORGAN RUNABOUT, driven by Mr Harry Martin. SEVEN STARTED – RESULT, MORGAN 1ST, at an average speed of 57mph.' In December that year they applauded

HFS's Cyclecar Trophy winning efforts: 'Once Again – The
MORGAN RUNABOUT has broken the well-contested HOUR
RECORD covering a distance of 59 miles 1120 yards.'

The advertisement, carrying a picture of HFS in the
vee-twin single-seater with the caption 'Only a Few Yards
Short of SIXTY MILES IN THE HOUR', explained what that
meant to the potential Morgan buyer: 'ON THE ROAD the
MORGAN RUNABOUT has been more successful than any
other cyclecar, gaining HIGHEST AWARDS in all the principal events of the year. Price 85 guineas – "Cheapest and Best"
– For full particulars and list of Agents, Apply MORGAN
MOTOR CO, MALVERN.'

There were indeed agents by that time, and they were
doing well out of Morgan's success, too. As well as that first
agency, Harrods, by late 1912 they included another famous
London store, Whiteleys, and car-only agents such as R James
in Sheffield and TA King of the City Garage, Hereford, sole
agent for the Morgan's home county.

As well as being chairman of the company the Prebendary
HG Morgan looked after its finances, and in 1913 the
company was able to declare 'a 100 per cent dividend'. A
handwritten letter in the archives, addressed to the Garage
and dated 21 February, reads, 'Despite the prophecies of
those whose mission it is to decry the Cyclecar, the above
dividend [100 per cent] has been declared by the Morgan
Motor Co. Evidently there is money in the Cyclecar business
for the makers of really good Cyclecars like the Morgan, and
not only for the makers, but for the agents too.'

'Incidentally,' it continues, 'the Morgan dividend provides
a striking answer to the question "Do competitions pay?".
The Morgan Co. has always supported both reliability trials
and races with an apparent disregard for the expenses
entailed, while the firms who have economised by holding
aloof from competitions are mostly heading for Queer Street
and the official Receiver.' And following some comment in
the correspondence columns of The Light Car and Cyclecar,
the Morgan Motor Co. Ltd responded, 'In reply to the letters
of "Growler" and Mr Bushnell, may we say that we are able
to pay a large dividend because, unlike some firms, we did
not start with a large capital and spend a great part of it in

unsuccessful experiments? We made our experiments first and then started with a very modest capital. We do not intend to give away trade secrets, but we may say that, if we adopted Mr Bushnell's suggestions and sold our cars at £60, we should lose about £30,000 in 1914! We should not benefit from the increased demand, for we are selling all that we can possibly produce. This seems to show that the public are satisfied that they get fair value for their money.' Some eighty years later, in 1990, when John Harvey-Jones visited Morgan for the BBC TV business programme *Troubleshooter*, his suggestions were to increase production dramatically and to put prices up substantially. Morgan were no more convinced by his arguments than they had been by 'Growler's' or Mr Bushnell's and on both occasions they stuck to their guns.

Small as it was and specialised as its products were, Morgan were now one of the most successful car makers in Britain. In 1914, not counting the runaway leader Ford, who built more than 8,300 Model Ts in Britain alone, the biggest output was Wolseley's, with some 3,000 cars, followed by Rover with about 2,000. Morgan had built close to 1,000 cars in 1913, and by 1914, with extended works, were in a position to build closer to 1,500, and sell all of them, until the war cut production right back. In the same year, Morris built just over 900 of its new Cowley, while Austin built fewer than 550 cars in total. Morgan's profits in 1913 and 1914 of £4,797 and £10,450 respectively also compared rather favourably with Morris's £5,400 and £15,000 in the same two years – especially if the relative sizes of the two undertakings were taken into account. Both were a long way behind industry leaders such as BSA and Rover, but their six-figure earnings reflected interests in bicycles, motor cycles and armaments as well as just cars, and all looked modest against Ford's massive $25 million.

There were other developments in 1913, including the launch of the Morgan Commercial Carrier, which was based on the Standard Runabout, with a rear pick-up-type box which could be removed to allow the car to be used as a passenger carrier. And there was a report in the press in 1913 about an even stranger Morgan than that. 'The Morgan Motor Company,' it said, 'has received an inquiry for a four-wheeled machine with a track of five feet, to run on the rails in India for the inspection of the line. It is probable that such a machine will be supplied, in which case it should achieve some terrific speeds. The Auto-Cycle Union will not recognize them as records!'

It was clear from all this that Morgan's expansion had to continue. Before the 1913 Motor Cycle Show, the local newspaper's preview reported that Morgan now had about seventy employees and would shortly employ one hundred. It referred also to negotiations for a new factory site, which it suggested was vital to the expansion of the company. After the show the local newspaper reported again. Morgan had taken more than seven hundred orders. The company now had more than fifty agents, and several of them had already sold all the cars they had contracted for during the show. Morgan, the report said, finally had to start declining further orders until they had finished the new works extensions.

That was one of the first references to the greenfield site at the opposite end of Pickersleigh Road from Chestnut Villa and the original garage-turned-factory. The land originally belonged to a local landlord, Lord Beauchamp, and in November 1913 Morgan arranged to purchase two acres of it, with a frontage of 240 feet – along what became Pickersleigh Avenue. Morgan immediately applied for planning permission and drew up plans with the local builder for the first of the buildings that still comprise the factory today, and which in 1914 would become the body finishing, upholstery and painting shops.

In the first instance, the Pickersleigh Road site would act as an annexe to the Worcester Road works, and it started a tradition of part-finished Morgans being transported between stages of the building process. Today they only need to be wheeled across the yard; in 1914 the chassis were taken from one site to the other, complete rolling chassis built in Worcester Road going to Pickersleigh Road for bodies (also built in Worcester Road and transported down to Pickersleigh Road), paint and trim, then back to Worcester Road for despatch. And then as now, while it may have seemed like an unneccessarily complicated way of doing things, it worked, and doing it this way allowed Morgan to grow gradually, without the need for so much investment at any one time that they had to resort to borrowing, which they never did.

Early in 1914 there was a 'motoring rally' in Great Malvern, and a picture in the local newspaper shows an AA man directing Dorothy Morgan and her father, the Prebendary HG, into the arena, HG smiling broadly in flat cap and tweeds. The paper reported 'a large turnout', and the accompanying picture shows a mix of motor cycles, cars and not surprisingly several Morgans. But the locals were not always so jolly. It seems there was still some dissension about noisy, smelly motor cars being manufactured in this small, essentially rural community and about the expansion of the works at Pickersleigh Road. But the Morgans, both father and son, were adept at dealing with such problems, as can be gathered from a letter sent on behalf of the Morgan Motor Co. Ltd in June 1914 to the Editor of the *Malvern Gazette*, after the council had announced plans to buy a plot of land adjacent to the Morgan site, for a rather different use.

The letter from Morgan read, 'Sir, – It is proposed to purchase a piece of land from Lord Beauchamp for the purpose of a burial ground for Malvern Link.

'The land adjoins our new workshops, and before it is purchased it may be well to consider the conditions of the purchase. We do not wish that complaints should be raised afterwards. The land will adjoin our new works. It will be quite impossible for us to stop work during the time that funerals are held, and the testing of machines, etc, will undoubtedly affect the solemnity of the service. The new burial ground will be approached over a narrow right of way, ten feet, on our property, over which cars, railway wagons, etc, will also pass. A road will have to be made at considerable expense, and as it will be over our land, and we and the public have an equal right to it when it is made, whereas we are in no way bound to maintain it. The land is outside the Malvern Urban District, and is in another parish.

'We wish to make these facts quite clear before further steps are taken, so that no blame can be attached to us afterwards. We purchased with the land the right to use it for a motor factory, and our buildings will extend to the extreme limits of our part of the property. The cemetry will, in fact, be a kind of backyard to our motor factory, we venture to think an unsuitable site for the purpose.'

Needless to say, the council did not proceed with its planned purchase, and the land today is a recreation ground rather than a cemetry. Morgan, on the other hand, did proceed with their plans for the expansion of the buildings on their own site, as well as continuing to improve the buildings at Worcester Road, which in later days included the machine shop, chassis brazing and assembly shops, the body-building shop (comprising carpenters' and sheet metal areas), and a repair shop for customers' cars.

Quite soon after the first Pickersleigh Road buildings were completed, however, and just as the system was starting to work, everything was thrown back into a state of uncertainty by the outbreak of war in August 1914. It did not bring an immediate halt to car production, but it left Morgan with a considerable amount of rethinking to do. Like Henry Ford, HFS was a pacifist, but he and his father were anxious that his company contribute to the war effort, and his thoughts are revealed in considerable quantities of wartime correspondence to the motor and motor cycle press. Much of it shows deep frustration with bureaucracy.

Towards the end of 1915, criticising plans for how profits would be taxed after the war, HFS revealed how loss of production was affecting the company. 'Is it intended,' he asked, 'that "profits divided after the war" should include profits included in the balance sheet of the year, but earned before the outbreak of war – even in cases where the war has entailed a direct loss? The firm which I represent has suffered heavily by the war, but it may be taxed heavily on "war profits". Our profit in 1911 was nil; in 1912, £1,314; in 1913, £4,797; in 1914, £10,450. The profits to be distributed after the war, in December 1914 [as a matter of fact they were invested in war loan] amounted to £7,455 in excess of the average profits of the three preceding years. But since the war profits have actually declined. In July 1914, our receipts were £6,089; in September they had fallen to £1,133. Since then they have recovered somewhat, but the first six months of 1915 show a decrease of nearly £13,000 as compared with the corresponding months of 1914. No doubt the same hardship would be inflicted on many others if the excess is calculated on the year's trading and not on the period of the war.'

The application for the patent for the Morgan four-wheeler had been filed in September 1914 soon after war was declared, and was granted in May 1915, but it would be another twenty-one years before a four-wheeled Morgan went into production. By 1915, Morgan had other priorities, finally switching most of their efforts from the much-reduced trickle of cars to government work, mainly making shells and other munitions while still building a few cars, including a prototype for a military model, which had three seats, one of them a rearward-facing passenger ahead of the usual one. It had very simple wooden bodywork, with a flat platform on the front for mounting a machine gun.

There was considerable military activity around the Malvern area during the war, with a number of camps, including those of the 16th Service Battalion Royal Works Regiment at Malvern, the Queen's Own Hussars on Malvern Link Common, and the 13th Pioneer Batallion the Glosters, who were visited by the Prime Minister, Lloyd George, in June 1915.

With the supply of new cars severely restricted by the war, second-hand cars – not least Morgans – were in great demand, often by army officers. A snippet from one late wartime magazine noted, 'A cyclecar is not yet worth its weight in gold, but we notice that two diamond rings, a typewriter, a gramophone and records and a two-speed Douglas motor cycle were recently offered in exchange for a Morgan . . .'

From 1916, the supply of petrol was restricted to those who needed it for work of national importance, and the restrictions were not lifted until 1919. That gave Morgan one of its main wartime advertising themes (and they continued to advertise more or less throughout the war) – economy. In June 1915 one advertisement was headed 'THE MORGAN RUNABOUT IS THE Car of Economy' and claimed '60 Miles per Hour, 60 Miles per Gallon'. In 1917 it was 'Use less petrol!', and 'The Morgan Runabout averages 50–60 miles per gallon'. There were advertisements depicting soldiers home on leave enjoying their Morgan with the family, including one in November 1915 showing the officer at the wheel, his wife and four children crammed into a two-seater with the line, 'See how happy they are on The Morgan Runabout – All Morgan Owners Are The Same'. The other side of the coin was the notice in the same month announcing, 'Up to the present we have not increased the price of our cars since the commencement of the war, but in consequence of the great rise in prices of all materials we are now reluctantly compelled to announce a rise in price of 5 per cent on all models . . .'

At much the same time as the petrol restrictions, from September 1916 the manufacture of cars and motor cycles was officially prohibited, except for military use and only where that was to satisfy orders already in place before the prohibition. HG Morgan was not impressed by that policy and argued that all it did (although not necessarily for Morgan) was to tie up stock and make factories idle. Nonetheless, between the reduced number of cars being produced and the increased amount of war work, Morgan showed a profit of £6,133 in 1916, the best it would achieve between its 1914 record and the start of the post-war recovery in 1920.

A lighter episode occurred in the early days of the war, when the local council set up a Motor Cars Committee to consider the purchase of two vehicles for official use. It shows just how little understood and how generally mistrusted the automobile was in Malvern, even then. Early in 1915 the council invited tenders for four-cylinder, two-seater light cars. They received twenty-two, ranging in price from £110 to £205 per vehicle and decided to buy two Swifts at £190 each. Before the decision was ratified, someone asked why they had chosen the Swifts; no one really knew, and could only say that Swifts had a good reputation. The committee asked whether they should seek something less expensive, such as a three-wheel light car, and after some discussion Mr Hayes said he had in mind something like a runabout, and 'strongly suggested that a local car should be obtained', adding that 'he knew of nothing that had ever been brought before the council that the public cared so little about'. Mr Foster seconded the suggestion and 'thought they ought to consider whether the Morgan Runabout would not be best under the circumstances. He knew they were economical and their speed was unrivalled. They could not run a small car with anything like the economy they could the runabout.'

Another member, Mr Santler, said, 'it seemed very strange that they should choose a car without expert advice. If they bought a horse they got the best advice they could, and now they had cars chosen by three gentlemen who had never driven a motor car.'

Two weeks later, the committee reported that it had further considered the matter and now recommended that two 'Malvernia' light cars be purchased, for £175 each, less a discount of 2½ per cent, from Messrs C Santler and Co. Ltd!

The Santlers were, in fact, Malvern Link's first car manu-facturers, preceding even Morgan. In the 1880s, Santler and Co. were based in Quest Hills Road, Malvern, and apparently making high-wheeler 'ordinary' bicycles and tricycles in a tiny factory of wooden and brick-built sheds, with just three or four workers. They were quite successful, and moved to the more up-market Northumberland Works, in Howsell Road, Malvern Link, the same road that ran alongside Morgan's original garage. There, before the turn of the century, Santler were building 'Malvernia' bicycles, and then they began to build 'Malvernia' cars.

According to one local guide book, Santler built the first four-wheeled internal-combustion engined car in Britain, in 1889, although it is hard to find another source that credits them with the same achievement or even lists the make. The origins of the claim seem to be that one of the Santler brothers worked briefly for Karl Benz, and presumably either modified one of his cars or copied one of his designs. Still, there is a picture of TC and WR Santler outside the Northum-berland Works in January 1904, sitting on a four-wheel Santler car claimed to date from around 1901, and sur-rounded by the entire company staff – eight men in all, including the Santlers themselves.

The council's motoring plans now descended to near farce. Explaining the decision to buy Santler's Malvernias, the chairman explained that he believed 'in some quarters the council had been rather blamed in the first place for getting motors at all, and in the second place for not getting the cheapest. There were motors to be had for less money than they proposed to give, but he wanted to emphasise with regard to the first point that the ratepayers did not seem to understand that the Council were almost driven to do something in this direction, for the reason that the question was mixed up with the market. They were giving up the market, and in doing so they gave up two stalls for horses there. These horses would have to be taken down to the sewerage farm every night, or stabling found for them in the town. They were useful in the town early in the morning,' he said, 'and late at night, and it was important that they should be suitably stabled in the neighbourhood. The trap horse used by the Gas Engineer was practically done for, and the other horse was over twenty years old.'

The chairman said that by having motor cars and putting the horses into the trap coachhouse, two stalls would be available for the horses from the market. Mr Prosser said the committee had chosen the Malvernia cars as 'fairly workman-like vehicles'. They had seen in this war how motor traction had taken the place of horses. As far as he knew, motor cars were the nearest approximation to being in two places at once, and that was what they wanted for their officials.

Now came the question of why not two Morgan Run-abouts, for only £169 the pair, and someone else thought they had agreed earlier on one Swift and one Malvernia. Mr Parker thought that before the Malvernias were purchased they should know how many of them were on the road at the present time. If they wanted to buy a steamroller they went to one of the best makers, and got a good article, not to a local maker. They knew nothing about these cars. He believed there were very few on the road, but as a council they ought to buy cars with a name and a reputation. He voted against.

It went on. Eventually they were told there were probably five Santler cars on the road in the neighbourhood, but that was all the Santler cars that were on the road anywhere. Mr Foster suggested the purchase of two Morgan Runabouts. 'It was the type of machine that was wanted for Malvern. They could pass him, get up the hills, were economical, the petrol consumed was low, there were only three tyres, and it would serve admirably. He had seen titled people riding in them.'

Dr Cowan retorted that, on a point of order, the Morgan Runabout is not a car'. Mr Swann said he had seen the Morgan in action and it seemed most suitable for the purpose. 'Possibly in some minds there might be a sentimental objection to a person holding an official position riding in a runabout, but that was absurd.' They decided on one Runabout.

There is a footnote to all this, a cutting in the Morgan archive of a letter from *Country Life* magazine in April 1987. It reads: 'Your "Town and Country" reference to Britain's first car, the Santler, brings to mind the last car that the Santler brothers built, in the early 1920s. This was known as the "Rushabout", and achieved some notoriety for being an almost exact copy of the very successful Morgan Runabout, also built in Malvern.

'Such mechanical differences as there were did not compare favourably with the Morgan, and it is not surprising that only about a dozen were made, in spite of the sales leaflet showing a handwritten price reduction of £165 to £85, which was the price of a Morgan. The commercial thinking behind this venture, hopeless from the start, may have stemmed from some sort of antagonism by Charlie Santler to the Morgan Motor Company. He may have been unduly sensitive by nature, as he claimed to have helped Benz to design his first car of 1885, and left him only because he was not given any credit for it.' There is a picture of the Rushabout. It is the Morgan's identical twin.

Just to think of Morgan quietly passing the war doing government work and waiting for the time when they could build cars in real numbers again is to underestimate how closely they watched the industrial situation and how seriously they took their business. By 1916, when they made a further loan of £3,500, the Morgan Motor Company Ltd had subscribed £20,000 to the War Loan scheme, but HG Morgan was very critical of the rules on the import of American cars to Britain, and especially Henry Ford's position. He wrote to *The Light Car*, 'I have read with the greatest interest your article on the English motor industry. The position is by no means a simple one. For the present, no restrictions on the import of American cars would have much effect. Probably every manufacturer can dispose of every car that he can make.

'Unfortunately he can make few cars, or none at all, because he is engaged on Government work, or because he finds it impossible to obtain materials. None of us who have Government work would wish to put it aside for other (and certainly more profitable) business; nor would a tariff on American products help us to obtain materials. The shortage of English cars is giving the American a huge advertisement. His cars are seen everywhere. It is possible that this may not, in the end, give him any great advantage. When war ceases there will be, I believe, an enormous demand for English cars from those who are at present unable to get them, not only in England but also in the Colonies and abroad. On the other hand, the trade will, to a certain extent, be disorganised. Skilled workmen who have been employed on other work, will have lost something of their old skill. Wages will be higher. Machinery will have to be re-adapted. The cost of production will be increased, and this will make it more difficult to meet competition. Certainly a Government which concerns itself with home industries (we have never had one yet) will take this into consideration. A tariff must come sooner or later, and the sooner, perhaps, the better. If it does not at present help the manufacturer, it will do something to keep English money from finding its way to America, or to relieve the English taxpayer.

'There is, I think, no question that, even if there had been no war, we should have had to meet a considerable "invasion". There would have been a large demand for the high-powered, low-priced car. The English car of this kind cannot hope to compete with the American until we can adopt American methods; and we cannot adopt American methods until we are sure of the American market. The English and Colonial demand is, by itself, insufficient, even with a prohibitive tariff. On the other hand, English manufacturers can, and do, produce cars which appeal to many who will not look at the American product. And here, I think, lies the best hope of the English manufacturer. He must produce something which the American cannot, or does not, produce

– something unique of its kind, or which has the advantage (which the American car does not possess) of perfect workmanship and finish. It is said that the Rolls-Royce finds purchasers in America itself. This is because the Rolls-Royce has a European reputation. We have sent some of our Runabouts across the Atlantic, because the Americans have not yet produced a light car so speedy and sporting as the Morgan.

'We have got to face competition, and we shall not do it by a blind and futile imitation of America, but by the perfection of English workmanship and inventiveness. A tariff will certainly be helpful, and it will come, but our industry will find salvation by producing something which America cannot produce, or cannot produce well.'

For a country churchman, HG Morgan's knowledge and understanding of the motor industry, world politics, economics and engineering were extraordinary.

The tariff did follow, and would have a major, long-term effect on the British industry. At the start of the First World War, America was neutral and could send its ships to Britain without the threat of attack. America, which mostly meant Ford, sent cars, to the extent that Britain's motor manufacturers officially asked the government to do something to restrict the imports. In September 1915, turning away from Britain's long-held policy of free trade, the Chancellor of the Exchequer, Reginald McKenna, imposed a 33⅓ per cent duty on a range of imported goods, including motor cars. It also applied to car components, and that hurt Ford's English operation, which essentially meant assembling Model Ts in Manchester from crated American components. Then in 1916 American imports were further restricted because shipping space was needed for more essential supplies, but at just about the same time Ford, following a suggestion from David Lloyd George, decided to set up a tractor factory – which could later be used to build cars – in Cork, in neutral Ireland. The factory did not reach full production until after the war but attracted criticism from some British manufacturers.

HG Morgan was critical of the way Henry Ford had manipulated the system, and wrote again to *The Light Car*: 'Your article on the Ford concession is most timely, and I trust that it will be widely read. The concession allows Ford to employ American capital in a manner in which British capital cannot be used. Apart from the restrictions on the investment of English capital, the Englishman have put their capital into War Loan. Mr Ford has lent this country nothing, and he did his best to prevent others from lending. He is allowed to use his capital in unfair competition with the British manufacturer. Ford is allowed to import thousands of tons of machinery and plant in ships which are sorely needed to import foodstuffs. No doubt he will be allowed to import petrol, which may not be imported for business in England. He will bring over thousands of workmen from America, and employ Irishmen who refuse to fight for their country. English workmen are not available for English firms. The result of this concession is that Ford will obtain for the time being a huge monopoly for agricultural machinery which it will be very difficult for the English manufacturer to break. And to what advantage? Even Ford cannot run up and equip an enormous factory in a few months. His enterprise will not enable the British farmer to grow a bushel more wheat this year or next. The Cork factory will not help us to win the war.

'Again, it is true that the concession does not give the American the right to manufacture motor cars till the end of the war. But as you point out, it does give him every facility to prepare in advance to manufacture. While English companies are devoting their energies to the production of munitions, the Ford company is devoting its energies to the manufacture of motors. It is obvious what the position will be at the end of the war. Ford is a keen businessman, with no great respect (as he has shown) for British interests. We may expect him to make use of the opportunities which the British Government has conceded.

'Another disquieting feature in the business is that Ford's agent in England has been made head of the new department for providing agricultural machinery. In some cases (as in my own county) his deputies are motor agents. In this way Ford will obtain (quite legitimately) a vast amount of information and experience, which will not be at the disposal of the British manufacturer. We may be quite sure that he will make the best possible use of it for his own advantage.

'No doubt the Government has acted from the best of motives; unfortunately, the best motives are sometimes most shortsighted. The Ford concession is, unquestionably, simply preferential treatment for the foreigner.'

The patriotism was clear but so was HG's eye to the future of his son's business, and in truth he also reflected the views of many other people in the British industry.

Morgan enjoyed other publicity during the conflict, thanks to some of the people who used their cars. Just as MGs and the like would be popular with RAF pilots in the Second World War, the Morgan was equally popular with their forebears in the Royal Flying Corps. RFC officer Captain Jack Woodhouse MC drove a water-cooled vee-twin Grand Prix model; Lieutenant Robinson VC, who had shot down a Zeppelin airship early in the war, drove a Morgan with an aeroplane mascot on its radiator cap; while most famous of all, the fighter ace, Captain Albert Ball, vc, dso, mc also drove, and was widely photographed in, a disc-wheeled, water-cooled MAG-engined Grand Prix. Captain Ball, sadly, did not survive the war, and there were many from Malvern who had joined the forces who did not return, including Ruth Morgan's brother Geoffrey Day. But those who did come back to Morgan found plenty of work waiting.

The Armistice was signed on 11 November 1918, and, once the war had ended, while Santler were making their handful of Runabout copies, Morgan were soon back up to full speed making the real thing. Exactly two weeks after Armistice Day, Morgan published their first post-war advertisement. It read, 'Not "Marking Time" But "Making Progress"'. It announced, 'An early return to something like the "Good Old Times". Holders of stocks of petrol or petrol licences,' it said, 'can use their Morgans for any purposes within 30 miles of their home or business address from the 1st December. In January, licences will be issued to all applicants, and motoring for any purpose will then become possible for all who have and can obtain cars. Those who require delivery of a "Morgan" in the near future should place their names on the list AT ONCE.'

When the war ended, Morgan was publicly calling on the government to base the return of men from miltary service to industry on the employment which could be made available for them, arguing that the motor industry had orders but not materials, and was still restricted by the need for anyone who did want to buy a new car to have a permit to purchase it. Morgan believed that making materials available to satisfy orders, and removing the restrictions, would create such employment. During the war, the company had acquired quite a lot more machinery, mostly at very low prices subsidised by the government, to fulfil official contracts, and most of it could be adapted to working on the cars. In fact some of that machinery is still working today.

Morgan were also in good financial shape, having worked very hard throughout the war on the government's fixed-profits terms, which were acknowledged as being quite generous. Once again, HFS was able to finance the next stage of expansion entirely from reserves, with no borrowing. The only sour note soon after the war ended was an accident which cost HFS Morgan two fingers from his right hand. Walking through the Worcester Road works one day in April 1919, he slipped on a patch of grease, put his hand out to stop himself falling and pushed it into a spinning capstan lathe, damaging his hand badly enough to necessitate the amputation of two fingers.

Other than that unfortunate incident, from which HFS recovered quite quickly, things were going almost entirely his way. Morgan were just entering the most prolific period of car building in the company's history. In October 1919 the *Malvern Gazette* reported the opening of the new works, accompanied by a speech from HFS. Peter Morgan suspects this might have been quite a difficult moment for his father, who preferred to stay in the background. As Peter has described him, 'he was scrupulously fair in all his dealings with people – family, friends, employees, industry associates. Morgan people liked what they knew of him, but they didn't know him well because he was excessively shy. This reserve made the idea of speaking in public abhorrent to him, so he just wouldn't do it.' He did it for the opening of the new works, however, and he did it again at another party just a few weeks later, in the Worcester Road works, to celebrate the birth of another new Morgan – Peter himself.

* * *

The first shop built (the one nearest the road), which had originally been the body shop, now became the offices and parts stores, which is how it remains today. It was extended along what became Pickersleigh Avenue with a new chassis brazing shop, the original upholstery and painting shop next door being similarly lengthened to deal with chassis building and finishing. The two additional shops, running parallel to each other down the gentle slope to what would have been the cemetry, were the same full length as the newly extended original shops, and they were used as the trim shop and the painting shop, respectively, for bodies brought in from Worcester Road.

The *Malvern Gazette* recognised the new buildings as a major undertaking for the area: 'The new works comprise offices, stores, brazing, erecting, finishing, upholsterers', painting and varnishing shops. They cover 38,400 square feet and are lighted throughout by electricity. The machine shop, carpenters' and tinmen's shops remain in the old building near the Link Station. The total area of the works is over 50,000 feet and they are thoroughly equipped in every way. From forty to fifty Runabouts will be turned out weekly, and to judge by the number of orders received the supply will be inadequate to the demand. Mr Morgan is already contemplating further extensions. The work of erecting the buildings has been admirably carried out by Mr Wilesmith.'

After a potted history of the company and its sporting successes to date, it ended by presenting a rosy picture of Morgan's future: 'There are agents in almost every country in Europe for the Runabout. During the War the works were given over for the making of munitions, and the number of cars manufactured was, therefore, small. There are now over 5,000 orders on hand, which gives some idea of the size of the industry.'

Morgan was ready to take full advantage. The company was one of the first car makers in Britain to resume full-scale production after the war, not least because of HFS's philosophy of simple design. Relying on craftsmanship rather than a heavily mechanised production process meant that little setting up of machinery was required, and they could work with limited supplies of materials that the big car makers needed in huge quantities. HFS had formally promised during the war that, when it was all over, he would provide employment for his workers on their return, and he kept that promise. He also kept a promise to present every one of them with a sovereign, and on a more social note, as things returned to normal Mr and Mrs Morgan provided a fleet of charabancs to take the factory employees on a day out in the countryside, with a substantial lunch laid on en route.

There were practical problems in getting back to work, as HFS himself recorded, in part of a letter to *The Spectator*. He resented an earlier reference to 'exorbitant prices' and suggested that the price of cars compared to before the war had increased by less than 75 per cent, while, '. . . the cost of labour has increased 100 to 150 per cent, the cost of materials 100 to 300 per cent, the cost of machinery at least 150 per cent. In point of fact cars can be produced at the present prices only by improved methods of production and decreased overhead charges. Even so, the manufacturer must be content with a decreased profit. Many people are obsessed just now by those blessed words "massed production". But massed production requires a different demand, an unlimited supply of labour and materials, and a vast capital – Ford's is capitalized in tens of millions. The first exists at present, but it is doubtful if it will continue in the future; the second may be found in the future, but it is certainly not to be found at present. As to the last, the manufacturer can hardly be blamed if he hesitates to risk millions (should he happen to possess them) on a mere possibility of success.'

In practical terms, the major problems Morgan had in the early days were shortage of engines ('if we could get twenty a week from one well-known English manufacturer at the present time,' he said, 'we would be delighted') and a shortage of tyres. But in business terms, for a while after the opening of the new works at least, HFS was more concerned that he had expanded too far, another sign, perhaps, of the cautious approach that had served him well so far. Soon enough, it was clear that he need not have worried. The company, even with its new factory, had to work virtually flat out now, because the immediate post-war period – in fact the five years up to 1923 – would be boom years for the Morgan. In those heady days, in spite of the difficulties, profits ranged from £28,573 in 1920 to a record £40,851 in 1923 when some 2,300 three-wheelers were sold as the world returned to something like normality, and the motor car in general finally became more widely accepted.

The car was also more widely coveted by now. The First World War had been the first mechanised war, and by the end of it the motor car was playing a major part in it. Hundreds of thousands of people who had never had any contact at all with motor vehicles before the war had become familiar with them. Tens of thousands had learned to drive, and having fought for and won their freedom, they now wanted to enjoy it; for more ordinary people than ever, that now included the desire to own a motor vehicle. If 'real' cars were still out of reach for most, cars like the Morgan were not.

Although Morgan had not made many cars in the later stages of the war they had not forgotten about them either, and when the fighting was over they were ready to launch new models that they had been working on during the conflict. The four-wheeler prototype had been quietly forgotten for now, but over the next couple of years they launched the sporty Aero and before that, most significantly given the way the market was developing, Morgan introduced the four-seater Family model.

Now a problem arose which would still be familiar to Morgan half a century later, as demand started to outstrip supply, although even at this stage the waiting list was measured in weeks rather than years. In 1920 Morgan had seventy-eight agents in Britain, including six in London, and others from Cornwall to Cumbria, as well as Scotland, Ireland, Wales, even the Isle of Wight. In December the company announced that between them the agents had taken bookings for all 1921's planned output; and a similar announcement was made the following year.

After the war there was demand for Morgans outside England, too, especially in France, where McMinnies' Grand Prix win of 1913 was still remembered. By 1920, Morgans were not only sold in France, they were built there as well, after Morgan granted a licence late in 1919 to his French agents Darmont et Badelogue, in Courbevoie, Seine, Paris, to manufacture the Darmont Morgan. Before long, Darmont were building several hundred cars a year, and they continued to build them until the market began to falter in the late 1920s. It was not only manufacturing capacity, however, that encouraged Morgan to grant the licence to Darmont; cars built in France also avoided the heavy duties which applied to imported vehicles.

But problems lay ahead. As the 1920s advanced, falling demand was a problem not only for Darmont but for Morgan in England, too, and it was inevitable, as the appeal of the cyclecar, even the few remaining good cyclecars, was presented with the challenge of Britain's most successful small car of the period, the Austin Seven.

The Seven, designed by former Wolseley man Sir Herbert Austin, was launched in 1922 and became to the British market what the Model T had been to America. Not that the Model T was not a big seller in Britain and just about everywhere else, but here its extraordinarily low purchase price was offset by Britain's peculiar tax system. The system that gave Morgan such an advantage presented the Model T with a serious penalty. The RAC horsepower rating on which the tax payable was calculated was based on the number of cylinders but also on the diameter of the cylinder bores, rather than on capacity. So British designs, even those with quite large engine capacities, used small bores and long strokes, and were horribly inefficient for it. The Model T, designed in America where there was no such artificial restriction, had a big, lazy engine with big cylinder bores. Unfortunately, that gave what was otherwise the ideal 'people's car', the Model T, a British tax rating of 22hp – twice the rating (and twice the tax burden) of some British cars of more or less the same size but far higher price.

The Austin Seven, on the other hand, was taxed at just what its name said, 7hp, and although it was not nearly as powerful or roomy as the Model T, once you'd taken the tax factor into account it could rival it on price. And small as it was, it was well suited to British roads and towns, small British garages, and expensive British petrol. It was also – and this was the big catch for Morgan – a 'real' car for cyclecar prices.

Worse, the Austin Seven (which Herbert Austin had designed on the billiard table at his home, because his colleagues thought the idea for such a small car was ridiculous) soon spawned rivals, and the rivalry started a price war. It went on sale, with four cylinders, four wheels and four seats, for £165, fully equipped. At the time, the cheapest Morgan Runabout, the Standard, with two cylinders, three wheels and two seats, cost £150, while the cheapest four-seater Family, with air-cooled vee-twin, cost £180. To most people it mattered little that the Morgan would run rings round the Seven for outright performance, and soon the Morgan was in trouble.

That did not happen immediately, however: the public was not entirely convinced at first that the Seven was anything more than a toy, and in the early days it did not sell particularly well. Ironically, the Seven, echoing the Morgan's first steps, turned the corner with some unexpected sporting exploits, right on Morgan's own patch, at Brooklands. In 1922, pioneer aviator EC Gordon England, recuperating in hospital with a broken leg sustained in a flying accident, saw the Seven and decided, however unlikely it seemed to anyone else, that it would make a good competition car, or at least the basis for one. He suggested to Herbert Austin the possibility of attacking the 750cc class records at Brooklands, with a specially developed Austin Seven racer. After considerable argument, a highly sceptical Austin agreed to let him try. Winning a bet with Gordon England, Austin had the car built before the plaster came off his leg, and once Gordon England had set it up as he wanted it, he took his records, including a mile at 72mph and a half-mile at over 75mph. Now the Seven started to sell.

In doing so, it killed most of the cyclecars that had survived this far, but although it damaged Morgan sales quite badly, HFS did at least fight back. In July 1922 the advertised price of the Standard Runabout was reduced to £135 and the Family to £165, the same price as the Seven. By November the Runabout was being advertised at 'Prices from £128', with a point being made of the £4 tax rate, which even the Seven could not match.

The timing was interesting in that 1922 was also the year in which HFS decided again to extend the Pickersleigh Road works, with two more rows of buildings (bringing the total to six of the present-day seven) so that he could move the body-building process from Worcester Road and put the whole production operation on one site; since the war, bodies had been ferried from one location to another on a wartime surplus Crossley truck. The two additional sheds at the bottom of the slope became the sheet metal shop with despatch department attached, and the body shop with its own wood mill, next to a new, separate wood store in the yard. The seventh row, incidentally, which brought the factory up to more or less its present layout, was added in the early 1930s, by which time Pickersleigh Avenue really existed, although all that surrounded the site even at this time was open farm land. By 1923, Pickersleigh Road had developed to the extent that everything was on the one site, except the machine shop which stayed in the original works until 1929.

In 1923, before the Austin Seven effect kicked in properly, Morgan built that record run of 2,300 cars – all of them, of course, three-wheelers. At this point, most of the other cyclecars of the pre-war era had vanished without trace, and Morgan would have picked up sales from customers who still wanted something of the cyclecar's ilk, but really Morgan survived and continued to sell because the Runabouts were actually good cars in their own right. Competition apart, an economic depression existed throughout most of the 1920s, and faced with that and the Austin Seven threat, HFS responded not only by reducing prices but by improving his cars still further. Nonetheless, after the record year of 1923, profits fell dramatically through the rest of the 1920s, to £27,351 by 1924, £21,060 by 1927 and just £12,343 by 1929, by which time the number of three-wheelers built had fallen to barely 1,000 a year.

There were several engine options over the years, the main ones being JAP, MAG, Anzani, Blackburne, Matchless and Precision, partly reflecting different customer preferences and power outputs but mainly showing that Morgan was not totally dependent on one source of supply. There continued to be all sorts of minor bodywork variations, on a range which ran, depending on precise date, from the

Standard (or Standard Popular as it was later called) to the Sporting, the Aero, the Grand Prix, the De-Luxe and air- or water-cooled variants of the four-seater Family model.

A quick-release rear-wheel mounting appeared in 1921, front-wheel brakes were offered as an option in 1923, electric starting in 1924, and electric lights were standard by 1925, all aiming to keep the Morgan in touch with the Austin Seven. Front brakes were standard by 1927, and geared steering replaced the old, direct type, finally answering one of the biggest criticisms, that the steering was too heavy at low speeds.

HFS was, as ever, trying to take a longer-term view and even when the order books were still healthy, prices continued to fall. By 1924 they ranged from £110 for the Standard to £160 for the overhead-valve Aero 'racing model', which was very quick indeed, the one area where Morgan continued to score not only over the Seven but over all-comers in its price range. By the beginning of 1925, prices ran from £95, and that now included electric lights, while the most expensive Aero with 10–40hp vee-twin was down to £142, with the advertisements promising 'early delivery can now be given'. And still they fell: from £89 in 1926, £85 in 1928 with even the Family from £102, or as little as £92 if you did not want side screens, electric starter or a speedometer.

But, save for a last ditch effort in the summer of 1931 when a 'Great Price Reduction' saw the cheapest two-seater advertised at £75, that was about as low as they could go, especially as output was now falling dramatically. Morgan was sailing very close to the wind. Profits had slumped to £4,080 by 1930 and in 1931 went into the red for only the second time since the company had been founded, staying there for the rest of the 1930s and just into 1940. Three-wheeler sales in the same period fell to just a handful by the turn of the decade. Yet overall, Morgan, thanks mainly to the factory's low overheads and flexibility, and partly to the well-established investment of capital outside the car building business, were not actually losing money even though they were occasionally doing no better than breaking even. But for all that, it seems that even now HFS was not blinded by sentiment about the product; if he really had been losing significant amounts he would probably have stopped building the cars.

Now, too, in an attempt to resist the inevitable, Morgan advertisements were increasingly emphasising the combination of economy, performance and 'luxury'. In 1929 they were selling, 'The Comfort of the Car – but at motor-cycle cost! . . . A comparison of actual costs and standard of comfort will result in a decided victory for the Morgan Runabout – it is the happy medium between Motor Cycle and Light Car, providing the Economy of the first and the Comfort of the second. Morgan Prices range from £86 upwards; all models are Taxed only £4 (no more than a "combination" pays), the average consumption is 50mpg, speed 50mph, and the Morgan's reliability is a byword amongst owners. Write for the Book of the Morgan. Your local Agent can supply any model for small Deposit and Monthly Payments.'

If this was an aggressive marketing policy it had to be: Morgan were now in a price war not only with the Austin Seven but with several other new rivals. In 1931 Morris could offer the Morris Minor, a sparsely trimmed, open two-seater but a real four-wheel car nonetheless, for an industry-leading £100, and in 1932 HG Morgan's nemesis, Ford, introduced its first small car, the 8hp Model Y, aimed directly at Europe. That too was a real saloon, reasonably equipped and even cheaper than Austin's and Morris's small car equivalents, at only £120. The price fell again, to £115, in response to the launch of Morris's excellent little Eight at £118, and finally, in 1935, to the all-important figure of £100.

Morgan's three-wheelers simply could not compete against this kind of price cutting and new product launches from far bigger rivals; and export sales, with no benefit of tax reductions in most markets, were virtually non-existent at this stage. The sales graph was in free-fall. By 1929 production was down to 1,002, by 1934 659, a year later just 286, in 1937 137 three-wheelers, and in 1939 a mere 29. By then, Morgan had tried to stop the rot with a four-cylinder three-wheeler, the Ford 8hp-engined F-type, introduced in November 1933, and which, with its new engine layout and pressed steel chassis, was by far the biggest departure since the first Runabout of 1910. But that was not the answer either, and by now Morgan was set to make the biggest change of all.

In October 1935 the wood mill survived a fairly serious fire but Morgan were able to carry on production by buying components in from local sources, until in December, almost phoenix-like from the ashes, there emerged what HFS had been dabbling with since long before the First World War – the first Morgan four-wheeler, as a production model.

It was really a four-wheeled version of the F-type three-wheeler with its Z-section pressed-steel chassis, and it was known as the 4-4 (later written as 4/4), meaning four cylinders and four wheels. Production proper started in March 1936, with an 1122cc Coventry-Climax engine rather than the 933cc side-valve Ford of the prototype, and although demand started slowly it picked up rapidly – in a repeat of three-wheeler tradition – after the 4-4 had started to prove itself with the first of its competition outings. It appeared on Morgan's stand, number 86, at the Olympia Motor Show in London in October 1936, and in November 1936, the advertisement read, 'Morgan made their name in the three-wheeler world and captured every prize worth having in the competition world . . . and here is a four-wheeler four-cylinder model that bids fair to capture the plums in the sporting circles of the motor car world . . . already winner of the International Ulster Trophy Race – an 80mph Sports . . . and its price only £210.'

Very soon the 4-4 was also available as a four-seater and as a drophead coupé, and it began to pick up sales. By 1937 it was selling almost as many as the nearly dead three-wheeler – 130 compared with 137 examples; by 1939, before the war intervened, four wheels were outselling three almost ten-fold, at 234 to 29. Furthermore, the change from F-type to 4-4 had been a straightforward and relatively low cost exercise, vindicating yet again HFS's original low-tech, hand-build philosophy. The final blow for the three-wheeler actually turned out to be a non-event, but it did its damage anyway. In 1936 the British government announced that the tax advantages for three-wheelers would finally be abolished in 1937, and, although it did not happen until some time later, the effect was much the same anyway. For all the problems, though, Morgan did survive, when all their former cyclecar rivals were long gone.

The 4-4 was the last new Morgan that HFS's father HG Morgan would see. He died in November 1936, and among the many tributes to a very popular man was an obituary, headed, 'A Pioneer Passes Away'. It was published in *Light Car & Cyclecar* on 20 November and read, 'With deep regret, we have to record that the Rev. HG Morgan passed away on Tuesday November 10, at Stoke Lacy at the age of 84.

'The Rev HG Morgan was the father of Mr HFS Morgan, and he took a deep interest in the welfare of his son's business, of which he was chairman. In the earlier days of Morgan history, he nearly always attended events in which Morgans were showing their prowess; he is included in the group shown on the front cover picture of our issue dated December 4, 1912, taken at Brooklands on the occasion when Mr HFS Morgan set out on his epic run with the object of covering as many miles in the hour as possible and as a result of which "HFS" became the first holder of the Challenge Cup for the Brooklands 1500cc local hour record offered by this journal.

'The funeral took place at Stoke Lacy, near Bromyard, Herefordshire, last Saturday morning. We are asked to thank, on behalf of Mr HFS Morgan and Mr GH Goodall, all their friends in the trade who have so kindly written sympathizing with their loss.'

HG was buried in Stoke Lacy churchyard. The family plot is just inside the front gate, and as well as HG Morgan, the brown and grey granite headstones commemorate HFS, his wife Ruth, sister Dorothy and several other members of the family and in-laws. The gate itself was erected in June 1938 by HFS and his sisters and dedicated to their father.

When he died, HG left all his shares in Morgan to his son. In July 1937 at an Extraordinary General Meeting of the board at HFS's home in Maidenhead, a special resolution was passed revising the regulations of the company, and after his father's death HFS Morgan succeeded him as chairman of the company, while in 1938 former works manager George Goodall took up HFS's former role as managing director. Goodall had joined Morgan in the late 1920s, from the service department of another local garage, after the premature death of Alfie Hales, the 'scraggy figure ... in a bowler hat and with a prominent nose' remembered by McMinnies in the 1960s. But however he looked, Hales had done a fine job for Morgan virtually from the start of car production, and like HFS he had been popular around the factory.

Hales and Goodall were very different in one respect, which also shows something about the way the company was organised at the time. For many years Alfie Hales had been paid on what amounted to 'piece work', with a bonus related to the number of cars built, so he had a very personal interest in keeping production to a maximum. When George Goodall took over he did not want the same arrangement but preferred a fixed salary deal, showing a degree of understandable caution given the rather parlous state of the market in the 1930s. When he was moving up in the company, though, HG Morgan had clearly been anxious to offer him the best options, and a letter from HG to HFS about George Goodall's position – undated but apparently from sometime in 1934 – reveals a good deal about the company structure, the way the 'reserve' fund was earning money from investment, and HG's thoughts on the future.

'I have been thinking,' he wrote to HFS from Stoke Lacy, 'about Goodall. In the first place I have tried to get at the actual assets of the company and find from today's share list that the stocks held by reserve are worth something over £215,000. Each of the 100,000 shares therefore is worth about £2 if the company were wound up, and much more if it goes on with even moderate success.

'The interest on the reserve is £7715 gross, less tax (4/6d) £5980 net. The interest on the 7 per cent preference shares takes £3500, so there remains in the reserve enough to pay nearly 5 per cent on the ordinary shares if there were neither gain nor loss. Of course this year we cannot pay a dividend on the ordinary shares as there was a loss. On the other hand you got £2000 as managing director, which is included in the loss.

'Now I wonder if something like the following would do for Goodall. (1) make him a director; (2) give him 500 ordinary shares; (3) give him say two per cent of net profits.

'The benefits to Goodall would be numerous. If the company went down, he would still have five hundred shares worth £1,000 to him from the assets of the reserve. If the company prospered, making, for example, an annual profit of £5,000, the company would distribute about 12 per cent of the ordinary shares, giving him a £60 tax-free dividend, plus 2 per cent on the annual profits. Goodall would certainly benefit from the shares; they would give him a stake in the company if it survived, assets if it folded and (ever caring) something for him to leave in his will. And such an arrangement would not be to the detriment of Morgan.

'Of course,' HG, concluded, 'this is only a suggestion and the figures are only tentative – you could give more shares or less, a bigger percentage of profits or a smaller . . . it would be possible to give a percentage on sales, but I doubt if that is advisable – at times you might be selling at a loss . . .'

He went on to explain to HFS in some detail various payments over preceding months both to himself and to his sisters, under the terms of their trust arrangement. It all showed HG's very firm grasp of the financial niceties of the company, his recognition that there was always the possibility that it could be wound up if the trading position slipped any further, and his natural instinct to be fair to all parties.

At the Annual General Meeting in July 1937 George Goodall, Harry Jones (with the company since 1912 and latterly in charge of the service department) and Major WJC Kendall as company secretary joined the 'newly constituted board of directors', each with a salary of £50 per annum. As chairman and governing director HFS was paid £2,000 per annum, a figure which remained unchanged for many years, which with his share dividends and investment income gave him an extremely comfortable lifestyle.

George Goodall would remain at Morgan even longer than Alfie Hales and well into the 1950s. In later years, with Goodall as managing director it was no longer necessary for HFS (who had moved house, to Berkshire, soon after the war) to be so closely involved with the everyday running of the company, or even to be at the factory every day. Through to the mid-1950s, he appeared at least once a week.

Even with early signs of success for the 4-4, as the Second World War approached, Morgan found themselves in a weaker position than they had been prior to the first war.

This was as a result of the erosion of three-wheeler sales over the last fifteen years, a decade of manufacturing losses, and especially the catastrophic collapse in the last five years or so before the war. In some ways, the war may have been Morgan's saviour.

This time, car production stopped completely and immediately, and Morgan lost many of their workers, some to the forces, others taken away for other government manufacturing work. Eventually, after a slow start, Morgan moved over completely to government contracts, although they were only able to use parts of their own factory. They mainly made shell cases, aircraft undercarriages, and components for anti-aircraft guns, while some parts of the works were used simply for storage and others were sub-let to other government contractors. Flight Refuelling Ltd, pioneers of in-flight fuelling systems, took space, and later added more of their own, next to the factory and Pickersleigh Avenue, on another piece of land acquired from the Beauchamp estate which up to then had been farm land. The buildings they put up there would eventually become part of the Morgan factory.

One other company – the Standard Motor Company – took space at Pickersleigh Road, its presence more significant in the longer term, for a longstanding relationship with Morgan, and even in attempts to buy the company out. Standard were run by John Black, who, thirty years earlier had produced Morgan's first patent drawings. Just before the war, Morgan had built a handful of four-wheelers with special Standard engines, supplied in part thanks to Black's associations with HFS. Now Standard took over two of Morgan's buildings to manufacture aircraft carburettors. After this war it would take Morgan much longer to get back into production, but when it did, the links with the Standard Motor Company would be vital to their future.

But now, inevitably, HFS Morgan's long stewardship of the company he founded was reaching a new phase, as he passed official retirement age and began to step back from the everyday running of the company, if only in his own way.

In 1960, WG McMinnies, recalling his association with Morgan, remembered how HFS used to enjoy his motoring way beyond driving his own cars. 'In later years,' he said,

'HFS's love of power was manifested in his ownership of such fine cars as Rolls-Royce (Silver Ghost and Phantom II) and Bentley, in which he would convey his now largeish family to resorts at home and abroad. This was one way in which he indulged his wealth, for he was essentially a family man and regularly used to take them all for three holidays a year, winter sports and so on. Also his place at Cannon Hill, Bray, near Maidenhead, was a large and lovely home in spacious and parklike surroundings, very different from the cottage where he had started at Malvern Link. From this home at Bray he used to drive regularly every week to the works, not using the Rolls or Bentley but one of his own stock models on which he might be testing some improvement. On one occasion in the 1950s, quite by chance I met him haring along, huddled up in the little car and evidently thoroughly enjoying himself.'

Writing about his own life in the early 1950s, HFS summed up his time as a motor manufacturer with some affection: 'Looking back through the years,' he wrote, 'seeing both errors and triumphs in their correct perspective, I feel I have enjoyed it all; the motor trade has been – so far as I am concerned – a most interesting business.' For his remaining years in this 'interesting business', he would be able to enjoy himself in a different way; the late 1940s brought a new face to Pickersleigh Road as HFS was joined by a valuable new colleague, his son Peter.

4 Sporting Life

MOTOR SPORT of one kind or another has always been at the heart of the Morgan way of life, for both the company and the customer. Morgan's reputation started with HFS Morgan's exploits in sporting trials in his very first cars; alongside his philosophies of simple design, craft-based production and commercial independence, HFS had two firm beliefs, that success in motoring competition attracted positive publicity, and that positive publicity sold cars. It was a view shared by his father, who supported all HFS's sporting exploits with great enthusiasm, by HFS's son Peter, who competed in trials, rallies and races for almost all his motoring life, and is a view still shared by his grandson Charles, whose circuit racing experience with the Plus 8 in the 1980s and 1990s led directly to the new generation Morgan Aero 8 in 2000.

Over the course of ninety years, Morgan's motor sporting achievements have covered virtually every area of the sport, from trials and hillclimbing to rallies, racing and record breaking, and Morgans have been successful in all of them. They have also covered the world, from the hills around Malvern to Le Mans and America, not only with factory supported efforts but also through hundreds of private owners, forming a bond between company and customer that Peter Morgan believes lies at the heart of Morgan's continuing success. Like everything else to do with the company's finances, the motor sports activities have always been carefully managed to achieve maximum effect without resorting to overspending or borrowing; when the funds were not available to compete, the factory cars simply did not compete – in distinct contrast, as Charles Morgan often points out, to the profligacy which saw Bentley go bankrupt. This chapter does not offer a detailed history of Morgan's sporting achievements, rather an outline of some of those most important and of direct relevance to the fortunes of the business, but it does start with some of the earliest outings of the first single-seater Runabout, in 1910.

Surrounded by hills as Malvern is, one of the key requirements of any early car (or indeed motor cycle) was for it to be able to climb them, even when the roads involved were little more than rough tracks. Not all early vehicles were up to the task, but with its excellent power-to-weight ratio, compact size and considerable agility HFS's Runabout was just made for scrambling up hills, and one of its first public appearances was at what became one of England's most famous speed hillclimb venues, Shelsley Walsh. Shelsley is not far from Malvern, a few miles north west of Worcester, via the fringes of the Malvern Hills. Reflecting the attitude of the British authorities to any kind of competition on public roads in the early days of motoring, Shelsley was conceived as a closed venue for motor sporting trials – going uphill fast.

The hill was discovered by the Midlands Automobile Club which was founded in 1901 and, like Morgan, is still going strong. In their early days they were among the clubs which organised hillclimbing contests on the open road, which, of course, was strictly illegal. They used to post lookouts on the approach roads but it was quite common for the local constabulary to turn up and call a halt to proceedings. One of the club's first venues was Sunrising Hill, on a public road in Warwickshire, and that gave the club its rising sun badge, but the idea of a legal, private venue led to the discovery of Shelsley.

The hill was set on the estate of a local squire named Taylor, and although it was soon tarmaced it was originally little more than a steep, unsurfaced farm track. Enthusiastically supported by Squire Taylor, the club had the idea of using it as a competition venue. The initial meeting was held in August 1905; the first legal 'speed' hillclimb in Britain, today it is the country's oldest motor sporting venue still in regular use. For the opening, Squire Taylor laid on a huge picnic in the cart sheds at the bottom of the hill which were bedecked with flowers for the party. The Worcester Civil Military Band provided the music and various Birmingham clubs supplied an army of uniformed waiters. The ladies wore long skirts and broad brimmed, veiled hats, the gentlemen wore stovepipe hats, high collars and deerstalkers. It was quite an occasion.

To put into perspective the challenge of motoring in 1905, the very first car to attempt the hill failed to make it to the top, and while the quickest climb of the day was made by a 35hp Daimler in 77.6 seconds, the overall winner (according to a formula devised by the club and based on car weight) was declared to be a 6hp De Dion which took a leisurely 289.6 seconds to reach the summit. Three months or so after opening his garage business and a few years before he built his own first car, HFS Morgan may even have been there to watch; it was also the day after his twenty-fourth birthday. Nearly five years later, HFS took the first Runabout to the hill, not to compete but to show it off in public, now that he was making plans to put it into production. His first competitive outing came a little later, soon after the Morgan's first appearance at the Olympia Motor Cycle Show in November 1910.

In December 1910, the Motor Cycle Club organised the first running of what is still a famous event, the London–Exeter Trial. It was held immediately after Christmas, on Boxing Day and on 27 December, when the weather was wet and the state of the roads atrocious. The entry list for the Winter Trial showed only two cars, Mr VH Brich Reynardson in a 10hp Cadillac and Mr CM Smith in a 15.9hp Thames, plus seventy-seven motor bicycles and passenger motor cycles, including HFS Morgan in his tiller-steered, vee-twin JAP-engined 8hp single-seater Morgan Runabout (CJ 743) at number 64. The rest ranged in size from NC Dear's 1½hp Wanderer to a number of 8hp Chater Leas with sidecars. The recently launched Morgan was up against a number of well-known, established (and to this day, still emotive) names, including Humber, Triumph, Indian, Douglas, AJS, FN, Rudge-Whitworth, Scott, NSU, Rex, Calthorpe, Zenith,

Clyno, Brough, Motosacoche, Enfield and Ariel, and a good number of more obscure makes. It was a time when men like HFS Morgan competed in vehicles they had produced themselves, and even from that list of marques you could pick out the names of company founders like William Chater Lea, Albert John Stevens of AJS, Alfred Angas Scott, George Brough, even James A Prestwich who made the JAP engines which powered Morgan's machine and many others, all of them competitors in events of various kinds.

HFS Morgan became as successful as any of them, and his reputation started with this first event. In spite of the appallingly wet and muddy conditions on the run to Exeter and back, and the newness of his design, he took a gold medal for a penalty-free performance. The motor cycle press, having only recently enthused over the newcomer at the Motor Cycle Show in November, were once again complimentary, reporting that the Morgan had more than held its own with the motor cycles. In itself, the achievement was significant, but even more so was the way in which HFS capitalised on it.

He recognised almost immediately that he had found the perfect means of combining the chance for development with the opportunity of publicity and promotion, and from here onwards every Morgan competition success was widely advertised.

There were plenty of competition successes, and before long they were not occurring only in trials. In June 1911, having survived a collision with a wall which knocked his front wheels out of line, HFS won another gold medal, in the London–Edinburgh Trial, and as soon as the two-seater Runabout was launched HFS started to compete with that too, recognising that even potential customers who wanted practicality were still impressed by performance. Its first outing was a disappointment because it had to retire on only the second day of the Auto Cycle Union's Six-Day Trial with a broken propeller shaft (no doubt the result of the extra weight finding an inherent weakness), but HFS even capitalised on that problem by learning from it and making appropriate improvements.

Competing with the two-seater brought another bonus – room for a companion on the testing long distance trials, and for HFS his companion more often than not was his future wife, the former Hilda Ruth Day, now Ruth Morgan. Ruth never drove in competitions herself but she accompanied HFS at every opportunity, in trials and rallies, and if she had been allowed to she would have been in some important races too.

Ruth was not HFS's only family supporter; his sisters were often in evidence as either spectators, passengers or occasionally drivers, and the enthusiasm of his father, the Prebendary HG Morgan, became as legendary as it may have seemed unlikely. Famously, both Ruth and HG were very much in evidence at Brooklands at the end of 1912 when HFS gave the Runabout the Blue Riband of that year's cyclecar competitions by capturing the hour record, and the massive kudos that went with it.

HFS had not been the first to race a Morgan at Brooklands, that honour had gone to Harry Martin who entered the international cyclecar scratch race organised by the British Motor Cycle Racing Club (BMCRC) in March 1912. Martin, an experienced motor cycle racer and TT rider, entered a two-seater Runabout with a special body which gave just about enough room to accommodate him and the obligatory passenger (or 'riding mechanic'). It was powered by an air-cooled overhead-valve JAP vee-twin of just under 1-litre. With this car, Martin lapped at close to 60mph during the short race and won by such a margin that all future cyclecar races at Brooklands would be run as handicaps. Soon after, Morgan were running advertisements under the heading 'The Pick of the Bunch', with the accompanying copy, 'The first Cycle-Car Race held, and run off at Brooklands, 27th March, resulted in a great triumph for the Morgan Runabout, driven by Mr Harry Martin. Seven started – Result, Morgan 1st, at an average speed of 57mph.' And proving beyond any doubt that success in competitions sold cars from the showroom, within days of that first cyclecar race win Morgan had received more than one hundred new orders, triggering HFS's final commitment to expanded production.

HFS's record breaking runs of 1912 were made in pursuit of a handsome silver trophy offered by the new magazine *The Cyclecar* to the holder of the one-hour distance record for cyclecars at the end of that year. The record was hotly disputed, and at least one other famous manufacturer would also do his own driving. That was J Talfourd Wood, the 'W' of cyclecar makers GWK – Arthur G Grice, Wood and CM Keiller. Coincidentally, both Wood and Keiller, like HFS Morgan, had worked with the Great Western Railway in Swindon, and their rear-engined friction-drive cyclecar was one of Morgan's chief rivals before the First World War, selling 52 cars in 1911, 150 in 1912 and almost 1,100 by 1915. GWKs were also a sporting rival, especially in racing and record breaking.

All the attempts on the hour-record, naturally, focused on Brooklands, the famous high-banked concrete oval near Weybridge in Surrey which had opened in June 1907 as the world's first purpose-built motor racing track, and also as a test facility and proving ground for the still-infant British motor industry. Uniquely, it allowed maximum speeds over great distances while also offering all the necessary technical support. That support ranged from trackside fuelling, preparation and repair stations to permanent (and officially recognised) timekeeping facilities, all overseen by the circuit's famous chief timekeeper, handicapper and official starter, AV 'Ebby' Ebblewhite. And because Brooklands was the first facility in the world for this kind of exploit, long distance records in particular set here were in most cases the world's best marks.

J Talfourd Wood's GWK set the early pace for the hour record during the summer of 1912 and by August had raised the mark to almost 50 miles in the hour, but Morgan was about to take it considerably higher – to within a few yards of 60 miles, or a mile a minute. He started his attacks on the record early in November, at a meeting organised by the BMCRC which included both races and time trials, including a one-hour race for sidecars and cyclecars. Before HFS himself took up the challenge of the full hour, other Morgan drivers had shown what was possible over shorter bursts, and in the time trials Warren Lambert had recorded flying kilometre and mile speeds of almost 59mph in his 1100 JAP-powered Morgan. HFS raced a single-seater Morgan Runabout, powered by a slightly smaller overhead-valve JAP vee-twin of just under 1-litre, with a rudimentary 'wind-cheating' body and a petrol tank sitting high on the tail behind his shoulders. He led from the start of the race, as Wood's GWK suffered electrical problems and the remainder of the eight starters (including one other Morgan, driven by Harry Martin) gradually fell back.

By the finish HFS had won the race by almost four laps, taken the 50-mile world record in 54 minutes 39.2 seconds, and put more than 55 miles into the hour. That was another world's best, more than seven miles better than Wood's existing mark with the GWK, and it put HFS and Morgan comfortably in the lead of the competition for the Cyclecar Trophy, with less than two months of the qualifying year left to run.

But the race for the record was not over yet, and the following week was one of high drama. In the middle of it, at Brooklands, Wood and his GWK took the record back from Morgan, with a run of more than 56 miles, but on Saturday 23 November HFS returned and put the record beyond reach, with a run of 59 miles 1120 yards. It was so close to the magic mile a minute, or as *The Cyclecar* splashed all over the front cover of only its second ever issue, on 4 December 1912, 'Nearly 60 Miles in One Hour'. At the same time HFS had reduced the 50-mile record to 50 minutes 28.6 seconds. No one tried to break the record again that year, and the *Cyclecar* Trophy was Morgan's.

The photograph on that *Cyclecar* cover showed HFS in the car just before the start, with timekeeper Ebblewhite standing by with his familiar bowler hat, pipe and stopwatch, and in the background HFS's father, the Reverend Prebendary HG Morgan with long black coat, bushy white moustache and formal top hat. HFS's wife Ruth was also around to lend her support, and appears in many other photographs of the day. Apparently the family solidarity was very important, because HFS was said to be a very nervous competitor, worried, Peter Morgan would recall, not so much about hurting himself as about the possiblity of damaging his cars' reputation with public failure.

Success, however, made all the anxiety worthwhile, and within a few days Morgan was using the achievement in the motor cycle press. 'Once Again – The Morgan Runabout has broken the well-contested Hour Record, covering a distance of 59 miles 1120 yards. Fastest Lap – Sixty-two mph. On the Road – The Morgan Runabout has been more successful than any other cyclecar, gaining Highest Awards in all the principal events of the year. Price 85 guineas. "Cheapest and Best".' HFS also displayed the *Cyclecar* Trophy in the window at the Worcester Road works, which were soon to grow, and the expansion was directly fuelled by these competition successes.

HFS ended a remarkable year by competing in three trials in quick succession in the few days either side of Christmas, including the London–Gloucester and the London–Exeter, where he had had his first success a year earlier. A local newspaper report revealed not only how much effort HFS was putting into competing but also what his successes were doing for the business: 'To show what ground can be covered in these cars,' it said, 'Mr HFS Morgan started from Stoke Lacy Rectory in his "runabout" on Christmas Day for London, ran it in the Trial from London to Gloucester and back on Boxing Day and from London to Exeter and back the next day, afterwards driving it back to Malvern. In this time he covered 800 miles, won a silver cup and a gold medal.

'Mr Morgan at his works in Malvern is turning two of these cars out every day – of course barring Sunday – and all these are sold for this season, and moreover he is enlarging the works with a view of a larger output shortly.' Although Morgan did not build cars on a Sunday, it seems the Reverend Morgan was not too worried about his Sunday services running a little late if his son arrived home from a competition outing in the morning with an interesting story to tell.

All this success in races, records and trials was adding considerable weight to the Morgan's reputation for durability, and in 1912 HFS had written to *The Motor Cycle* to say that by that time he had driven his own cars for 'probably 30,000 miles, including all the chief reliability trials'. In response to one of the recurring fears of the day, he said he had never had a rear tyre failure. In 1913 the reputation spread even further, with Morgan's first big success abroad, and one of the most famous in Morgan's history.

The event that heralded this success was the French Cyclecar Grand Prix and the central character was that staunch Morgan supporter W Gordon McMinnies – also known as 'Platinum'. Late in 1912 McMinnies acquired his own Morgan, an 8hp JAP-engined single-seater which he nicknamed 'Jabberwock', after the fierce creature of the Lewis Carroll poem. In *The Cyclecar* of 8 January 1913 he reported how he had covered almost five hundred miles in the car before it was a week old, and thereafter he used it more or less continuously for reporting on trials, and before long for competing himself, initially in hillclimbs, then in races. He would be one of the Morgan team for the Cyclecar Grand Prix, and specifically for that race HFS also produced a special competition car, which would become known as the Grand Prix model. By lengthening the wheelbase he was able to move the two seats from on top of the bevel box to in front of it, and much lower down, both changes contributing to much improved high speed cornering stability. He also made the chassis a bit stiffer with larger side tubes, and tested the car in the London–Edinburgh Trial, with an air-cooled, side-valve JAP vee-twin and four gears.

Having been proved in various trials, the Grand Prix model was given a special water-cooled overhead-valve JAP engine and improved bodywork, tested again at the Shelsley Walsh hillclimb and Porthcawl Sand Races, then entered for the French Cyclecar Grand Prix (which supported the French Grand Prix proper) on 13 July as part of a four-car Morgan team. The press reported, 'Mrs HFS Morgan is most anxious to accompany her husband in the Grand Prix Race in France. Unfortunately, however, lady passengers are not allowed.' Instead HFS would be partnered by his brother-in-law, Geoffrey Day, while the rest of the team would comprise another 'works' car with a 1000cc water-cooled Precision vee-twin for Rex Mundy, a side-valve Blumfield-engined car for NF Holder, and a second water-cooled JAP-engined car (essentially like HFS's Grand Prix save for the body) entered by the new Cyclecar Club for McMinnies.

In the event, Holder failed to start (in fact he failed to appear at all, having stayed in England to compete at Brooklands a few days later), HFS suffered a broken piston before the end of the first lap, one of Mundy's front wheels collapsed on his second lap, while McMinnies, with Frank

Thomas, survived to take a famous victory – but not an easy one, as the inevitable Morgan advertisement after the race reported, under the heading, 'The Speediest Cyclecar in the World Beats Every Other Competitor in the Grand Prix.

'The famous British Morgan driven by Mr WG McMinnies, a British driver, won the race at an average speed of 42 miles an hour, in spite of a certain amount of bad luck. Starting fourth, it was not long before Mr McMinnies forged his way into the leading position. But he was not to hold it for long. Tyre trouble delayed him, and he started again to find that he had dropped from first to fifteenth place. The Morgan was asked to accomplish what looked like a hopeless task – and not in vain. The temporary leaders were overhauled, one by one, until Mr McMinnies, though hampered by another delay, had recaptured the place of honour and romped home an easy winner.'

McMinnies was 'an easy winner' in as much as he was a long way ahead of any other competitor after the one hundred and sixty-three rough and hard-fought miles but not so easy when it came to beating French chauvinism. After the race the organisers decided that his Morgan was not a cyclecar after all but a sidecar, and they awarded first place in the cyclecar category to a Bédélia. A *French* Bédélia. This was not the last time the French racing authorities would juggle the rules to produce the 'correct' result, as the Mini team found out in the Monte Carlo Rally in the early 1960s, and Morgan, amongst others, discovered at Le Mans on various occasions.

But to the French public, if not the race organisers, the Morgan had proved itself and orders boomed. Morgan's French agent (and later manufacturer under licence), Darmont et Badelogue, could sell all the Morgans they could get hold of and the press reported, 'In 1914 the Paris agents for the Morgan are taking 150 machines, while for 1915 they have ordered 500 machines'. And Morgan's competition exploits had apparently spread the word even beyond Europe. In 1914 it was reported that 'an American champion motor cyclist named Coes has been so impressed by the running of the Grand Prix Morgans in trials that he has decided to take one back with him when he returns'. By then,

Morgans were already winning races in America, including four in just one meeting in July 1914, at the two-day cyclecar race meeting on the Michigan one-mile dirt oval, a track right in the heartland of the American motor industry. Those American cars would have been some of the first exports to what eventually became Morgan's biggest market, and they had clearly been sold largely because of the exposure of, and the success in, competition.

The famous French win was celebrated by a commemoration dinner at Frascati's restaurant in London on 30 July, hosted by McMinnies and Thomas, and before the dinner the chairman read out telegrams of congratulations from HFS Morgan and JA Prestwich. Less happily, the most famous Grand Prix model and certainly one of the most significant of all early Morgans, the Grand Prix winning car, did not survive in its original form for long, and McMinnies was fortunate not to expire with it. A few weeks after the race he was using the car to report on the Scottish Six-Day Trial when he had what he later reported in *The Motor Cycle* as 'a marvellous escape'.

He described the incident with a certain unsouciance: 'When going along the wide, main road between Falkirk and Edinburgh I suddenly felt the steering fail. We were doing about 35 to 40 miles an hour, and I told my passenger what had happened. He had three seconds warning in which to dismount. The machine deviated slightly from its course, and I saw that we were making straight for a telegraph pole. I could do nothing whatever, and when, within two yards of the post I made sure that I was going to be killed. Bang! There was a frightful shock, my passenger disappeared, and I realized that I was still alive. I shouted to him "Are you all right?" and he said "Yes". I got up and found that the tail of the machine, on which were placed two heavy bags, the coats, and tarpaulin, tools, etc, had been hurled twenty yards down the road, where it was lying upside down. All the spare parts which had been carried in the receptacle were also scattered about. Sprockets, chains, screws etc lay in confusion around us.

'My passenger limped up and took photographs of the scene. I inspected the machine, which was a perfect wreck, and resembled a crumpled-up matchbox more than anything else. With the help of the crowd which collected we lifted the debris on to a laundry cart which happened to be passing. What happened to the laundry baskets I have no notion, but somehow I imagine both they and the wreckage reached Falkirk and were then sent home.

'Mr Proctor, the father of one of the competitors, very kindly gave us a lift to the finish on his Hupmobile car, and then my passenger discovered that he had a clicking inside, which was diagnosed as a broken rib, whilst injuries to his legs had also resulted. Mercifully I am unscathed, but the poor old Jabberwock de Picardy will never again take the road, its promising career having been cut short in its infancy. Luckily the engine is untouched, and I hope will soon be running again.' It was, and the remains of the two-seater Grand Prix winner were soon rebuilt as a successful single-seat racer, which occasionally carried a passenger on the tail, with legs tucked down into the cockpit alongside the driver, until the sporting authorities took a dim view of that.

In the meantime, Morgan's successes continued. The list of wins is far too long to detail, but one could chart the course of the most important achievements quite closely by following Morgan's advertisements in the specialist press, which were updated every few weeks and always recorded the latest competition exploits. They included numerous gold medals and other prizes in the major trials – in every discipline from the acceleration tests and hillclimbing to restarting and fuel economy – and no longer only for HFS but for many other Morgan drivers. There were fastest times and class wins in numerous speed hillclimbs, which was another area where McMinnies now excelled, alongside the likes of Morgan agent and racer A Warren Lambert, WD South and many more. There were wins in speed trials and sand races, multiple successes at Brooklands in everything from short sprints to long-distance, high-speed reliability trials, and to cap it all there was the record breaking.

By the beginning of the war, Morgan could advertise the Grand Prix Model, at £106, as 'the car which in 1914 won 11 cups, 12 gold medals, and 21 firsts in speed trials and hill climbs'. Also by the outbreak of war, Edward Bradford Ware,

Above: Stoke Lacy Rectory, the Morgan family home, at the turn of the century

Left: The family at much the same time. HG and young HFS at the back, Freida and Ethel's future husband Willie Cowpland on the left in the middle, with Ethel second right, Dot cross legged at the front, with Aunt Siddie and HFS's mother Florence on the right

Bottom: cycling enthusiast HFS helping Mr Davison to master the bicycle, in around 1913

Left: Chestnut Lodge, with the Morgan & Co Garage to the left

Below Left: the commercial breakthrough – HFS at the tiller of the first two-seater, with Willie Cowpland, in 1911

Below Right: William Stephenson-Peach and the single-seater prototype of 1909

Bottom: HFS at the wheel of the early four-seater, in about 1912. Ruth is the front passenger, HFS's sister Dorothy and Geoffrey Day are in the back

Right: HFS and Ruth in familiar pose in about 1913. They were married in 1912 and Ruth acted as HFS's enthusiastic co-driver for many years

Below: the essence of the three-wheeler twin — light weight plus ample power equals speed, as here at SUNBAC's Angel Bank hillclimb in July 1923, where HFS won the 1100cc class

Below Left: celebrating the hour record at
Brooklands, 1912, HFS at the wheel, HG in top hat

Below Right: the chassis and machine shop,
Worcester Road, 1912. HFS is in centre in cap, Alfie
Hales next to him on the right

Bottom: Captain Albert Ball VC, DSO, MC, in Grand
Prix Morgan

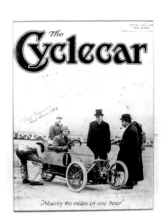

Below Left: Ruth in an early Grand Prix Morgan at Stoke Lacy

Below Right: HFS, nearest camera, watches preparation work on the 1913 French Cyclecar Grand Prix cars

Bottom: Herefordshire Auto Club Reliability Trial, May 1913

Above: Lieutenant RT Messeroy in the Birmingham Trial shortly before the First World War

Right: a rare piece of Morgan understatement from a 1920s advertisement - without a mention of competition exploits

Opposite: clockwise from top. EB Ware in the pits at the 1921 Cyclecar Grand Prix at Le Mans, rear damping for 1920s racer, Matchless twin holding its own in later life, and Ruth and HG at a Malvern gathering in 1914

The Morgan Runabout

The Morgan Motor Co. Ltd.,
Malvern Link.

Above: three Morgan generations in the 1920s, HFS in the centre, schoolboy Peter in front, and HG smiling on the left

To Peter Morgan
from
GMB Stewart
22/3/30

Top: Gwenda Stewart at Montlhéry, where she raised the 1100cc flying kilometre record to 115.66mph in August 1930

Above: Peter's sisters Sylvia and Stella, left at Donington for an ACU Rally, and right heading for the golf course

Right: from the 1919 catalogue

THE MORGAN RUNABOUT

Special Features.

Extreme Simplicity and Strength of all working parts.

Very Light on Tyres.

Special System of Springing, giving great comfort.

Motor Cycle Tax.

Over 50 miles to One Gallon of Petrol.

No Belts or High Speed Chains.

Freedom from Side Slips.

Accessible position of Engine, etc.

Above: HFS at the wheel of
the chassis which served as a
test bed for the larger Standard
engine, leading to the Plus 4
in 1950

Right: the Ford engined 4-4
four-wheel prototype, built in
1934 with the F-type three-
wheeler as its starting point

WP 7490

Top: a choice of
configurations, using
sporting achievements
to introduce the 4-4
in 1936, and the
F-Type alternative

Above: the classic
flat-radiator look of
the early post-war 4-4,
typical of the period
from 1947 to 1952

Right: the 4-4's 1267cc
overhead-valve four-
cylinder 'Standard
Special' engine

Top: the Pickersleigh Road paint shop in the late 1920s

Left: the Ford-engined F-type in 1937, shifting the emphasis from sport to low cost leisure

Left: Peter Morgan on leave from the army during the Second World War, with his first wife Jane, who he married in 1940, and with blackout lamps on the 1937 4-4 that he had campaigned in pre-war trials

a former motor cycle racer turned Morgan man (and also an experimental engineer for JAP), held a string of records with his streamlined Morgans, notably those for cyclecars in the under 750cc class, from one hour at just over 47mph to the flying start kilometre at more than 65mph, and some of his long distance records survived into the mid-1920s. On 28 March 1914 he had broken various middle distance records in the BMCRC 100-mile high speed trial at Brooklands but retired after twenty-seven laps when, shades of Isadora Duncan, his passenger's scarf became caught up in the chain.

One of the few flies in the Morgan ointment in this period had been the strangely ambivalent attitude of the authorities towards the three-wheelers, a reluctance to define them once and for all as either car or motor cycle-and-sidecar combination. In 1914, for instance, the RAC banned three-wheelers from its Light Car Trial, and various other organising bodies declared the Morgan to be a motor cycle, which led to a great deal of correspondence in the specialist press, not least from the Morgans, father and son. Either way, the Morgans kept winning, and the beneficial publicity kept coming.

After the war, many of Morgan's cyclecar rivals failed to reappear, but the three-wheelers from Malvern Link took up where they had left off. The controversy over definitions continued, however, with some juggling of names and affiliations. The Cyclecar Club became the Junior Car Club, which accepted cyclecars for membership but with weight and capacity limits, and for competition purposes they were governed by the Auto Cycle Union while light cars were the province of the Royal Automobile Club. At Brooklands, the Brooklands Automobile Racing Club had excluded three-wheelers from its motor car meetings, so the Morgans, which ironically were quite capable of beating most of the light-weight four-wheelers, were restricted to racing either under the auspices of the British Motor Cycle Racing Club against the sidecars, or in mixed-club meetings. In 1921, HG Morgan was still criticising the system, as in a letter to *The Motor Cycle*: 'The three-wheeled runabout has been the Cinderella of the motor house . . . All cars had four wheels, therefore the three-wheeler was not a cycle car. It was equally true, of course, that no cycle has four wheels, therefore the four-wheeler was not a cycle car. Therefore there was no such thing as a cycle car. QED.'

Not long after losing two fingers in his workshop accident, HFS completed the 1919 London–Edinburgh Trial with another gold medal performance. He then made fastest time for a passenger car at the Stile Kop hillclimb, and soon after took another gold in the ACU Six-Day Trial, while in France P Houel won the cyclecar class of the Circuit de l'Eure. When Brooklands reopened, Morgans resumed their winning ways there, too. EB Ware was the driver to beat, with his spectacularly compact and streamlined single-seater, his closest rival, also Morgan mounted, being Douglas Hawkes.

The gold medals from trials kept building up, as did the race wins, while all the time the speeds kept increasing, and, in the difficult period after the war, competition exploits kept Morgan sales afloat. The technical lessons learned through competition – not least the option of front brakes for the sporting models from 1923 – were fed back to production models too, which meant that the Morgan was not only faster than most but also far more reliable. By 1921 EB Ware had raised the 1100cc flying kilometre speed to more than 86mph, but Hawkes was also starting to set records, which the two regularly traded into the mid-1920s, with Hawkes getting into the 90mph-plus bracket during 1923. It was yet another driver, though, who achieved the next momentous Morgan milestone, one that is still impressive even seventy-five years on. On 24 July 1925 Harold Beart with an 1100cc Blackburne vee-twin engined two-seater, and intrepid passenger, set a flying-start five-kilometre record of 100.4mph. That was the first ever 100mph-plus record for a three-wheeler cyclecar.

This was a high spot after what had been a difficult time for Morgan, following an accident involving EB Ware which changed the whole face of British motor racing. Early in 1923 Ware had demonstrated the all-round abilities of the standard production Morgan by making the best overall performance in the Junior Car Club's General Efficiency Trial, held, inevitably, at Brooklands. The tests measured not only speed but hillclimbing ability on the famous Test Hill, acceleration and fuel consumption. Ware lapped at almost 56mph and recorded 56mpg (nicely symmetrical numbers), and the

Morgan beat not only the other cyclecars but also the Austin Seven, which would have given some satisfaction. He repeated his success in the same event in 1924.

A few months later, however, Ware became the centre of a major drama. Racing at Brooklands on 20 September 1924 in the JCC's 200-mile race, his JAP-powered car had a number of minor problems early in the race, then a single catastrophic one. After thirty laps, lapping at around 85mph and fighting to catch up, he began to experience rear-wheel or possibly tyre problems and a couple of laps later the Morgan went out of control and veered across into the fence, spinning the car around and throwing Ware and his passenger, Allchin, out before overturning. Allchin, ironically, was only in the passenger seat because the wife of Ware's intended passenger, Church, had had a premonition of the accident the night before and refused to let her husband race. Both Ware and Allchin were seriously hurt but both recovered, though the accident marked the end of Ware's racing career – and the end of an era for Morgan and the other three-wheelers. After this incident, the JCC immediately banned them from racing alongside four-wheelers, and other sanctioning clubs supported their stance, so the three-wheeled Morgans would never perform their giant-killing acts in mixed races again.

There were other repercussions for Morgan. Ware, who was also a highly respected experimental engineer with JAP and had other motor cycle and even aviation interests, was sufficiently badly injured to need extensive surgery, steel plates were inserted in his arms and elbows, forcing him into a long convalescence. He took legal action to try to recover his medical costs, against tyre makers Dunlop, engine supplier JAP, and against Morgan. None of them would admit liability, however, and after a long legal battle Ware lost the case and most of his own money. He rebuilt his career as a consultant, including working for BMW in Germany, became chief scrutineer for the Auto Cycle Union, was a consultant in the design of the new racing circuit at Castle Donington, and he appeared in both advertising promotions and university lecture tours, until his death in 1939. In the end, it was a sad and rather acrimonious close to a very fine relationship.

With all this drama in the background, Morgans continued to do well in the races they could still enter, were as successful as ever in trials, and by 1927 they could boast 18 gold medals and 8 silvers in the Colmore Cup Trial alone, and since 1920 another 15 golds and 11 silvers in the post-war Victory Trial. They were also as successful as ever in hillclimbs and speed tests. The Darmont- and Sandford-Morgans in France paralleled most of what the Malvern Morgans did in Britain, and Morgans continued to dominate the record-breaking arena – topped by Beart's 100mph achievements with his water-cooled, Blackburne-engined streamliner in 1925 but including less extreme records in other classes, often holding every possible record in an individual class.

In an effort to put three- and four-wheelers back on an equal footing in post-war competitions, a new club, the New Cyclecar Club, was created out of what was originally the Morgan Club. EB Ware, perhaps surprisingly in view of his on-going litigation with Morgan, was on the committee alongside the likes of Harold Beard and Captain Archibald Frazer-Nash, the latter of Morgan's four-wheeled cyclecar rivals Frazer-Nash. In August 1928 the club organised its first races at Brooklands, on a course combining the track and what we would think of today as various 'chicanes', finally pitting three-wheelers and four-wheelers against each other, after almost four years' break. Morgans won several of the events including the main one, the Cyclecar Grand Prix, and, ironically, the only major incident of the day saw a four-wheeled Austin Seven overturning.

The Austin Seven was giving Morgan a torrid time in the commercial marketplace, but the Morgan's competition successes helped keep the demand up, and it was a rare Austin indeed that could beat a Morgan in its natural habitat at Brooklands. In fact it usually took the works-entered Austin Seven racers to beat Morgan, and once they were able to race together again in events like the Light Car Club's splendid relay races at Brooklands it was almost always the Morgans that were Austin's main rivals. And it was not only the men who were achieving miracles with the Morgan, as was superbly demonstrated by a run of records in 1929 and 1930 for Gwenda Stewart.

Gwenda Stewart was one of the greatest of the lady racing drivers to compete at Brooklands in the inter-war years. The daughter of war hero Sir Frederick Manley Glubb, sister of John, better known as 'Glubb Pasha' of the Arab Legion, from 1937, after she married Douglas Hawkes (her third husband), she became Gwenda Hawkes. It was Hawkes who prepared Gwenda Stewart's record-breaking Morgans, with which she took a whole catalogue of records at Montlhéry, the French answer to Brooklands on the outskirts of Paris. In September 1929 with a 1-litre air-cooled JAP Super Sports model running on alcohol fuel she took the Class K hour record to over 101mph – the first time any three-wheeler had put more than 100 miles into the hour – and in November she raised the five kilometre mark for 1100cc three-wheeler cyclecars to more than 106mph. With different engine capacities, from as small as 350cc, she took almost every other record available, and the ones that Mrs Stewart did not hold, Mr Hawkes mostly did. In August 1930 they took up where they had left off on the high-banked Paris track, Gwenda Stewart, with a 1086cc JAP engine in her car, finally posting a speed of 115.7mph over a flying kilometre. That would never be beaten by any other classic three-wheeler Morgan in its original two-speed format, or indeed by any other three-wheeler of the period. Morgans now held the outright record in every available three-wheeler class.

In a way, it was the end of an era, because the three-speed three-wheeler introduced in 1931 was never considered by purists to be as much of a competition machine as the old two-speeders. Similarly, when the F-type four-cylinder three-wheeler arrived in 1933 it was not remotely as sporty as the original vee-twin, tubular chassis cars. In particular, the four-cylinder Ford engine could not match the low speed torque of the motor cycle-engined big twins (which now included a range of powerful Matchless engines as well as the mighty JAPs), and in trials events in particular that slogging power was one of the Morgan's great strengths. But for all that he still loved competitions, HFS Morgan knew when to emphasise them and when to take a different tack. It was noticeable, for instance, that in the first advertisements for the F-type four-cylinder, published around the time of its unveiling at the Olympia Show in November 1933, Morgan included one reassuring paragraph for the high-performance faithful: 'We would stress the fact that the new and extra model in no way replaces the twin-cylinder model on which the reputation of the name "Morgan" has been built.'

But the promotional emphasis for the original F4 four-seater, four-cylinder was 'Family Motoring to suit the Family Purse', while in contrast the classic twins were still advertising other attributes, as in the 1934 offering headed, 'If it's sheer performance you want ... high maximum speed, breath taking acceleration and high speed hill climbing – make it a Matchless-engined Morgan'.

It was 'thoroughbred' versus 'de luxe'. Nonetheless, both 'new' types, three-speeders and four-wheelers, soon appeared in competitions, and George Goodall, quite often partnered by his son Jim, did a reasonable amount of development driving for both the three-speed and four-cylinder cars in trials, while HFS was still active, too.

The four-cylinder three-wheeler did become more sporting with the launch of the two-seater version, and for a while there were a number of 'four-wheeler' Morgans running in trials in the early 1930s, but the twin rear wheels actually comprised two tyres mounted very close together on adjacent rims carried on a single hub, which in the eyes of the law (as confirmed by the civil courts which had been asked to clarify the licensing position) still made the Morgan a three-wheeler.

And then came the true four-wheelers, and a completely new competition era, heralded appropriately enough by HFS Morgan himself. On Boxing Day 1935 he reappeared as a driver in the London–Exeter Trial, where his first car had made its debut in 1910. This time HFS would be entered officially in the 'veterans' class, confined to those, like himself, who had competed in the very first running of the event. There was nothing veteran about the car he was using, however, because it was the Coventry-Climax-engined four-wheeler which went into production immediately afterwards. The prototype had already been extensively tested by both HFS and George Goodall, and had even been tried out at

Brooklands during the summer, quite successfully. In the London–Exeter, where the weather in 1935 was just about as wet as it had been back in 1910, HFS was the only veteran to gain a Premier award, and the new car, having passed the competition test, went into production in 1936.

By this time, Morgan had largely given up using lists of competition successes in its advertising, but it was not ready to give up competition itself. In that 1935 London–Exeter Trial, HFS had had a new partner, his son Peter, who was only seventeen and had recently learned to drive with the other Ford-engined four-wheeler prototype, around the grounds of the family home in Berkshire. Peter was to become as much a mainstay of Morgan four-wheeler competition exploits as his father had been with the three-wheelers, and just as convinced, in his own way, of the commercial value of competition success. The truth of the matter is probably shown by the fact that the 4-4 initially sold quite slowly from its production launch in March 1936, but started to be far more popular as soon as it began to accumulate a few results in trials, speed tests, rallies and races. The company started entering 'works' four-wheelers in all kinds of events, with HFS Morgan, George Goodall and Harry Jones (the works manager and test driver) usually doing the driving, and often taking awards. As well as providing publicity, these early outings also provided valuable testing mileage for the four-wheelers, whose detailed specification was still quite flexible, and, thanks to Morgan's way of doing things, relatively easy to modify.

There was one major difference with the arrival of the 4-4: there was no longer any argument about where it fitted in the grander scheme of things, no worrying about cyclecar and sidecar definitions or what kind of events it was allowed to be entered in. The 4-4 was a 10hp sports car, and that is how it was allowed to compete, full stop.

In March 1937, three 4-4s appeared in the RAC Rally, an event which had first been run in 1932 and which – comprising long, timed 'navigation' sections punctuated by special tests – was rather different from today's all-out forest-racing format. It was tough and competitive though, especially when the weather was as wintry as it was in 1937, and it was already a real car tester. HFS and the Goodalls, father and son, were in works cars and ED Bowman and WH Acock (of Bowman and Acock, the Morgan agents who had taken over the original Morgan works as well as Chestnut Villa as their premises) had their own 4-4. The Goodalls, never having contested the RAC before, won their class, and added another kind of award to the string of trials medals the 4-4 was beginning to pick up. In a golden age for this lower-key end of British motor sport, where much larger rival manufacturers like MG, Austin and Singer also had their official teams, Morgans were still quite capable of holding their own against all comers.

The biggest early success for the first four-wheeler Morgan, however, came on the racetrack, in a slightly unusual race in Northern Ireland, the Ulster Grand Prix. In 1937 the province's most famous race, the Tourist Trophy, came to the mainland for the first time, to be held at Donington, the circuit for which former Morgan three-wheeler star EB Ware had acted as a consultant. In place of the TT, the Ulster Automobile Club organised its own event, the Ulster Trophy, on a new road circuit near Ballyclare.

The 150-mile race was run as a handicap event, and the twenty-three starters included some very high quality machinery with an international flavour, including Alfa Romeo and Maserati racing cars, plus the very fast, supercharged MG sports cars. It was a Morgan that won it, however, driven quickly and extremely consistently by Robert Campbell, who had taken on the drive at the last minute because his boss, the Belfast Morgan agent Jack Parish, had not received his own competition licence in time for the event.

Only a few weeks later another 4-4, driven by Des McCracken, won another prestigious Irish road race, the Leinster Trophy, again against strong opposition. Very quickly, such achievements were being used in advertising the 4-4 as a new generation of successful sporting Morgan. 'Morgan made their name in the three-wheeler world,' one advertisement ran, 'and captured every prize worth having in the competition world ... and here is a four-wheeler four-cylinder car that bids fair to capture the plums in the sporting circles of the motor car world ... already the winner of the International Ulster Trophy Race. An 80mph Sports . . . and its price only £210.' It was back to business as usual.

In 1938 HFS and Peter Morgan continued the trials story by both taking triple gold medals in the 'big three' Land's End, Exeter and Edinburgh trials, while the 4-4 was pitched into its biggest race yet, at Le Mans, and acquitted itself remarkably well for a first-timer, leading to another famous Morgan model. The Le Mans effort was, strictly speaking, a private one, with the backing of one of Morgan's most energetic agents, the Winter Garden Garages in London's Holborn. The Winter Garden was opened in 1930 by an enthusiastic rally driver, Lance Prideaux-Brune, who usually competed with his wife Constance and who already had some experience of Le Mans. Appropriately for the Morgans, with a love of family holidays in Cornwall and in particular HFS's great uncle's endowment of the Padstow lifeboat, the Prideaux-Brunes were an old Cornish family which could trace its roots back to William the Conqueror and Edward I and who had lived in the Padstow estate of Prideaux Place since 1535. As four-teenth-generation head of the family, Peter Prideaux-Brune says, 'politically unlucky, the family always backed the wrong side in, for example, the English Civil War in the 1640s, and Monmouth's Rebellion of 1685 – but somehow we managed to survive'.

In the 1930s, Lance and Constance Prideaux-Brune backed another seemingly lost cause but this time helped it to survive. In 1932, while keeping a very low profile, the Prideaux-Brunes in effect bought the struggling Aston Martin company, for which the Winter Garden Garages held an agency, and kept it alive until they sold it on to Sir Arthur Sutherland shortly after, while continuing to provide finan-cial support. Through that association they went with Aston Martin to Le Mans in 1933, working with the pit crew, alongside Dick Anthony, Winter Garden's works manager and a skilled race engineer and regular Aston Martin racer. Anthony was also at Le Mans in 1934, and Winter Garden became a Morgan agent in 1937; soon after, they were approached by a potential customer looking for a suitable car and team to contest the 1938 Le Mans race.

That customer was Prudence Fawcett, a sports car enthusi-ast who had little experience of racing but who wanted to contest Le Mans, and had the funds to do so. She approached Morgan about the possibility of a car and HFS came up with one developed from the 1937 TT racer, while suggesting that the Prideaux-Brunes should organise the effort. The 4-4 was powered by a specially tuned version of the 1098cc Coventry-Climax engine and among its other modifications it had a large capacity fuel tank and cycle-type front wings. It was capable of close to 100mph, but once Miss Fawcett and her co-driver Geoffrey White (the Winter Garden sales manager) had established a comfortable pace during practice their first aim was to complete the race, the second to put up a good average speed. In the end, by running to a disciplined schedule, they achieved both. For a while they even led the under-1100cc class, but in spite of falling back from that position later in the race with minor engine problems they kept going to finish thirteenth overall of the fifteen finishers from forty-two starters. That was fast enough to satisfy HFS Morgan's secondary target, to qualify for the Rudge-Whit-worth Cup, a competition taking into account two successive years' performances in the race. Early in 1939, to celebrate the success, Morgan introduced a tuned version of the 4-4, with cycle front wings, as the Le Mans Replica, with HFS's usual eye to good publicity.

By 1939, Prudence was engaged and had promised to give up racing, but the Morgan was entered again for the second leg of the biennial cup and Prudence's place in the factory-prepared 4-4 was taken by Dick Anthony. This time the further modified car ran in the up to 1500cc class and after a promising start struggled in the later stages of the race with a familiar malady for 1930s' Le Mans racers, persistent misfires almost certainly caused by dubious fuel quality. They finished though, fifteenth overall this time, second in their class and the highest placed British car in the biennial cup competition.

In between the two 24-Hour races the Le Mans car raced again in the Tourist Trophy at Donington but struggled to be classified in twenty-fourth place from thirty-one entries. Other Morgans fared better in lesser races and in the many trials they were still regularly contesting, while Peter Morgan, at his father's insistence, was playing his way gently into the circuit racing discipline by learning his craft in trials, before making a successful track debut in the high-speed trials at Brooklands in September 1938.

Peter Morgan looks back with obvious pleasure on all his days competing in Morgans in various forms of motor sport. 'It's quite interesting that over the years, I took virtually every model into the MCC trials and I won triple awards with the 4-4 Series 1 before the war, with the Plus 4, the Plus 8, and I think I got a triple with the Plus 4 Plus – the only one I think I didn't get a triple with was the 4/4 after the war. My first triple was quite good; it was 1938, with the 4-4, and father got one the same year. He'd made me go in for that when he'd said, "you're not going on the race track until you can handle a car well on the really steep hills and in the rough."

'So I did trials first but I always really wanted to go racing more than anything, I loved it, but unfortunately it was interrupted by the war. I did Donington once before it, quite successfully, with two races during the day, and I did the one-hour trial at Brooklands in 1938. It's sad that that was towards the very end of Brooklands. I was actually entered for the Campbell Circuit event which I think was going to take place in September 1939, but that was cancelled, and I was so upset because I was really looking forward to that one, on what was really a semi-road course.

'I used to go and watch the twins racing, of course, but I never saw my father race. When I was born he more or less gave it up. There's a lovely story, that's quite true, that mother was with him in the Scottish Six-Day Trials in 1919, around June, and I was born in November – so I say that one of the reasons why I've always been able to put up with Morgan suspension is that my mother carried me through six days of it even before I was born, and if that didn't teach me all about it, nothing would.

'After the war, once I got more involved in the business side of things, I was always rather the way father had been in competitions, very concerned not so much about the driving itself but about doing justice to the car. You know it can do this, you know it can do that, so you know you've got to do well with it – and that always slightly spoiled it. Before the war, even at the high-speed events at Donington or Brooklands, I didn't have a care in the world, it was just great fun, but the war made a big difference, I was five years older, with more to think about. It was a shame really because I could have had a great time on the circuits, and the 4/4 was very successful then . . .'

Peter continued to accompany his father in trials and rallies, their results including a class win with the Coupé in the 1939 RAC Rally, alongside the Goodalls who won the 10hp open-top class. But for now there would not be much more motor sporting activity in Europe, as war was declared in September 1939 and other priorities took over, with the Morgan factory turned over to war work rather than worrying about cars much less about motor racing.

Morgan eventually struggled back into business against the same restrictions as the rest of the British industry but did at least discover that the war had not affected either Morgan owners' or the general public's enthusiasm for motor sport of all kinds. What was possible was severely restricted by petrol rationing and other materials shortages – notably of tyres – but as the trials and hillclimbs scene drifted back, Morgans were still very much in the forefront. HFS – now with Peter by his side in the factory as well as in trials – still competed, and as ever he used competitions both as proving ground and promotional vehicle. With petrol rationing still in force, the late 1940s dragged on with only a limited number of events on the mainland and a few more in Ireland where the restrictions were not so severe, until the first post-war race in England took place in September 1948, at the new Goodwood circuit, a former airfield in Sussex. One of the few things not in short supply at the time was disused airfields . . . Peter Morgan, resuming his racing career, briefly led the 1100cc sports car race at Goodwood but eventually finished second to an MG, and that inter-marque rivalry was to become one of the big features of post-war competition, in America as well as Britain.

At about this time, one particular young man who was to become a very famous racing driver bought his first car:

Stirling Moss's choice was a Morgan three-wheeler. As he told the *Daily Express* many years later, 'I learned to drive when I was six. I used to sit on my mother's lap and drive round our farm in Berkshire. She was a rally driver and father was a racing driver before the war. So driving was in my blood.

'When I was fifteen [in 1944], I wrote in for my licence for a three-wheeler, which you can drive at sixteen. I thought if I wrote in early, I would get it well in time. But they obviously did not match up the ages and sent me back the licence!

'I bought a Morgan three-wheeler. It was blue and cream with a 1000cc Matchless Super Sport engine – and I paid £50, which I had won riding. Nowadays one would fetch over £10,000. It could do up to 70mph and I kept it for a year until I could drive a proper car on the road. The only serious scrape I had in it was when a back tyre burst. The car overturned, but only suffered a flattened windscreen. I was OK, but I was most concerned about the ferret I had with me: he only had a little mark on his nose.'

If the type of enthusiast who bought the Morgan three-wheeler was clear, one thing was changing and that was the level of direct dealer involvement for Morgan in the motor sports scene. In the glory days of the three-wheelers, many dealers competed themselves, in everything from trials to record breaking, or if they did not they helped with cars for other drivers. When the emphasis switched to four-wheelers, the number of dealers directly involved in motor sport fell dramatically at first, partly because the four-wheeler was a more expensive car to race, partly because it could not hope to match the virtually guaranteed success of the three-wheel twins. It was not so much that it was not a good competition car, more that the whole scene had become rather less easy going.

The Morgan factory, on the other hand, became, if anything, even more involved in all branches of the sport. It entered its own 'works' cars, entered teams of cars in the major events, and prepared cars to the individual specifications of many highly successful customers. As ever, the company treated all its motor sports activities as both potential publicity and as an opportunity for valuable engineering development. They did particularly well in rallying during the 1950s, not least with Peter Morgan himself. Having helped develop the Vanguard-engined Plus 4, and with his father having resisted the advances of the Standard Motor Company to take over Morgan, Peter Morgan gave the Plus 4 its competition debut in the Exeter Trial at the end of 1950, winning a Premier Award with his Coupé version. In 1951 he led the Morgan team (of two- and four-seater Coupé Plus 4s) to the team prize in the RAC Rally, and for a while threatened to snatch the over-1500cc open car win from Ian Appleyard's Jaguar XK120. The factory celebrated the occasion with a special advertisement in the motoring press, as usual, and the Morgans repeated the RAC team prize victory the following year.

Through the mid-1950s, Morgan drivers scored several impressive results in other rallies, including wins for private owner and former Jaguar driver Jimmy Ray in successive London Rallies in 1952 and 1953, and this was prehaps the golden age of British sports car racing on the numerous former airfields turned race circuits around the country. In America, too, the Morgan was a popular, relatively inexpensive racer, and again widely advertised as such by the American agents, who could advertise first and second places in the under $3,000 series-production category of the Sebring 12-Hour Grand Prix of Endurance in May 1955, among many other strong performances. But it was not easy to do consistently well in America against the likes of MG, Healey, Triumph, Jaguar, Allard, the homegrown Corvette, and new European star, Porsche.

Nearer home, the Morgans saw out the 1950s with first and second places in the 2-litre production class of the 1958 RAC Rally and welcomed in the 1960s with a win for Brian Harper in the 1960 Welsh Rally. But with the face of rallying already beginning to change, the most important results for Morgans would now start to come from the racetrack; and the most important of all would happen in June 1962.

In 1961, Morgan had planned a return to Le Mans, prompted by successful racer and Morgan tuner Chris Lawrence. Nearly forty years later, Chris Lawrence ran the engineering programme for the new generation Morgan Aero

8, but in the early 1960s he was better known as the proprietor of Lawrencetune; based in Acton, west London, it specialised in making the TR-engined Morgans go faster. In 1961 Lawrencetune had introduced the 116bhp Sports version of the Plus 4 as a customer road car and it was a race-prepared version of that car that he intended to take to Le Mans that year. Just as they had been for the Cyclecar Grand Prix in 1913, the French race organisers were being awkward, and this time they refused the Morgan entry on the grounds that they thought the car was simply a pre-war model which had been fitted with disc brakes, which in their opinion would not be suitable for the race.

Peter Morgan admits that he did a 'bit of spadework' for the 1962 entry, which was officially backed by the works, because the privately entered 1961 car, the one the authorities rejected, was, in his own words, 'rather scruffy'. He says now, 'it should not really have gone. But the two cars we had the following year were immaculate . . .' And in February 1962 the Morgan board had allocated a budget of £750 'for competition activity'.

Chris Lawrence still believes there may have been more to the 1961 rejection than that, and is convinced that part of the reason for the rejection was pressure on the organisers from the works Triumph team. They intended to contest the 1961 race with special twin-cam-engined cars but had good reason to believe that the Lawrencetune Morgan, even with its 'ordinary' TR3 engine, could show them up. And there was reason to believe that they had threatened to withdraw their works entries (which were a lot more prestigious than a single privateer) if the Morgan raced.

Either way, the 1961 Lawrencetune entry was turned down, but in 1962 they returned, with the works-prepared Plus 4 Super Sports (the same car that had been rejected a year earlier!) registered TOK 258, with Triumph TR3 power. This time the French authorities managed to contrive a reason for rejecting two 'experimental' Lotus entries, but Morgan finally persuaded the Le Mans organisers that the Plus 4 was a serious, modern entry. And today Peter Morgan credits his French dealers with helping to smooth the way with the race organisers in 1962. 'Jacques Savoye, the father, competed for many years at Le Mans in the Singer, and he was well known there so he had quite a bit of pull. He said a few words in the right ears . . .' But in any event, if the Le Mans officials had not been entirely convinced of the Morgan's pedigree and abilities before the 1962 race, they certainly would have been by the end of it.

New rules had permitted the entry of 'experimental' sports cars of up to 4 litres, prompting a head-to-head contest for the overall win between Ferrari and Maserati, with outsider challenges from the prototype Aston Martin 212 GT and several Jaguar E-type coupés. The race was a hard one, with almost all the 'experimental' cars retiring, but Phil Hill and Olivier Gendebien kept their Ferrari 330LM together for long enough to win the race overall. The Morgan was entered in the 2-litre GT class and Chris Lawrence shared the driving with Richard Shepherd-Barron. The only other entries in the class were a Bristol-engined AC Ace and an MG-engined TVR, from Morgan's specialist sports car rivals in Blackpool, but that did not detract from the ultimate result. At the end of the 24-Hours only eighteen of the fifty-five starters were still running, and the Morgan had finished thirteenth overall, while comfortably winning its class. It was a spectacular achievement and Morgan celebrated in familiar style, splashing the news across the specialist press. The advertisements read, 'Le Mans 1962: First in the 2-litre Grand Touring Class. During the 24-Hours the car covered 2,565 miles at the average speed of 94mph'. There is a large, framed picture on the wall of Peter Morgan's office of the car on its way to that famous win, and even now Peter remembers it as one of the greatest moments in the company's history.

He would obviously have liked to have competed at Le Mans himself sometime in his career, but never did. 'I would have liked to have done it, yes, because you know I used to do battle with the likes of Ian Appleyard and his Jaguars in things like the driving tests and the rallies, and I could give him a good run for his money. But when it came to things like Le Mans father said "no". That was the one I really wanted to do, but Liège–Rome–Liège was very appealing too, and the Alpine was ideal for Morgans . . .'

He has no doubt, though, that competing in Morgans taught him a lot about both the cars and the customers. 'I enjoyed myself and I also believe that the years of rallying were very important to me – because if you were in a rally and sitting in the car all night, or perhaps two nights and a day, you knew how uncomfortable the car was. And if you did not, the next guy who came along in a Morgan would certainly tell you.' Such experiments also give Peter Morgan a certain credibility as a man who knew about his own cars: 'I think it was one of the Reeces who broke a steering damper, or something else came adrift, and I got under there and put it right. They were absolutely amazed that here was a car manufacturer who actually knew how to do something on his own cars . . .'

He says now that at one point during the night at Le Mans Chris Lawrence had just about had enough and did not want to continue, 'but he was very glad that he did. It was a great achievement for him and a very important one for us. We would really have loved to have gone back the following year, because I said, "come on Chris, let's go and average 100mph – there's no cheap sports car that's ever done that". He looked at me very carefully and we talked about it and he said first of all that he did not think that we could get any more out of the engine reliably and the only way we could possibly do it was by changing the body style. He did that himself, of course, with the SLR, but I was not ever interested in that really because I was still keen on running a car that people could actually go out and buy. Le Mans had had a hell of an effect for us because at that time people could say, "look, I've got one of those and it won its class at Le Mans", and it was just about at that time that Le Mans really started to change . . .'

Peter also remembers with considerable amusement what Chris Lawrence did after the 1962 win, and laughs about how he can still see shades of it today when Chris is so closely involved in the development of the latest generation of Morgans. 'He's a very clever engineer, and he does some terrific things, but with finances he's a disaster. He really is, he's hopeless – I tell him to his face. I mean, when he won his class at Le Mans, what did he do? Instead of coming back and making something of his own business he swanned off down to the Mediterranean, chartered a yacht, sailed around the Med for six weeks and got rid of all his winnings – because I'd given him the winnings, and in fact the standby car, although the actual car was already his . . . I'm sure he's done similar things since, but then, his mind is on engineering, and he's very good at it . . .'

Le Mans 1962 was an important moment, too, because the result had a marked effect on sales, at a time when they badly needed a boost. It was the time when the American market was nearing rock bottom and leading up to the time when the Plus 4 Plus showed that Morgan people still wanted traditional Morgans. The special versions produced by Lawrencetune were still very much traditional Morgans, but with more power, and the option of many other performance tweaks, many of them proved on the racetrack. The Plus 4 Super Sports was the 'factory' version of Lawrence's aftermarket offering, built between 1961 and 1968, initially with the 1991cc TR3 engine, then the 2138cc TR4 engine, extensively tuned by Lawrence. In that time Morgan, with Lawrencetune, built just over a hundred cars, most of them two-seaters, but a few with four seats or the two-seater coupé body and the lower type body of the 4/4 rather than that of the bulkier Plus 4. They mainly used light-alloy bodies and wider wire wheels, and Lawrencetune added hotter camshafts, gas-flowed cylinder heads, twin-choke Weber carburettors and free-flow exhaust manifolds, while the engines were also balanced (by Brabham's engineering workshop) and generally beefed up internally. With up to 125bhp depending on the engine and its state of tune, in less weight than the standard car, they were among the fastest Morgans around in the 1960s.

Those and other people's modified versions of the regular four-cylinder, four-wheeler Morgans kept the flag flying in club level motor sport right through the decade and beyond. The general increase in sophistication – not to mention the considerably greater expenses – of motor sport as it was now developing meant, however, that Morgan were no longer regular competitors at the higher levels, where technology had moved on.

But there was life in the Morgan still. In 1975, Chris Alford won the British Production Sports Car Championship with a 4/4, winning his class in all seventeen championship rounds with his Ford-powered car. Then, with the coming of the Plus 8, with enough power and performance to make up for at least some of the chassis' lack of sophistication by modern standards, there were more successes to come. Mostly they were in national series now, because on an international level, even with the abilities of the Plus 8 with its light weight and reasonably strong Rover V8 power, a Morgan was no longer a match in terms of handling dynamics to some extent and aerodynamics in particular for a more modern generation of slick-bodied, stiff-chassised sports racer. Nonetheless, Charles Morgan played his part in the continuing saga, and in keeping the motor sport momentum going even when it seemed that the cars really would eventually have to be pensioned off. In 1978 he won the Production Sports Car title outright, amazingly with a car developed from the very first production Plus 8.

That car was prepared by Rob Wells' Libra Motive tuning company, whose name was writ large on the highly success-ful car, and Charles clinched the closely contested title on one weekend at the very end of the season with back-to-back wins at Silverstone on Saturday and Cadwell Park on Sunday. As ever, the win was celebrated in Morgan's advertising, and was even being mentioned in despatches as late as 1984, under the heading 'We've learned a lot in 75 years', with the copy adding, 'Since HFS started it all in 1909, we've added another wheel and a host of technical refinements that we feel would have made him proud to see applied to his original design. If we were to ask him now, "What do you think of the competition?", he'd probably say "We'll win".'

Charles Morgan took a Production Sports class win in 1979, while Rob Wells and Steve Cole gave the Plus 8 two more outright British Production Sports Car Championship wins in 1981 and 1982, and even then the Plus 8, already fourteen years old, was not finished. Wells turned one into one of the most extreme Morgan racers ever, with space-frame chassis, 300bhp Rover-based engine and huge rear wing on its one-piece, lift-off, glass fibre body, and he used it to take the

British Modified Sports Car Championship in 1982, to back up Steve Coles' Production win. In 1987 Grahame Bryant, Tony Morgan-Tipp, David Raeside and Rob Wells were outright winners of the Birkett Six-Hour Relay race at Snetterton with their 3.9-litre Plus 8 beating three Porsche teams and setting fastest lap of the race. After one hour they were a lap ahead, after two hours, two laps, and after three hours three laps, where they stayed to the end of the race. And it was not only the new cars that had racing successes. In 1990 Bill Wykeham and Ludovic Lindsay (who was more usually to be seen in an historic ERA single-seater racer) went to the rerun of the Classic Carrera Panamericana road race with a 1961 Plus 4, which the racing press enthused had 'covered itself in glory'. They were leading their class by the second day and stayed there until the end of the seven-day, 2,000-mile marathon, also finishing a quite remarkable sixth overall, in an event won by a far more exotic C-type Jaguar.

For many years there have been Morgan-only race series in Britain and around the world, for everything from virtually standard cars to outright racers, and going into the twenty-first century those series are as popular as ever. The most significant Morgan racing programme of all in recent years, however, has been the Plus 8's journey through the International GT Championships, led by Charles Morgan in the famous blue and yellow racer which, as described in Chapter 6, was the catalyst for the Aero 8. That car's debut was announced at the end of the 1994 season as the return of the Morgan factory to top level racing after an absence of fifteen years, with the most advanced Plus 8 yet.

That was the car through which Charles Morgan and Chris Lawrence began to develop the aluminium honeycomb chassis which eventually led to the Aero 8, and even back then *Autosport* said 'it will form the basis for a new customer sports car for both road and race track – the Plus 8R'. They were very close to the mark, but even they probably could not have imagined how technically sophisticated the Aero 8 would turn out to be at its February 2000 unveiling. And the inescapable fact of the Aero 8 is that it shows yet again that racing still does improve the breed. It may also have a future role beyond attracting a whole new generation of Morgan customer. If Charles Morgan has anything to do with it, a racing version of the Aero 8 will eventually take Morgan back to Le Mans. The Plus 8 road car became a racer that led to another road car, the Aero 8, that could become a racer. HFS Morgan would have loved the symmetry of that.

5 Peter Morgan: the Man in the Middle

IN NOVEMBER 1999, Peter Morgan celebrated his eightieth birthday, with a large gathering of family, friends and Morgan people. A couple of days after the party, he was back behind the paper-strewn desk in his jumbled, homely office at Pickersleigh Road, as he is for at least a few hours on several days each week.

Nobody is particularly surprised that he is still around so much. Just before his seventieth birthday, in 1988, he talked about 'slipping into retirement' once that milestone had passed. 'There wouldn't be enough to do if I packed up completely,' he said then, 'but I intend doing less and less. I have quite a nice time now, to be honest, thanks to delegating the duties I don't enjoy, such as public relations and advertising. I still like doing vehicle regulations and a certain amount on the financial side.'

In the early months of 2000 he had both hips replaced, but on each occasion he was back behind his desk as soon as he could get there. Peter Morgan is not the retiring type. Twelve years on from pondering the possibility, having seen not only seventy but also seventy-five come and go, he is still here, as happy as ever to keep an eye on things while his two collies wander around the office and the stores, and while his son Charles does the majority of the everyday running, in much the same way as Peter worked alongside his own father in the late 1940s and much of the 1950s.

And if the company would never have existed but for his father's initiative and his grandfather's financial savoir-faire, it certainly would not have survived beyond the 1960s without Peter Morgan's total commitment – which has included weathering the trauma of his father's death, resisting more overtures for takeover, challenging and beating the Inland Revenue, totally restructuring the company at great personal risk, and at the same time creating new cars and new markets. Through more than fifty years with Morgan, Peter has made the second phase of the company what it is, and he now supports the genesis of the third phase, through Charles Morgan.

Looking back now, a few months beyond his eightieth birthday, it remains clear that Peter Morgan has never lost his admiration for his father as a role model. 'I've lived through a very interesting period, I was young at the time but I knew that the late Twenties and early Thirties were damned difficult for my father. It was a struggle for everybody, particularly for father with the Austin Seven coming on the scene, which, no doubt about it, really did hit the three-wheeler and the twins very badly. So having been through that and also with his teaching, I say to people I was probably the luckiest person on this earth because I had the most wonderful teacher. You know it was very, very rare to find a good engineer who's also financially sound . . .'

The only son of that 'good engineer who was also financially sound', the founder, HFS, the father of current managing director Charles, and the man who steered Morgan through some of its most difficult days, Peter was born into the Morgan way of life on 3 November 1919, in Chestnut Villa, next door to the Worcester Road factory, which celebrated his arrival with a party in the carpenters' shop. Nearly three weeks earlier, on 16 October, his father had organised another, even grander party, to celebrate the opening of the new paint shop, the first extension to the pre-war buildings at Pickersleigh Road, with a dinner and dance for around three hundred people – Morgan employees, their families and friends. Seven months before that, on 5 March, Peter's older sister, Sylvia, then aged five, had laid the foundation stone for the extensions, and placed a silver half-crown under it.

In the few years that they had been building cars between the launch of the Runabout in 1910 and the outbreak of the First World War, Morgan had grown steadily; after the war, they had to resume normal production as rapidly as possible, to meet a demand for Morgans which picked up again very quickly because the three-wheelers were affordable and, with fewer materials needed than for larger cars, they were available.

With the combined facilities of Worcester Road and Pickersleigh Road (which by the time Peter was born was already almost twice the size of the much expanded original works), Morgan now had the capacity to build around forty cars a week – and they were able to sell them all. Furthermore, for now at least, demand was growing.

HFS had also arranged for the Runabout to be built under licence in Paris by his French agents Darmont et Badelogue, so by around 1922 he was confident enough to start another substantial expansion of the factory at Pickersleigh Road, soon to bring it up to six rows of shops including the original building from immediately before the war. True to Morgan tradition, the work was all funded from reserves, without the need to borrow. That was an even braver and more important decision than it might seem, because the next few years would be vital ones in the company's survival, in the face of tough new competition from low-cost cars like the Austin Seven (launched in 1922) and many others.

HFS had responded by reducing prices while improving his cars. Never wavering from his fundamental philosophy, he resisted tooling for big increases in production, with the short-term investments that implied, even when the order books were full. That helped him to hang on while others were failing all around him, through the Depression years of the mid- to late 1920s, and to survive even when three-wheeler sales were falling catastrophically into the late 1930s.

This was the ever-changing background of Morgan fortunes against which Peter and his four older sisters, Sylvia, Stella, Brenda and Barbara, grew up in Chestnut Villa, part of an extended Morgan 'family' which included long-serving members of the workforce as well as HFS's many visitors from the sporting world, and keeping a close eye on what was happening both in the workshop next door and in the expanding new factory in Pickersleigh Road.

Peter remembers his grandfather, the Reverend HG Morgan, teaching him to play chess on Sundays, and his primary schooling was close to home, at the Link School, Malvern. While he was there, in 1925, the family moved a little way along Worcester Road, to Fern Lodge, a much larger house than Chestnut Villa, with good-sized gardens rather than a factory on the doorstep. The garage, though, was never short of an assortment of cars, ranging, in the late 1920s, from the inevitable three-wheelers to HFS's first Rolls-Royce Silver Ghost, and a tandem-two-seater pedal car built at the factory for young Peter – with four wheels, long before that was the norm for the company.

HFS loved all kinds of cars, not only Morgans, and he was wealthy enough to indulge his interests. His £2,000 a year director's fee from the Morgan Motor Company was substantially supplemented by his income from an extremely broad investment portfolio, and by the beginning of the 1920s the company's annual profits were already climbing past the £30,000 mark, peaking in 1923, before the Austin Seven effect kicked in, at almost £41,000. After the Eagle and the Star of his pre-manufacturer days, HFS drove the Wolseleys and Darracqs for which the Morgan Garage held the agencies. He drove Lanchesters, a Hupmobile for a while, then a sporty Prince Henry Vauxhall, and in 1922, with the company booming, he bought a Rolls-Royce Silver Ghost tourer, and later still a Bentley. He collected older cars, too, and in the mid-1930s apparently had various rival light cars and cyclecars, including an AJS and a Carden. Strangest of all, he had a Pennington three-wheeler from before the turn of the century.

He made the most of Morgan craftsmanship, to produce exactly the cars he wanted, to his own body designs. As well as the four-wheeler pedal car for Peter, the Morgan works later made bodies for Ruth Morgan's Alvis, and for HFS's next Rolls-Royce – a Phantom II which he bought in 1930. HFS's father and sisters had a wide assortment of cars as well, while the family would regularly go on motoring holidays – first to Wales, as Peter remembers, and later to the north coast of Cornwall in the 1930s, with an assortment of Morgans and other cars. Peter even remembers seeing the Padstow lifeboat endowed by his great uncle. 'The *Helen Peele* was the last steam-driven lifeboat in the world I think, and it used to keep steam up all the time,' he says, 'just ticking over so to speak.

I remember it well, it was still going when we used to go down there for family holidays, at the lifeboat station along the coast.'

But Peter was never quite as interested in boats as his father had been as a boy, and given the family business there were other obvious distractions. Once he was old enough, Peter used to drive cars of his own, first a two-seater, three-wheeler F-type, later the first of the four-wheelers; that was the motoring-orientated backdrop that Peter grew up against. There were some restrictions, however, and for all that Peter is more the first of the 'four-wheel' generation, he still hankered after the early three-wheelers when he was learning to drive, but that was one place where his father drew the line. Later, he also made sure that Peter did not go too far too fast with his motor sporting ambitions. 'Father would not let me go on the tracks until I'd shown that I could do some good in trials. And after the war I said to father, the Plus 4 is quite a good rally car and I reckoned it could be pretty good in something like the Alpine; he said "sorry Peter, I do not care how fast you go up the passes but you're not racing coming down them . . ." and I know why he said that, because in 1922 or thereabouts he took a three-wheeler to Switzerland and went round all the passes, and I knew he'd had some hairy moments coming down, and that's the sort of thing that would go in there and he would not forget – it was purely that. I know it was.'

While Peter was growing up, although he loved cars his main interest was in locomotives and model railways, and his father was happy to encourage that. 'I used to spend hours watching the trains going through Malvern Link, because my walk from the Link School to Fern Lodge was along the path that went by the railway line and the Link station. It's no longer there now, but there was a little pathway from the back of the house through to the station, by the up-line. Father always kept his love of trains, he loved locos and if ever we went anywhere by train he would invariably take me to have a look at the engine. I had a model railway, a Basset Loake O gauge, until Charles came along and I changed it to OO gauge. In fact I've still got bits of it now, tucked away in a room somewhere in fairly sad condition . . .'

The family left Fern Lodge in 1935 and moved to Berkshire, to an even larger house with larger grounds, at Cannon Hill, Braywick, near Maidenhead. The way that HFS bought Cannon Hill and the sheer scale of the house and the surrounding grounds shows that he was a pretty tough bargainer and by now a very substantial businessman. Given the climate, his success should not be underestimated. The mid-Thirties were a difficult time for the car manufacturing side of the company, with 1935 itself showing a loss of more than £4,000, in the middle of a decade which saw only two years in profit. But there was always the safety net of investment incomes from the company's reserves, more than £8,000 gross returns in 1935, which more than offset the manufacturing losses, while HFS's own shares brought him almost £8,000 gross over and above his usual, long-standing £2,000 director's fees. In 1935, too, although production had fallen to just three hundred and nine cars and was still in virtual freefall, the assets of the company were shown as some £260,000, all controlled entirely by the family.

The new house was described by the agents as 'a fine family mansion dating from the reign of Charles II, designed by the brothers Adam'. It only gave half the picture. The estate included the house, which had twenty one principal bedrooms, plus a lodge, gardens, kitchen gardens, outbuildings and around 25 acres of parkland. Obviously taken by it, HFS only looked seriously at one other property in the neighbourhood; Cannon Hill was the one he wanted. The vendor was asking for £8,750, and HFS – having set himself a budget of £7,000 – originally offered £4,000. The vendor said he might accept £6,000, HFS offered £5,000 and the deal was done; payment was made in full, in typical Morgan corporate style with no outside borrowings but all from available funds.

Peter Morgan says the reasons for the move from Malvern to Berkshire were largely to do with improving family life, and the social prospects of the children. 'My mother thought father was doing too much and she was doing too much herself, with all her various good works and so on around Malvern Link. The third reason was a worry that my sisters would not meet up with suitable people to marry. In the end the big joke was that the two eldest ones married Malvern people anyway. The two younger ones and myself married people from Berkshire, or who we met in Berkshire, so that rather backfired. But as ever it was a practical decision, and whether the marriage part is true or not there was certainly more going on in Berkshire than there was in Malvern . . .'

Now in his mid-fifties, HFS was a long way from retiring, but he was beginning to step back. He still visited the works every week, usually driving himself there, often testing something new. In the early days he would stay for a night or two with the new owners of Chestnut Lodge, next door to the original factory. In 1936 that had reverted to being a garage with a Morgan connection, proprietors ED Bowman and WH Acock being Morgan agents and regular competitiors in Morgans. Bowman and Acock still have the Ford garage on the corner of the site, but Chestnut Lodge now has a filling station outside and the original Morgan Garage building was demolished in 1984. In the late 1930s, HFS gradually began handing over the everyday running of the Pickersleigh Road works to George Goodall, who had become works manager early in 1927 and would become managing director in 1938, having been joined in the factory in 1936 by his own son Jim – yet another regular motor sport competitor.

By the time HFS and Ruth Morgan moved to Berkshire, Peter, having finished his early schooling at the Link School in Malvern, had moved to Oundle public school in Northamptonshire, where he stayed until 1936. His move to Oundle was prompted by a number of HFS's business connections as well as by Peter's choice of engineering as a chosen career. 'I went to Oundle mainly through friends within the business. Burman's children went there, the Owens of Rubery Owen went to Oundle too, and quite a few other engineering people. Father particularly liked the idea that every week during the term you went into one of the workshops – it might have been machining or whatever, but they even had a foundry there. That was great fun, they had a forge where you could learn to shoe horses (at least I knew how to), and then of course there was the carpentry. It was pretty good, it taught you quite a lot. The foundry side was especially intriguing, I used to make little brass aeroplanes and things like that . . .'

During that time, as well as pursuing his academic subjects, he learned to drive; this often involved hacking the Ford-engined four-wheeler Morgan 4/4 prototype (after it had served its main purpose) around the spacious grounds of the new family home. His father brought it home one day after the decision had been taken to go with Coventry-Climax rather than Ford power. He presented it to his fifteen-year-old son, telling him that he could learn to drive around the garden. But even as a car-maker's son, Peter did not have carte blanche with what he was allowed to drive. 'The four-wheeler prototype was really an F-type three-wheeler with another wheel on the back,' he says, 'but just because I learned to drive on the first four-wheeler and joined the company when the four-wheeler was taking over, that didn't mean I was strictly a four-wheeler man rather than a three-wheeler man.

'I was rather pushed into it by my father more than by anything else. Before the war he would not allow me to have a three-wheeler twin, and I wanted a twin more than anything else – naturally. But he just would not allow it. And the reason why all came out one time when we were all on holiday in Cornwall.

'I used to tell him everything. I never kept secrets, and one day when I was driving an F-type three-wheeler I said to him, "I had a bit of a turn today coming up the hill. I was on the adverse camber and I was lucky that there was nothing coming the other way because I had to drive across, because the inside front wheel came up and I nearly went over". He didn't say much; he just said "ah well, now you know why I wouldn't let you have the twin; with that you really would have gone over", and he was probably right. All that had really happened was that one front wheel had come up and there was a lot of graunching [sic] at the back where the chassis member had gone down on the road and held me up. But he was good about things like that . . .'

Leaving Oundle, with its reputation for promoting engineering subjects, Peter was faced with a choice between going to university or going to engineering college. He admits at the time to not really having a career plan, but he did have the unswerving support of HFS. Asked by his father if he would prefer to go to university or do a practical training, he opted for the latter; to his father's evident delight, he went to the Chelsea College of Automobile and Aero Engineering to study for a BSc in automobile engineering.

He was at college in Chelsea from 1937 to 1940 and received a Full Diploma (First Class) in Automobile Engineering, a National Certificate in Mechanical Engineering and in January 1940 became a Graduate of the Institution of Automobile Engineers. From then to July 1940 he did outside work experience with the British Ermeto Corporation, but as well as having a successful academic stay in Chelsea he had a busy social life, meeting people like Duncan Hamilton. Hamilton became a very fine racing driver, and winner of Le Mans in 1953 for Jaguar, but as well as being a great driver, he also had a reputation as a bit of a rake, and Peter saw early evidence. 'We drove down to Brighton together once and wound up in a rather shady club where Duncan went off with the mother and I went off with the daughter. I left Duncan there on his own; I'd got him there but I do not know how he got back. We used to meet up after the war but we lost touch before it when he went into the Air Force and I went off into the Army . . .'

Before that happened, Peter had graduated from Chelsea with the intention of going into the motor industry, probably with either Rolls-Royce or Rover. He admits that he always intended eventually to join the family firm, but the onset of the Second World War meant that none of this would happen for a while yet.

At first he tried to enlist in the Royal Navy, as an artificer (the military term for an engineer by any other name), but he was rejected – he has always assumed because of his sight. He then went to volunteer his services to the Army and was selected for the Royal Army Service Corps. 'After I'd been turned down by the Navy,' he says, 'I did not hear anything for a few days, maybe a week or so afterwards, then an old school pal of mine rang me and said "what are you doing?"' The answer was 'nothing', as a result of which we went to the HAC and I ended up with a job in the workshops. In the RASC Peter's engineering background brought him a first posting as a workshop officer for a transport company, in the motor coach workshops. 'We had the First Coldstreams and the First and Second Grenadier Guards and the responsibility to move the Southern Command – Monty's lot, although he was not head of it at that time – anywhere in the country if an invasion had occurred.' He found plenty to keep him busy, because most of the coaches needed new engines before they went anywhere. 'Someone had requisitioned a lot of coaches and they were ghastly – they all had cracked cylinder blocks and God knows what. They'd really taken the Army for a ride as far as the cost of requisitioning the coaches was concerned. When I got there I think about twelve were runners out of thirty-three and when I left thirty-one ran, which I thought was pretty good. Mind you I spent a hell of a lot. I used to be going up to Bristol buying new engines every weekend . . .'

It was good practice for life at Morgan. 'I remember going up to Ashchurch with one of the coaches and bringing back a Ford V8, and that was how things used to work. But I was not there for all that long, I think for about nine months, and then I got a posting to Sierra Leone – to Freetown . . .'

That was to the workshops of the Royal West African Frontier Force, and it was the beginning of a West African spell that Peter Morgan loved. From Freetown he went on to take charge of the Army workshops in Nairobi, where he stayed until the end of the war. 'I always think it's quite funny,' he says, 'that while I was there I finished up in charge of more people than we've got here now – and some very different people, too. We had British Other Ranks, I had Italian prisoners of war – under a colonel, a charming chap who I remember used to make damned good spaghetti; then I had Indian Sikhs and Indian Hindus, who were always at each others' throats, I had Chinese carpenters, West Africans and East Africans – it was quite a mixed lot and they were all good in their own departments.'

While Peter was away, the Morgan factory had been given over to war work and the rest of the family had been temporarily displaced from the house at Cannon Hill, which HFS had offered as a wartime base for a company involved with Morgan. They moved into a smaller, rented house nearby, where Peter would occasionally visit when on leave, and catch up with driving various Morgans.

Demobbed from the Army towards the end of 1946, having reached the rank of captain (or, more accurately, substantive captain, acting major), Peter Morgan was again faced with a decision about his future; but that still did not automatically mean going back to the family business. Nairobi had been an enjoyable posting and on leaving the RASC he was offered a job locally, similar to that of his Army role, looking after a vehicle fleet for the United Africa Company which specialised in logging.

By this time, however, he was married. His wife Jane, who he had married in December 1940 when he was twenty-one, was living in Malvern in the house that Peter had first rented, then bought, in St James's Road. Jane was proof that HFS's policy of moving to Berkshire had been at least partly succesful; she came from Maidenhead and had been at school with the Morgan sisters. When HFS saw Peter's letter to Jane explaining the United Africa Company job, he hinted strongly that it was time his son came home. If he returned, there would be a job waiting for him with the company. Peter says now that the episode was an exercise to get his father to offer him a reasonable salary, even though that would only be around half his captain's pay.

'It was really just a bit of a joke,' he says. 'Father kind of blew his top and said "no, we can't have that". But I wouldn't really have done it because I loved the cars and I'd already had a great time with them. Remember I'd been racing before the war, so I'd had some pretty good experiences already, and I'd been to Brooklands, been to Donington, been all over the place really, more or less from the time I had a licence.'

Taking up the option of coming home, in 1947, at the age of twenty-seven, Peter Morgan joined the Morgan Motor Company. He did so with a broad range of responsibilities, from general run-around to development engineer. Although much of the factory was unionised (as was most of British industry at the time, and by a very wide range of different unions) he could work in the areas that had non-union labour. And when the previous incumbent left, he became the company's draughtsman, working closely with his father. It was a great experience.

'Father was a talented engineer, a very good artist and a magnificent tutor. He was a remarkable man, too, in almost forcing you to find things out for yourself. In later years I used to criticise the play in the steering on the Plus 4 in particular, which was due to a bad steering box. But as well as that there was this wheel tramping problem, and I thought this must be friction, so I reckoned I'd try one without the steering damper. The steering was much lighter, and I thought "yes, this is very good", until I went down the road and it started shaking like mad. I said to my father, "you know it was terrible", and he said to me "well yes, I knew that it would be but I thought you ought to find out for yourself". You know, it was so typical. Then there was another time when I brought him a drawing that was really very like an early Healey, in the early 1950s, some time before that car came out. I made a model of it, just in wood, put some wheels on it, and it had a full width body and so on. I took it to him and he looked at it and said, "oh yes, that's quite nice. Now run along and do the four-seater". And of course he knew I could not. Bang, he was clever like that . . .'

Peter arrived at the factory in February 1947, during that particularly bitter winter. He joined the Morgan board on a salary of £9 a week. Times were difficult for the company; its survival was by no means a certainty, principally because of big changes in the market following the war. Circumstances were, in many ways, worse than those that followed the first war, when Morgan had been able to restart production quickly, before almost any other car manufacturer in the country. This time it was out of the question.

Peter freely admits that the future was uncertain, but he was adamant that the company would survive. 'I never thought that it wouldn't. And of course I was aware that it had a lot of complexities. When father died it was virtually an investment company. It had so much invested, I don't know what it would be in modern terms but I suppose it would amount to about seven to ten million pounds in investments outside of the car building . . .'

The Inland Revenue had apparently noticed this some years earlier too. In November 1940 Morgan were negotiating with them as to whether the main business of the company should now be regarded as the management of financial resources rather than the manufacture of motor vehicles, with Morgan refuting the suggestion. In December Morgan won their case; the Inland Revenue decided not to redefine the company's main business although it must have been a close run thing, given that the company lost £1,826 making cars that year while making £9,209 gross on investment income, albeit at a time complicated by wartime production changes.

By the time Peter arrived after the war, that dispute had been resolved, and the company did have one other major advantage, a recurring Morgan theme. Although three-wheeler sales had already gone into serious decline long before the Second World War, the new four-wheeler, the 4/4, had been announced at Christmas 1935 and introduced to the market in 1936. It had cost very little to develop as an evolution of its three-wheel, four-cylinder cousin (as Peter said, an F-type with an extra wheel at the back), building it involved few changes from the process of building the three-wheeler, and it had started almost immediately to sell well, overtaking three-wheeler production even before the war. It had made money, not least because Morgan bargained hard with its suppliers and watched costs extremely carefully, bargained as hard and cost-controlled every bit as assiduously as much larger companies, as is clear from pre-war minutes.

In November 1937, 'Mr Morgan reported that negotiations with the Standard Motor Company for the supply of engines for the four-wheeler were nearing completion, but this engine would have overhead valves and would be similar in type to that fitted to the SS cars. The price would be approximately £25 and a demonstration model was now on test. It was noted that the company was under contract to take delivery of a further 250 Climax engines at a price of £29 rising to £36, and it was resolved that the possibility of negotiating an amendment on this contract should be reviewed as soon as a definite decision had been made regarding the stability of the Standard engines.'

Over the next few months the negotiations continued, and played a central part in pricing the cars, at a time when price cutting was propping up sales. By June 1938 they were discussing actual costs versus estimated costs of the new four-wheeler (as well as other cars in the range) and came to the conclusion that there would be a substantial reduction in estimated profits. At the same time they discussed reducing the price of the four-wheeler by £10 once the cost saving of the Standard engine became available, to bring its price below £200 for the first time, in time for the 1938 Motor Show. In August they decided not to cut the price of the three-wheelers but to go to £199 10s for the 4/4 two-seater (cutting profits per car from £24 3s 6d to £15 17s 6d) and £215 for the 4/4 four-seater (trimming profits from £31 1s 0d to £23 6s 6d). They did however note that profits would improve again once the remaining stock of one hundred and fifty of the more expensive Climax engines from the last order of three hundred and fifty had been used. And in November HFS reported further interviews with John Black where he had been given a 'reasonable assurance' that Standard could deliver a £10 cost saving per engine compared with the Climax unit, while bringing their engine to the point where it could offer comparable performance to that offered by Climax, which was still an important point.

By July 1939, with war imminent, the estimated profits per car were £38 on a Coupé, the same on a 4/4 four-seater, £31 on a 4/4 two-seater, £23 on an F Super and just £8 on the basic three-wheeler F4. With the usual sales ratio between models, that was reckoned to represent an average profit of £26 10s per car, a return of better than 10 per cent, which most other companies could not even dream of.

Morgan entered the war years still looking financially healthy. By the time Peter arrived on the scene, there were the considerable sums Morgan had earned during the war, on the government's fixed-profits schemes, plus funds from sub-letting parts of the factory to other companies, and the advantages of being able to purchase machinery installed during the war at favourable rates, then adapting it to making car components.

Set against that in 1946 were many obstacles to an immediate resumption of car production. Much of the pre-war workforce had been taken away by the war, some of them into the forces, others relocated by government order for wartime production elsewhere. Some of them, sadly, would never return, but even the ones who did would filter back slowly, as post-war military demobilisation in a still volatile political period would take a considerable time. 'At the time the whole industry was struggling,' says Peter now; 'the factory had not really got back from the war work and we had not got everybody back. For the past three years or so I've been the oldest one here. People came during the year that I arrived, and there are one or two still with me now who came late in 1947, but I was actually the first.' Some of the workforce did not return until more than a year after the fighting in Europe had stopped; even if they had returned earlier they would have found parts of the works still housing their wartime occupiers from other companies, some of whom did not leave until well into 1946.

Finally, like every other manufacturer in Britain, Morgan faced appalling materials shortages, and most unhelpfully a return to an atmosphere of official antagonism to the motor car. In 1946 the British motor industry officially celebrated its Golden Jubilee, but for manufacturers and motorists alike there was little to cheer about. Petrol was still rationed, and would be to a greater or lesser extent until 1950, at which point the ration was removed but fuel tax doubled. Nor could you simply buy a new car, even if you could afford one: to order a new vehicle you had to acquire a Ministry of War Transport Licence – and then wait your turn. When you finally took delivery you had to sign a covenant agreeing not to sell the new vehicle for at least a year, to prevent a black market trade. Far from going away as post-war production restarted, in 1950 the new car covenant was extended to two years and was not abolished until 1953.

In the immediate post-war years, the new Socialist government did not consider a return to motoring for the masses as one of its priorities, and selling sports cars even less so, unless they were sold abroad. All cars for the home market were subject to purchase tax, which had been introduced during the war to discourage the sale of 'luxury goods'. The tax remained on cars even though it was soon taken off such things as household appliances. Government policy on the motor car, and its antipathy towards it, was summed up by the Chancellor of the Exchequer, Hugh Dalton, who said, 'There is too much congestion on the roads at home . . . the industry should concentrate on exports . . . I have been asked to take purchase tax off cars sold in this country, but regret that I cannot do this now. I have been told that the trade want a definite statement, and I shall give it. I cannot hold out any hope of removing the tax for some time to come . . . The motor industry and would-be purchasers of private cars in this country should, therefore, proceed on the assumption that the purchase tax is here to stay.'

He went on to make the position on exports abundantly clear when he said, 'I hope that the motor industry is going to export a lot more than it sells at home. There is a great block on the roads at home and great opportunities for trade abroad. There is today a sellers' market for cars, as for other British exports, in many different parts of the world, and I hope that the motor industry will fully exploit it. This is a time,' he said, 'for exporters not only to renew contacts with old markets but to find their way into new ones – and there is, of course, no purchase tax on cars which manufacturers export. To this extent, therefore, the export trade is stimulated, as it should be . . .'

In February 1945 the Morgan board had decided they should plan to build 300 three-wheelers and 500 four-wheelers as soon as possible. In July 1945 they received official authority to build just 50 three-wheelers and 75 four-wheelers by the end of the year. Standard, in the meantime, accepted an order for 200 engines, and the orders started to mount up. In January 1946 the board heard that there was 'good progress' on resuming car production for export to Australia, and that there were now around a hundred orders in hand from home and abroad. This was good news in view of the fact that monthly income from the machine shop on outside work had already fallen to around £1,300, compared to wartime peaks of more than £4,000 a month. By February 1946 there were 193 orders pending, and Morgan were aiming to start building a car a day as soon as possible. By March there were 270 orders, by April 428 – and the deal with Standard was extended to cover 380 engines at £61 per engine – which, tellingly, was 75 per cent more than the unit cost of essentially similar engines in 1939.

The numbers of cars ordered, however, and the numbers delivered, were two very different things. By May 1946 the former was 549 cars (and remarkably perhaps, 300 of those orders were for three-wheelers), but at the beginnning of the month Morgan had delivered exactly a dozen cars – seven 4/4s for export, two coupés and three Supers for the home market; by the end of May they had delivered just another five. By June 1946 there were 864 orders, by July 994, and Morgan had delivered exactly 22 of them, which had crept up to 47 by October 1946, as output reached a heady two a week.

So when Peter Morgan came to the company in February 1947, any meaningful production had only barely resumed, and the adage, as everywhere in British industry, was 'export or die'. By the end of 1947 Morgan were trading with the USA, Canada, South America, Australasia, South Africa and many European countries. It was not the last time that Peter would have to face the problem of pursuing new export markets.

HFS Morgan was now into his late sixties, and not permanently on site, but he was still very active in steering the company's policies. In 1952 he faced one of the sadder episodes of his working life, when he had to accept the end for the three-wheeler. Quite simply, there was no market for it anymore and, other than in tiny numbers there had not been since just before the Second World War, when the government had first announced its intentions to change the tax system in a way that would remove the three-wheeler's tax advantages, albeit without implementing the changes as planned because of more pressing problems. Post-war restrictions had made the situation worse. To qualify for supplies of steel and other materials, Morgan had to export; in mainland Europe and the USA there were no tax advantages for the three-wheeler, and no longer any export market for it, which meant in effect that Morgan were not allowed to build it, even if there had been a home market. Although the end was delayed, it was inevitable, and while HFS was reluctant to make the decision, ever the pragmatist he did what he had to do, and concentrated all his efforts behind the four-wheelers. The very last of the three-wheelers, a Ford-engined F Super, was completed in July 1952.

Peter Morgan's era became that of the four-wheelers, a time to rebuild a Morgan market. He believes the changeover from three wheels to four could have been more damaging, save for the timing. He argues that the break in production during the war let Morgan distance itself, more easily than might otherwise have been the case, from the image of being only a maker of three-wheelers. When they did make the break, the four-wheeler was well enough established to fill the gap. Furthermore, if there was an export market for anything in the post-war years, it was for sports cars.

The late Forties and early Fifties were some of the most difficult years the company ever faced. It was one of the rare periods when Morgan's car manufacturing operation actually lost money, and although the losses were quite small (£1,551 in 1949, £618 in 1950, £2,683 in 1951 and £372 in 1953 after a profit of £3,543 in 1952), and offset by earnings from Morgan's other interests (as ever, the broader investments), they did leave HFS and Peter Morgan with some difficult decisions. Most importantly, those decisions included whether to accept a takeover bid for Morgan from a close associate, the Standard Motor Company.

Standard was controlled by Sir John Black, the same man who, in 1910, working for a patent agent, had produced the patent drawings for the first single-seater, three-wheeler production model. He had had no real contact with HFS between the time he produced those drawings and a chance meeting with HFS at a party some time before the Second World War, leading to the agreement over engine supplies, but in the meantime he had built his own career in the motor industry, joining Standard in 1929 after working for Hillman, and becoming managing director four years later.

Black was knighted in 1943, partly for his stewardship of Standard's own war efforts but largely for his role as chairman of the Joint Aero Engine Committee, which put him in charge of Britain's 'shadow factory' network. Immediately after the war, Standard's associations with Morgan grew closer again, largely because of the rekindled personal connection between Sir John and HFS, although this time Peter Morgan would be closely involved in the process too.

Later, the links presented Morgan with some difficult decisions, but initially the association with Standard may well have saved the company by removing the temptation for HFS to build his own engines. As long ago as 1914, he had experimented with a 1-litre four-cylinder side-valve Dorman engine – tried out in the prototype four-wheeler of the period but, like the car, quickly abandoned. And, just as he had always relied on proprietary twin-cylinder engines from a variety of makers, for several years between the wars Morgan had used other people's four-cylinder engines, first in the three-wheelers from 1933, and since 1936 in the new four-wheeler. Those had included engines from Ford and from Coventry-Climax, but in the late 1930s the supply of Coventry-Climax engines in particular had become uncertain. That led HFS, quite uncharacteristically, to look at whether it might be preferable to make Morgan independent of outside suppliers by building his own engines, even if the cost of tooling and small-volume production would be considerable. By 1939 that idea, and any such others, would go no further.

HFS did not abandon his ideas completely. In May 1942, discussing post-war plans with JA Prestwich of JAP, there had been the suggestion that JAP might mass-produce a car similar to the existing Morgan, to be marketed as the Morgan Car. HFS did not want to pursue that arrangement – and whether Prestwich saw it as a partnership or a takeover is unclear – but at the time HFS did say he would be interested in a four-cylinder JAP engine. Nothing came of that either, and by December 1944 HFS was talking to the board again about Morgan building their own engine, and immediately after the war he went as far as to commission drawings for an engine.

That engine was a small capacity, four-cylinder, overhead camshaft unit, designed by Harry Hatch of the AJS Motor Cycle Company, which by then had been taken over by Matchless, whose twins had appeared in many of the early three-wheeler Morgans. In the 1920s, Hatch had also designed the 1100cc Blackburne vee-twins, as used in many other Morgan three-wheelers, and the racing version of which had been particularly successful for Morgan in record breaking. The post-war project, however, only went as far as the drawings (which are still in the Morgan archives). They were delivered in October 1946, a few months before Peter Morgan took up his new job, but no engine was ever built. Hatch's estimate for his work on an 1100–1300cc engine was £250 for the drawings, plus a consultancy fee for its development, and a royalty of 5s per engine once it went into production, although this, of course, never happened.

Many times since, Peter has said that Morgan's decision not to build their own engine was one of the most important in the history of the company. He is quite certain that if his father had gone through with the project, it would have killed the company, just as the huge investment needed to take this major manufacturing step has killed many other overconfident small car makers.

The temptation to revive the Morgan engine project after the war had already been much reduced, thanks directly to Sir John Black, who provided HFS with the alternative that he needed, and under very attractive terms. It was largely Peter Morgan who brokered that deal and planned the new car.

In 1939, Morgan had built a small number of 4/4s (fewer than thirty cars) with engines supplied by Standard. They were more than simply off-the-shelf units; they were produced specifically for Morgan and were rather more exciting than the side-valve, Flying Ten engine on which they were based. They were four-cylinder 1267cc units, with overhead valves and a cylinder head design using lessons learned from the overhead-valve engines that Standard had built for William Lyons' SS Jaguars. They produced 40bhp, which was a little more than Morgan's regular Coventry-Climax offering of the time, and enough to boost both the 4/4's performance and Morgan's image. Following those pre-war cost negotiations between HFS and John Black, the Standard engines were ultimately considerably cheaper than the Climax.

After the war, Sir John Black was happy to continue supplying this special engine exclusively to Morgan, without ever using it in one of his own cars. In 1946, with supplies of Coventry-Climax engines now virtually unobtainable, the Standard-engined Morgan 4/4 reappeared, again using the familiar 1267cc overhead-valve four.

It saw the first generation Morgan four-wheeler to the end of its days in 1950, but the car that followed – the Plus 4 – continued the relationship with Standard. While in many ways the design of the new engine was not as good as the old one, what it lacked in mechanical sophistication it made up for with capacity. It was a four-cylinder, overhead-valve engine again, this time with the substantially larger capacity of 2088cc (at least by the time it reached full production form), and it was taken from the new Standard Vanguard saloon. It also brought a leap in power output, to 68bhp, so the transmission and other areas of the recipient Morgan were uprated to cope, and the whole car was made slightly larger, making room for the bigger engine but adding a bit more cockpit space. It was a quicker Morgan again, and very successful, which prompted the next pivotal moment in Morgan history.

Sir John Black urgently needed a sports car in his portfolio. As outlined in Chapter 6, American servicemen's affection for European-type sports cars had prompted an import boom, with British marques like MG and Jaguar very much in the forefront. Black had a sporting marque in his armoury, but not a sporting car. The marque was Triumph, which, like so many early manufacturers, had started with bicycles, and in this case progressed to motor cycles before branching out into cars. The motor cycles, introduced in 1902, were massively successful both commercially and in competition, giving Triumph a deservedly sporty reputation. The first car, which appeared in 1923, was a fairly ordinary light car of its day, a 10/20hp four-cylinder, designed for Triumph by Lea-Francis's designer Arthur Alderson, and rather expensive alongside most rivals. That was joined by a larger model in 1924, the 13/35, which was the first British car to have Lockheed hydraulic brakes on all four wheels. Then in 1927, Triumph introduced the first of the more sporty models which would in future define the company's character.

It was another light car, the sort of opposition the three-wheeler Morgans were faced with on all fronts in the late 1920s, and it was called the Super Seven. It only had an 832cc engine and 21bhp, but not unlike a Morgan it had light weight on its side and even the ordinary, tourer versions performed well. There were also Sports models, including a supercharged type, which performed better still, and the Super Seven family became big sellers in the late 1920s and early 1930s. Triumph, however, was suffering as badly as most from the Depression, across all areas of the company. The bicycle business was sold, and in 1931, with motor cycle sales down by almost a third, Triumph was unable, for the first time in thirty years, to pay an ordinary shares dividend. In 1936, the motor cycle business was sold off as well, for around £50,000, although production continued in the original works until they were destroyed by bombs during the Second World War, leading to the start of two-wheeled Triumph's Meriden era.

The car operation, meanwhile, was underlining its sporty image with a new line of larger cars, and the next few years in Triumph's history form an interesting contrast with Morgan's approach. Where Morgan were cautious and self-sufficient, Triumph were more profligate. But in hindsight, this was where their paths began to converge.

The Triumph range grew, with four- and six-cylinder cars, topped by the exciting 2.3-litre eight-cylinder Dolomite sports model of 1934, which, sadly, was dropped after just a handful were made. Like Morgan, Triumph built a good reputation on sporting exploits, but unlike Morgan they did not control their costs. In 1935, a year in which Morgan built just two hundred and eighty-six three-wheelers in the final year before the birth of the four-wheeler, Triumph bought a new factory. But in 1936, while Morgan were just about holding their own, Triumph, already suffering from several successive years in the red, lost some £212,000. And in 1937, while Morgan were cautiously but effectively building sales of the new four-wheeler alongside the fast-declining three-wheelers, Triumph (having raised capital by issuing £200,000 worth of new stock) came out with the biggest range of cars it had ever produced. The range was again topped by a sporty model, the controversially styled 2-litre, six-cylinder Dolomite, and it helped Triumph make a small profit in 1937. In 1938, having seen a small trading profit wiped out by large investments into yet another new model, it was back to making losses. That, however, did not stop Triumph bidding to take over Riley, which had gone into receivership. Nor did the new model stop Triumph following them, in June 1939.

Triumph's sporting credentials were bringing them into the Morgan story. With war approaching, sales of parts of the

Triumph Car Company had been arranged on the receiver's behalf by Triumph's former technical director Donald Healey, who would set up his own sports car company after the war and become one of Morgan's greatest rivals. Two elements of the deal were selling the Triumph name to a Sheffield steel maker, the Thomas Ward Group, and leasing one of Triumph's factories to the Armstrong-Whitworth Aircraft Company. That factory was also heavily bombed during the war, but in 1944, what remained of it was bought by Sir John Black for £77,000, along with the rights to the Triumph name. Black did the deal after another of his engine customers, William Lyons of SS Cars, had turned down the offer of the Triumph Company from the receiver, on the grounds that his resources would be better utilised in expanding his own, successful marque, rather than trying to rebuild an unsuccessful one in Triumph. Black obviously saw more potential.

The deal, first broached in October 1944 and signed and sealed by November, was a good one. Ultimately, by selling off the bombed out factory in 1946 for almost as much as he had paid for the whole package, Black had acquired the still highly regarded Triumph badge for almost nothing. As part of the Standard organisation it gave him the platform for the sporty cars he believed he could sell in the post-war market, in competition with Lyons' new Jaguars, which had now evolved from the Standard-based SS. Black's initial thoughts did not involve Morgan.

The plan did not start brightly, because the first Standard-built Triumphs, launched in 1946, were frankly not terribly exciting: they included the rather bulbous, alloy-bodied 1800 Roadster with its throwback dickey seat, and the interestingly styled but under-powered Renown saloon, forerunner of the smaller 'razor-edged' Mayflower, launched in 1952. The Mayflower would use the ordinary version of the smaller engine used by Morgan in the 4/4, but strangely, although it would have been improved by its extra zip, it never adopted the uprated Morgan version. Both Roadster and Renown started with the 1.8-litre, four-cylinder engine that Standard had supplied to Lyons for his first Jaguars, and both graduated in 1949 to the 2.1-litre Vanguard engine of the type soon to be supplied to Morgan. It was an engine that did Standard proud, not so much because of its role in the Vanguard, successful though that car was, nor for its use in the Triumph Roadster, which also did quite well commercially, with sales of around 4,500 cars in 1,800 and 2,000 guises over the next four years, and certainly not for its relative handful of sales in the Morgan. It played a successful part in a rather different role.

In August 1945, Sir John Black signed an agreement with Harry Ferguson for Standard to build Ferguson's small, low-priced tractors, and in 1946 they started production, soon switching from imported engines to the Vanguard engine and creating a most useful economy of scale. The tractor operation was so successful that in 1947–8 Standard built more tractors than cars, and made considerable profits in the process, to the extent that Black briefly talked of switching production completely to tractors, and forgetting all about cars. He did not, of course, and before the end of the 1940s he started to think about reviving a real Triumph sports car.

His thoughts were of a car for the booming American market, to sell somewhere between the MG TC (and its successor the TD) and the Jaguar XK120, launched in 1948. In the UK market that would also put it head-to-head with the Standard-powered 4/4. Back in 1944, after Lyons had turned down the possibility of taking over Triumph, Black had had talks with Lyons about forming a partnership, and it was only after Lyons declined that Black committed himself to the Triumph deal, with the express intention of competing with Jaguar's sporty saloons and sports cars.

His problem with launching a Triumph sports car in a hurry was simply that he did not have one to launch, and that was when he turned to Morgan.

At the London Motor Show in October 1950, Morgan unveiled the new Plus 4, with its 2.1 Standard Vanguard engine, closely related to the unit in the big-selling Ferguson tractor. Morgan showed both a left- and a right-hand-drive roadster plus two coupés and a four-seater 4/4 to represent the four-seat option, because the four-seater Plus 4 was not yet ready. The Plus 4 was well received by the press, and it clearly impressed Sir John Black. Standard's new 'sports car' offering for the show, following on from the Triumph Roadster (which had ceased production at the end of 1949), was the Triumph TRX, or 'New Roadster'. Although the underpinnings were an unmodified Vanguard chassis plus most of that car's running gear, the TRX, like the original Roadsters, had an all-alloy body, this time with a much more modern look.

Styled by Walter Belgrove, the TRX had a sleek, all-enveloping shape rather than the Roadster's old-fashioned separate wings and headlights. The dickey was gone, the headlamps were hidden behind retractable panels in the wings, operated electro-hydraulically, as was the fold-away hood, and even the seat adjustment. It had a twin-carburettor version of the 2.1 Vanguard engine, but the TRX, which retained the three-speed gearbox and column change, plus the three-abreast bench-seating of the old Roadster, was far less overtly sporty than the Morgan, and rather more tourer than genuine sports car. With all its creature comforts and double-skinned body construction, it was quite an attractive car, but it was heavier, slower and considerably more expensive: at £975 it was nearly twice the price of the cheapest two-seater Plus 4, which cost £510. Three TRX prototypes were built in 1950, but although the TRX appeared at the Motor Show it never went into production, scuppered by a mediocre public reception and by Standard having more profitable cars to worry about. It had, however, provided the final link in the Morgan connection.

The TRX project was not officially cancelled until 1951, but Sir John Black probably gauged the reaction at the 1950 show pretty well, and before it had ended he was talking to the Morgans. In a meeting on Standard's show stand, he sugges-ted that an amalgamation of the two companies could be a good thing, combining Morgan's clearly attractive Plus 4 design with Standard's production capacity to build a car that could sell in substantial numbers in America, against MG and Jaguar. HFS did not immediately commit himself either way but both he and Peter went away to consider the offer. That included a promise from Sir John that, if the amalgamation was rejected, it would not jeopardise future Vanguard engine supplies, and if it was accepted, Peter Morgan would have a role within Standard Triumph. Their answer, delivered some weeks later, was no; Peter confirms now that, from the outset the answer was always going to be no. True to his principles, HFS, having considered all the possibilities, again opted to remain independent, a decision supported unequivocally by his son, then and now.

The Morgan minutes of November 1950 report the episode: 'Interviews with Sir John Black: Mr Morgan reported that during the course of the motor show Sir John Black had invited both him and his son to meet him and discuss the possibilities of a sale of the Morgan Motor Company Ltd to the Standard Motor Company Ltd. Mr Morgan indicated that he and his son had given very careful thought to this proposal but felt that in all the circumstances it would be desirable for the company to postpone any further negotiations on those lines until the company had had an opportunity of testing the value of its post-war research and development on the Plus 4 car. After discussion it was resolved that the greatest possible effort be made to step up production and to defer any further discussion with Sir John Black for at least a period of one year.' In December 1950 Black was informed of the decision and told HFS that he would be happy to reopen negotiations at a later date should it ever be appropriate. And with those statements Morgan summed up one of the biggest and most far reaching decisions of the company's life – to stay independent.

The answer was not what Standard either expected or needed. As Harry Webster, then Standard's chief engineer, revealed in an interview in 1990, 'Sir John decided he wanted a sports car to export to America. He tried to buy Morgan, to whom we were supplying engines, but under no circumstances would they sell out. I know he was very angry and he decided immediately to go into opposition.'

Having failed to take over Morgan (because for all the talk of partnerships, the offer really amounted to a takeover) Sir John Black started the hugely successful Triumph TR range, while continuing to allow the Morgan connection.

Early in 1952, Triumph produced a car coded 20TS and known originally as the Triumph Sports Car. It was created on a very tight budget, using as many off-the-shelf compo-

From top: Peter racing his ex-TT 4-4 at Silverstone in August 1949, HFS remained active in trials after the war, and a different shape, in the pretty Drophead Coupé

Opposite: Peter Morgan at Bournemouth with Drophead Coupe in the 1951 RAC Rally, en route to the famous team prize victory - and an even more famous win, as the flag falls on the Chris Lawrence, Dick Shepherd-Barron Morgan at Le Mans in 1962

Top Left: Peter and Charles at Blue Hills, Cornwall, on the Lands End Trial with the Plus 4 Plus

Left: Peter Morgan and Tommy Thomson contested the 1958 RAC Rally, which finished here in Hastings, but Morgan could no longer repeat their pre-war class wins or Peter's second place finish overall in the 1951 event and the team prize in 1952

Below: testing a Ford-engined Series II 4/4, launched in 1955

Above: Peter Morgan in the original Plus 8 prototype,
outside the main entrance to the Pickersleigh Road
offices and works

Man Enough?

Choosing a Morgan means you demand more than most. Stepping out from the crowd. A Morgan man expects — and gets — vivid acceleration (0-70 in 7.5 seconds in our latest plus 8) ; safety up to 125 mph assisted by impeccable handling and big servo-discs up front ; plus the ability to show off his natural panache.
The Morgan 4/4 is also a delightful 100 mph sports car.
Both cars are attractive — not only to you !

First of the real sports cars

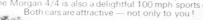

MORGAN MOTOR COMPANY LIMITED, Pickersleigh Road, Malvern Link, Worcs., WR14 2LL Tel : 06845 3104

Top: very much the early 1970s way of advertising the Plus 8, not exactly PC by the year 2000

Above: not a trial but throwing a Plus 8 around in the dirt for a mid-1970s publicity shot

Right: perhaps the most famous four-wheeled Morgan of all, the 1962 Le Mans T class-winning TOK 258 at Brands Hatch for the launch of the 2-litre Rover engined Plus 4 in May 1988

Left: Charles the learner driver with Peter the teacher and grandmother's F-Type, in Cornwall in the late 1960s

Below: the original Plus 8 in the Snetterton 24 Hours, where Charles shared with Rob Wells and Graham Bryant but lost a wheel while leading

Opposite: the way it used to be. Cars being assembled in batches in the 1970s - with a mix of four- and eight cylinder models

Right: Chris Alford's 1975 prodsports win allowed Morgan to indulge in the kind of advertising they always loved

Below: a mid 1960s flight of fancy from teenaged Charles

Bottom: Charles as cameraman, with 'fixer' Jamshid, newsman Martin Lewis and soundman Chris Squires

MORGAN WIN
1975 PRODUCTION SPORTS
CAR CHAMPIONSHIP!

Chris Alford, driving the
John Britten All-British Racing Team Morgan 4/4,
is outright winner of the 1975 BRSCC Production Sports Car Championship.
(Subject to official confirmation)
The 1600cc 2-seater, with only the minor
safety modifications permitted by the regulations,
won the up to £2500 class of every race it entered,
at circuits as varied as Brands Hatch, Silverstone, Castle Combe,
Croft, Rufforth, Llandow, Mallory Park and Snetterton.
John Britten, in the team's Morgan Plus 8,
had several outright wins and finished second in the
up to £4000 class of the championship.

THE JOHN BRITTEN ALL BRITISH RACING TEAM

Above: the old way, pre Harvey-Jones, with tin snips and hand formed wings; now it's laser cut blanks and superformed wing panels

Right: another of the *Troubleshooter's* pet hates in 1990, wheeling part finished cars around the yard. That still happens, but now they don't make so many trips

Opposite: the details may have changed in recent years, but hand crafted coachbuilding is still at the heart of the Morgan tradition

Top Left: starting point for the body frames, early 1990s style, well seasoned hardwood and a steady hand

Left: the wooden frame - even for the Aero 8, it forms the foundation for any Morgan body

Below: John H Sheally II, one of America's greatest Morgan enthusiasts, and a prolific winner in US sprints with this early Plus 8

nents as possible, notably the chassis from the Standard Flying Nine, which had been out of production for some time, but several hundred of which were in storage. That was a bad decision, because that chassis simply was not strong enough for the job, so a replacement was hastily designed and fabricated in time for the car's first public appearance, at the London Motor Show of October 1952. As Harry Webster told the story '[Sir John] directed me that he wanted a sports car, in a very short time and with very little money involved. We took a Mayflower front suspension, a Vanguard engine and gearbox, and a Mayflower back axle, put them on the floor and literally drew a chassis round them. We carried out some stiffness tests, and it was pretty obvious that the towers of the front suspension were far too weak, so we put in a tie-bar and that was our chassis. Walter Belgrove designed a very stark body. We carried out some test work and showed the car confidentially to certain members of the press, who criticised the styling, particularly the short arse end with the external spare wheel, so we designed the longer tail, and that's how it went into production.'

The important difference here between Triumph and Morgan is not in the way the cars were designed, but in the final execution, and the way it confirmed the value of the Morgan philosophy. HFS did very little by way of formal drawings but would apparently sketch body designs over pictures of the chassis, or sometimes draw a body shape in chalk on the factory wall, to be converted into working drawings by someone else. So Morgan also took the low-tech design route, but where Black's Standard-Triumph now had to commit to expensive mass-production tooling, HFS and Peter only had to change the drawings and reprogramme the craftsmen.

The original car that Webster describes, powered by a mildly uprated 75bhp, twin-carburettor, 2-litre version of the inevitable Vanguard engine, retrospectively became known as the Triumph TR1, but the only example built was the 1952 show car. By the beginning of 1953, with the changes that Webster outlines, it had evolved into new prototypes for the virtually identical looking (save for replacing the 'short arse end') but more thoroughly developed production reality, the

TR2. Interestingly, at the start of the project Black had told Walter Belgrove, who also did the final styling, that he could design a traditional looking sports car, in the same mould as the MG – or the Morgan. Belgrove, however, chose to do something more modern, albeit simple to tool for and to build. With its restyled, more angular tail and an increase in power to 90bhp, the car reappeared at the Geneva Show in March 1953 and went into production in late summer as the TR2, offering considerable performance for a very reasonable price.

In fact at £555 without tax before the end of 1953, or £595 from the start of 1954, it was in direct competition with Morgan's Plus 4, to a far greater degree than the TRX ever could have been. Remarkably, even now the relationship between Morgan and Standard-Triumph was not completely compromised, and from 1954 Morgan's Plus 4 was available with the 2-litre, 90bhp Triumph TR2 engine, alongside the Vanguard-powered version. Still, it was a slightly odd relationship; mass-production meant the Triumphs could sell in much larger numbers, while the Morgans – thanks to the age-old recipe of good power in minimum weight – were the faster cars, and quite capable of embarrassing the TRs in competition. That still irritated Sir John Black.

Fortunately, although he was well known as a ruthless boss within his own organisation, he was perhaps by now too close to HFS Morgan to withdraw supplies of Standard and Triumph engines completely. But as it transpired, his days at Standard, and his days in the motor industry itself, were approaching a rather sad and acrimonious end.

In November 1953 he was involved in a road accident near the Standard works, as a passenger in the prototype of yet another Triumph TR-engined sports car, the Swallow-Doretti. His injuries were at first described as minor, but it soon became clear that he had problems. He had even bigger problems politically within the company, where his totalitarian style of management was causing concern to other board members, especially when he assumed the chairmanship, and in effect total control, in mid-December 1953, only weeks after his accident. The accident gave the other board members a chance to act, and early in January 1954, after meeting in private over the New Year, they presented Sir John with his own letter of resignation. It admitted that the effects of the accident were affecting his ability to run the company, and that his doctors had recommended an extended period of rest and recovery. He had little option but to sign it, and the fifty-eight-year-old Black was replaced by thirty-seven-year-old Alick Dick, who inherited bigger problems than Standard's relationship with Morgan.

Morgan, however, did start to notice that the numbers of engines available from their old mentors were not always what they had been. To make up for the shortfall, which obviously dictated the number of Plus 4s that Morgan could build, in 1955, under Peter's guidance, they reintroduced the 4/4, not in its original shorter-wheelbase, narrower-track guise but in effect as a smaller-engined Plus 4 – with power by Ford.

The crux of all this was another example of Morgan's on-going dilemma about engine supplies. Searching for an alternative to the specially made 1267cc Standard engine had been one of the first roles that Peter Morgan had been given when he joined his father early in 1947, and before the company went with the larger Vanguard unit which had brought them this far (and which HFS at first thought was too big and heavy), it seems that Peter had spoken to most of the industry about a replacement.

By then, Coventry-Climax could no longer supply engines at all, because they were fully committed to supplying forklift trucks and small, high efficiency fire-pump engines, one of which subsequently formed the basis of the first of a famous line of Coventry-Climax racing engines, the FPF – standing for 'fire-pump four'. Ford could have supplied more of the side-valve 1172cc 100E engines used in the three-wheeler type F, but HFS wanted something more up to date for the 4/4, with overhead valves. General Motors told Peter Morgan it was not their policy to supply engines to other manufacturers, and Morris were not even considered because of their MG connections. Peter spoke to Morris rivals Austin about using their new A40 engine, but was told by Austin chairman Leonard Lord that, while they would have no objections to Morgans using Austin engines, they did not expect to have any supply beyond what they needed for their own cars. In the end, Peter had persuaded his father at least to consider the larger Standard engine, and HFS allowed him to acquire one of them and try it in the 4/4 chassis.

It turned out to be a good piece of delegation on HFS's part, and good judgement from Peter Morgan. Standard lent Peter an engine to work with, and in its original 1850cc form it fitted reasonably easily into a 4/4 chassis with a mildly modified engine bay. When HFS tested it on some of the more severe climbs in the Malvern Hills he was impressed enough to agree that it should go into a production model.

Until supplies of the Vanguard engine became available, Morgan continued with the 4/4. When it did become available they replaced the 4/4 with the Plus 4, the new name reflecting not only the fact that it had a bigger engine and more power but also that it was a slightly bigger car. In fact a 4-inch stretch in the wheelbase not only made room for the bigger engine, but it also offered that bit more space for driver and passenger.

Standard finally put the Vanguard into production in the middle of 1948, with a slightly enlarged version of the engine, because that year saw the introduction of a £10 flat-rate tax system, irrespective of capacity or rated horsepower, and Sir John Black reasoned that the rather heavy, beetle-backed Vanguard needed all the power it could reasonably be given. As the increase came from an increased bore size and did not affect the external dimensions of the engine, Morgan had no problems with the planned fit into the new car, but did have a problem in that the new capacity, of 2088cc, took them outside the 2-litre competition class. The car went ahead, however, and Peter Morgan had made the first of his major contributions to the future of the company.

It preceded a policy statement by Morgan's board in June 1952, under the heading 'Long Term Policy of the Company', which said 'Some discussion ensued regarding the Company's long term policy and at the conclusion of this discussion Mr HFS Morgan summed up his views by saying that he believed the Company's success in the future would continue to rest upon its ability to produce the fastest car of its class, produced at as high a standard of production as was consistent with public demand.' In November 1953, they were investigating 'the possibility of a Morgan car at a popular price for the home market, possibly with a Ford engine and gearbox'.

The Vanguard-engined Plus 4 survived, alongside the Triumph TR-engined versions, until 1958. That same year, following the death of George Goodall, Peter took over as managing director, and a year later, when his father died, he became chairman.

Ruth Morgan, Peter's mother, had died in February 1956, aged seventy-one, at the Chelsea Women's Hospital in London; she was cremated in Wandsworth and her ashes taken back to Stoke Lacy. Ruth Morgan left money in her will to each of her thirteen grandchildren – three of Peter's children, three of Sylvia's, three of Barbara's, two of Stella's and two of Brenda's. She left a substantial sum to family friends, Mr and Mrs Newman, who looked after the household, and the remainder of her quite substantial estate was divided equally between Peter and his sisters. HFS himself died on 15 June 1959, only a few months before the fiftieth anniversary of the Morgan car, at the age of seventy-eight. He had been working up to the end, and only three days before he died he had driven from Maidenhead to the factory in his four-seater Drophead Coupé. He died in Malvern, and is buried in the churchard at Stoke Lacy alongside his father and beside many other members of the family, including his younger brother Charles George who died in infancy in 1887. His gravestone reads, 'HFS Morgan, the founder of the Morgan Motor Company of Malvern Link. Born Stoke Lacy 1881, died Malvern 1959.' He left a total of £250,287, of which £146,349 was taken in death duties. The will had been drawn up in February 1957, when times were not easy, and before he died he had taken steps to ensure that the company would remain firmly with the family. In 1970, in an interview with *Motor* magazine on the eve of Morgan's sixtieth birthday, Peter Morgan explained, 'The firm had been operating in times when it was possible to put by more resources than now, and my father transferred the business to his family so that it was not affected by death duties.

'We did, however, have what might be called an unscrambling with the family by means of a voluntary liquidation as I intended to buy out my sisters' interests and run the firm as a proprietary business. I would not say we've got vast resources but we have reasonable finance to carry on in the way we are going, and this does not exclude bringing out new models as and when necessary . . .'

His father's brief, rather moving, handwritten will had made the changes in the company's affairs as straightforward as such things can ever be. He wrote, 'I have made this will as simple as possible and hope it will give my dear family the least possible trouble . . .

'I bequeath to my son, Peter, rather more than to his sisters, as he has had the trouble and worry of running my old business (now under the control of my family), which may have to be sold owing to the increasing difficulty of running a private business. I have had a long and happy life, and words cannot express my thanks to my children, in-laws, and grandchildren for their love and kindness to me. May you all live long in happiness together. God bless you all.'

The company would not, as HFS apparently feared, have to be sold, but it needed to be restructured. It had been left under the terms of HFS's will in trust to Peter and his four sisters. Peter was now in everyday control of the company, and he was one of the trustees, alongside Major Kendall, the company secretary. Although the overall financial position was quite sound, it was another difficult period in terms of sales and profits, and the company's affairs were again under close scrutiny by the Inland Revenue, just as it had been in the 1940s.

The first mention of a restructuring of the company was in November 1960, but before any of that could be resolved, Morgan had to answer to the Inland Revenue's concerns – not, this time about the relative importance of car manufacture versus investment but about the way the trust had been structured. The legal arguments were immensely complex, the case would ultimately continue for several years, and would only be resolved on appeal in the High Court. The central question was about HFS Morgan's control over the assets held in trust. HFS's principal concern, as ever, was to be fair to all the members of his family who were the ultimate beneficiaries, and while he did not have any access himself to the funds of the trust he had the power to decide how it would be split between the five beneficiaries – his children – and that gave rise to some ambivalence over the duties ultimately payable.

In the early 1950s, the structure of the company was exactly as it had been from the day it was set up as a limited company in 1912. It had a paid-up share issue of 100,000 shares, nominal capital £100,000, comprising 50,000 ordinary shares, 49,500 B preference shares and 500 A preference shares, all of £1 each. By the time HFS died he had already given away virtually all the ordinary shares which he originally owned in the company to other members of the family. Amongst those transactions, in January 1949 he had transferred 24,000 ordinary shares in total – 6,000 to his wife Ruth, 6,000 to Peter and 3,000 to each of his daughters. In July 1952 he transferred another 24,000 ordinary shares to Peter and Major Kendall, as trustees of the deed of trust that had first been set up in February of that year. In March 1954 there was a proposal to increase the capital of the company, and authorising capitalisation of £50,000 of the company's reserves, which was transferred from the reserve account to the capital account, with 50,000 previously unissued shares now being issued in proportion to existing shareholdings – all of it within the family. In March 1957, following the death of their mother, a further 24,000 ordinary shares were transferred to Peter and his sisters, this time with 12,000 going to Peter and 3,000 to each sister.

All this meant that by HFS's death all his ordinary shares had already been given to the younger members of the family, and what was left to be distributed was the preference shares of various types. Some of those had already been transferred before his death but the majority of them were the subject of the trust. The trust itself was set up in February 1952, with Peter and Major Kendall as trustees. The Inland Revenue's initial question was whether the capital of the trust fund (then valued at approximately £90,000) had become liable to estate duty on the death of HFS. Had the answer been yes the duty payable would have been some £57,000.

The complication arose because in May 1957, having been advised that duty might be payable if HFS died before any of the children (which was highly probable), each of his off-spring had signed 'Deeds of Irrevocable Assignment'. The dispute with the Inland Revenue basically came to the question of whether the terms of the trust amounted to a taxable interest in the case of each of the beneficiaries. And the ultimate verdict of the High Court, before Mr Justice Cross in April 1962, was that the terms of the trust had been properly met and that the duty was not payable. Morgan had stood their ground and won an extremely important victory.

If the verdict was a considerable relief to all concerned, it was only the beginning of the unravelling process. A decision could now be made about the future of the company, which essentially meant a decision between Peter and his four sisters, with the help of the other trustee, Major Kendall. Peter knew, too, that although he had the largest single share, he did not have a majority shareholding and that Kendall (who had been awarded the MBE for his war work) also had the power to make decisions for the good of all the benefici-aries. Peter's comment is to the point: 'If I'd misbehaved myself I could have been cut out, and the Revenue attacked that but they lost. In theory my sisters could have taken the company over when father died but in reality they could not because within the trust the trustees were myself and Major Kendall who actually had the voting right. Fortunately he said he thought it best not to sell the company, but if he'd said it was best to sell it would have been sold.'

In the end, the company *was* sold – but to Peter. But the road to that ultimate solution was still one fraught with difficulty and, in Peter's case in particular, it was very risky.

Peter's sisters had now joined the board of the Morgan Motor Company Ltd, but once the negotiations started in earnest they tended to be represented by proxy by their respective husbands, led by Sylvia's husband John Hardwicke, who was a Lloyd's underwriter in the City. In February 1961 it was proposed that the company should be restructured. A new company would be registered, taking over sufficient assets to continue production, while the original company would be liquidated. All its shareholdings would be sold (they ranged from Guinness to Marks & Spencer, via several other breweries, tobacco companies, BMC, Hawker-Siddeley, ICI and dozens more) and any proceeds surplus to the production requirements of the new company would be reinvested. But it was not that simple.

In March 1962, they discussed ideas for redistributing the reserves, which they estimated to be around £188,000 but which were finally assessed at £210,864. If these reserves were distributed among the shareholders (Peter and his sisters) the freeholds and other assets would still be sufficient to cover the value of all the issued capital of the company 'by a safe and sufficient margin'. A distribution of the reserves was recommended but there was still argument from some quarters that the company should simply be sold and the entire proceeds divided; this was a solution which Peter naturally resisted and which led to a protracted round of further investigation into the company's true value, further complex legal advice and a degree of friction between Peter and his brothers-in-law, with his sisters rather standing on the sidelines.

Not until early 1964 was an acceptable division of the shares finally agreed, and the shares transferred, with Peter acquiring the largest proportion. In January 1965, with Peter's intention to run the company and pay off his sisters' interests himself now clearly established, the board discussed the possibility of a voluntary liquidation, with Peter continuing as sole trader. It was 'a matter of expediency between the shareholders' and would not affect car production, trading, or anything else other than the legal status and ownership of the company, although the shareholders still had not made a formal decision.

Things were now clearly accelerating towards a conclusion, however, and by February 1965 there were even suggestions for a name for the new company that would rise from the ashes of the old: Pickersleigh Motors Ltd, Pickersleigh Road Motors Ltd, or Three Wheeler Cars Ltd, or perhaps Runabout Cars Ltd. That month, the deed was actually done, when a special resolution unanimously agreed, 'that the company be wound up voluntarily and that Derek Ronald Andrew ... Chartered Accountant ... is hereby appointed liquidator for the purposes of such winding up'. As the liquidator, he was 'authorised to allot to Peter Henry Geoffrey Morgan, a member of the Company, the freehold properties of the Company, its fixed and moveable plant, machinery and tools, its stock in trade, its products completed and in the course of manufacture, its goodwill and book debts and all its other trading assets whatsoever and also all or any stocks, shares and other investments of the Company in specie by way of satisfaction or in part satisfaction of his share and interets in the Company's assets'.

And that, as far as the original Morgan Motor Company Ltd was concerned, was that. Now it was the Morgan Motor Company (Proprietor PHG Morgan).

One side of Peter's father and grandfather would have been immensely proud of his commitment and faith; another side – the cautious, pragmatic side – would undoubtedly have been very concerned about the risk. Because now, and as it transpired for the next five years, Peter Morgan would be running the company, in times which included the collapse of the American market and the launch of the Plus 8 among other things, totally exposed – without the safety net of limited liability, and totally responsible, personally, for the company's finances and potential debts.

Looking back, Peter Morgan has no doubts that it was what he had to do if the company was to survive, and he was adamant that it would: 'It was not my sisters who wanted to sell,' he says, 'but my brothers-in-law. They never had any faith in me, you see, that's why I bought them out in the end.

'I came through with just the firm but no money while they had just over £100,000 each. But I'd retained the company. In fact I had a little bit in reserve, enough to run it, and I remember saying "the holiday's over, now we've got to start to work and make some money". Before that it did not matter, and it never had. It had not mattered in George Goodall's time because in George Goodall's time the manufacturing side of the company was not very successful, not financially very viable. Before that Hales had been an excellent works manager and we made a lot of money in those days. But the difference between Hales and Goodall was that Hales took the option of working for bonuses based on production, where George never did. Really it was because not many people other than father and myself really had faith in the thing. And of course my sisters never had any interest in running it, they were very much the old school

'But it was all quite amicable, even when we were unscrambling it. It was my wife, my ex-wife, who thought the restructuring was a good idea, even when I thought it was a ghastly mess. Father had always said to me – because he did not have any inkling of what was going to happen – if you are going to run the company it will be a difficult thing and you have to be very careful. You'll have good years but you'll certainly also have very bad ones, too, and what you need to do is have backing.

'I suppose that's why, in a way, people have criticised me for being overcautious. Of course I *was* in a way, and I'm sure that came out in the episode with John Harvey-Jones where I said it was easy for him, he was not playing around with his own money at ICI and here at Morgan I was playing with my own . . .

'For many years, at least five, I ran it as an unlimited company. I could have made the shares over to my wife but I did not – and during that time, when I was just the proprietor of the company, I could have lost everything. We did not become a limited company again until 1 June 1970, when it was completely reformed. It had been a very long time since my father's death in 1959. Litigation had come first and had taken four or five years, and then we had the restructuring. But we came through . . .'

While all this was happening, the Morgan car, perhaps more than at any time in its history, was being written off as an anachronism. Its styling, and to a lesser extent its engineering, was a relic of earlier days, while all its main sporting competitors (and there were now many) had moved on to a 'modern' look. While its traditional styling would eventually prove to be one of Morgan's big selling points as retro became popular, in the motor industry of 1959 nostalgia was still a thing of the future. If this sounds like a contradiction in terms, it is somehow appropriate to Morgan.

By now, Morgan sales were lower than was comfortable and manufacturing costs were higher. For most of its life the Morgan, for the performance that it offered, was an extraordinarily cheap way of buying a sports car – usually significantly cheaper than mass-produced alternatives, even when they had inferior performance. To some extent, that changed in the late 1950s, when smaller 'mainstream' sports cars like the Austin-Healey Sprite and the new generation MG Midgets came along, followed by Triumph's own offering, the Spitfire, from 1962. All of those could offer the sports car image, albeit without too much sports car performance, for very aggressive prices, made possible by selling in what, to Morgan, were vast numbers. And different though the products were, they inevitably took away some Morgan sales. Peter Morgan had to change the balance, and needed the cooperation of the workforce to achieve it. He explained the situation to them without disguising the fact that things were not good. He outlined his plans for balancing production with reduced costs, and they backed him to the hilt, but he still needed to revitalise the Morgan image, which led to one of his few failures, the Plus 4 Plus. The story of that car is short but revealing.

By the early 1960s, the reorganisation of the company was in hand and Peter had made the policy decision to rebuild the European market to ease the disproportionate and dangerous reliance on the American market, urgently so, because that market was falling apart by 1961 or 1962 as America faced recession. But the affordable sports car market was perhaps more competitive than it had ever been, and Morgan faced a tough time against mass produced models from the likes of MG, Austin-Healey, Triumph and Jaguar, cars which might not have the Morgan's hand-built cachet but in some cases could rival it for performance, and increasingly leave it behind on modern styling.

In the saloon car world, the era of separate wings and running-boards was all but over by the end of the war, with the smooth-sided looks pioneered by men like Raymond Loewy, Harley Earl and Virgil Exner in the USA quickly spreading to Europe. Sports cars followed the trend, the As and Bs replacing the T-type MGs, the XKs replacing the SSs and ultimately the E-type replacing the XKs. By the late 1950s, Morgan was the only serious survivor of the old school, and for the first and perhaps the only time Peter Morgan began to think Morgan had to follow fashion.

His scheme for bringing Morgan into line was the Plus 4 Plus, a very untraditional Morgan. It was based, admittedly, on a more or less standard Plus 4 chassis and running gear, but it had a modern, streamlined body and it was built not with hand-shaped panels over an ash frame but moulded entirely in glass fibre – another Morgan first. The Plus 4 Plus also revealed that Peter Morgan was well aware of other Morgan rivalries in the early 1960s, especially from Colin Chapman's increasingly successful Lotuses, and to a lesser extent from the likes of other glass fibre specialists including Marcos and TVR.

Also most un-Morgan-like, it had a fixed roof on its two-seater coupé body, and the shell was not even made in the Morgan factory. It was made by specialists, the Edwards brothers, of EB Plastics of Tunstall, Staffordshire, and in 1962 the total cost of developing the prototype was recorded as being £3,000. One good thing about it was that it disproved a theory that HFS Morgan had had about the new material several years earlier when Peter had first suggested to him that they might investigate its use. HFS (and others) was not convinced that glass fibre, still a new material in his lifetime, would stand up to use as a Morgan body without cracking, on what he readily admitted was a more than usually flexible chassis. Peter only had the chance to prove it worked after his father's death, but says there was no problem whatsoever. Early in 1963 Peter and his wife took the prototype Plus 4 Plus for a fourteen-day, 3,000-mile 'trial' tour through France and Spain; minor damage to a front wing was repaired by a French garage, proving that repairs were easy enough to carry out even away from the factory but it was later remarked that the final repair had cost about 50 per cent more than it would have for comparable damage on a metal body. Peter even used a Plus 4 Plus himself in trials and other events as well as using the car extensively on the road, and never had any breakages, not even any need to rehang the doors because of sagging hinges.

The Plus 4 Plus was also a good performer, with the same 2.1-litre, four-cylinder Triumph TR4 engine as the Plus 4, and the usual Morgan advantage of low weight. It was launched at the London Motor Show in 1963, and soon afterwards it

appeared in Morgan advertising under the headline: NOW –
THE NEW MORGAN SPORTS CAR PLUS.

Interestingly, this advertisement and some later ones,
showed a female driver with the car, perhaps indicating
hopes for another expanding market sector. The first advertising copy read, 'The new Morgan Plus Four Plus, developed
from the successful Morgan Plus Four, is the latest addition to
the Morgan sports car range, with new smooth sweeping lines
and providing ample room for two. This elegant sports car is
powered by a four cylinder 2138cc engine developing 105bhp
at 4750rpm and fitted with a four speed syncromesh gearbox.
Girling front disc and rear drum brakes, independent front
suspension, a weather protected body with wind-down side
windows and a heater fitted as standard equipment. The
enthusiast will find this the ideal sports car for tireless long
distance travelling. Price £1275 including purchase tax.'

In 1964, when sixteen Plus 4 Pluses, the best annual figure,
were built, the ad-men tried again with one headed, 'Make
Friends with a Morgan Plus Four Plus', and the copy, 'Drive
well and influence people with your new Morgan Plus Four
Plus. They will be influenced by the surging power of the TR4
engine, by the grip of the Girling front disc brakes, by the
comfort, by the individuality of the man who chose
Morgan . . .'

The last gasp, in 1966, screamed, 'Definitely a Morgan Girl!
Speed, she likes. Comfort, she appreciates. She admires men
sensible enough to choose the rather exclusive Morgan Plus
Four Plus and occasionally let her drive. 2138cc. TR4A
engine. 110mph. Front Disc Brakes. And superb Morgan
controllability. Try one for ever – this week.' Two things in
this piece were true. For one thing, she genuinely was a
Morgan girl – the model throughout the Plus 4 Plus advertising campaign was Peter's daughter, Sonia, appearing as Lady
Jane Colwyn. For another, the Plus 4 Plus really was rather
exclusive: unfortunately for Morgan, the enthusiast did not
want to know, and the critics were not very impressed either.

One of Peter Morgan's friends said it reminded him of a
midget submarine out of the water; others thought it looked
like a cross between a Lotus Elite and a Jaguar XK150.
Looking at it now, aside from the Humpty Dumpty roof and

a windscreen that Peter Morgan says he would have liked to have moved forward a few more inches, it is quite a good looking car; but the market was not interested, and only twenty-six were sold before production stopped in 1967; of these only eight were sold in Britain.

Peter believes that the Plus 4 Plus did not fail because it was radically different; the only radically different thing about it was the styling, and he reveals some of the thinking behind it. 'It was brought out really because of all this hoo-hah about open cars; that was partially my reason. There was quite a strong suggestion that the open car would be abandoned – not banned, abandoned. America had given it up, but it's ironic that America was the first to take it up again – and they never actually did legislate against open cars, but at the time it certainly seemed they might. I think the story was mainly put out by people in British Leyland as an excuse to allow them to get rid of the MG, because that was the kind of thing that happened there then.

'There were also questions of quantity. People saw that open two-seaters were never going to be a volume car, so its future didn't look all that bright. Even MGs didn't have huge sales in the home market; most of them went to America. That's why people wanted to take us over, because the American market was so keen on cars like ours. If you seriously wanted to build open two-seaters you had to be selling in America.'

The other change was to a glass fibre body, and Peter has his own thoughts on that. 'Glass fibre was not popular then; it smelt. It still does I believe. I'm told that people do not like going to the TVR factory because of the smell. It's also difficult to get comparable quality with a hand-made aluminium body, but the people who did ours, the Edwards brothers, they knew their stuff. That was one of my briefs; I said "I don't want one of these flimsy paper-thin glass fibre cars which will be cracking all over in six months. I want a decent job". The only one I knew on the market at the time was the Jensen, although at the time that wasn't a particularly light car. They said, "well, yours won't be particularly light" and I told them I did not mind that but I did not want lightness at the expense of it being so thin that it would crack and distort.'

What would have happened to the coachbuilding tradition at Morgan if that car, glass fibre body and all, had been a success? 'We would have gone ahead with it but very soon after it was launched one knew that it wasn't going to be. It didn't take long, and I suppose in a way the fire at EB Plastics was – I can't say a godsend – but it was wonderfully timed because it was at a time when quite frankly I wasn't in a position to take a lot more bodies. But they never pushed me. They were very good like that. We never had a real written contract. I'd always said, "we have to see how people react to it", and they fully appreciated that. They weren't fools; they'd made their own Debonair, of course, so I think they knew the ups and downs of marketing cars and from that angle it worked out very well and there were no hard feelings at all. I think that even today if I met either of them I'm sure we'd get on fine. It was a mutual understanding; they didn't lose money and I didn't lose a lot. It was done purely out of what profits we were making at the time . . .' No change there then.

Peter does not think the demise of the Plus 4 Plus was lamented by everybody in the factory. 'Nobody here much liked the idea of the glass fibre. I remember announcing I was going to use it and the look on the faces in the sheet metal shop. They were called the Little Tin Gods – and they were tin gods; they were very off about it because it would have cut down so much of their work. There would still have been sheet metal work to be done but nothing like as much and they could see this didn't do much for them. Plus there was dear old Cec Jay [Cecil Jay, also a well-known former competition driver who had been with Morgan since 1927] who ran the spares department, very successfully, and he didn't like glass fibre at all. When my own car was crashed they never repaired it – and I suppose it was not really necessary because by then I'd moved on to the Plus 8, and jettisoned the Plus 4 Plus . . .'

The irony of the Plus 4 Plus, however, is that while Morgan owners had given it a big thumbs down, in rejecting it they had rediscovered the fact that far from wanting to go with fashion, they still preferred the traditional style of the classic Morgan. Peter admits that his early 1960s conviction that Morgan's looks had to change if they were to compete with 'modern' rivals was wrong, but he is certain that he learned a valuable lesson from the exercise: do not change for the sake of it; only change what needs changing. In 1970 he talked to *Motor* about the practical aspects of design in a market already becoming constrained by emissions and safety legislation. 'Once you've crashed your car,' he said, 'and made sure it conforms, you must have quite a few thoughts about introducing new ones. As to generally developing the Morgan, we are not averse to this but at the moment it is extremely popular in the present style and, as other people have said to me, it would be suicide to change. We experienced this when we brought out the Plus 4 Plus, which many people thought was not in the Morgan image – it is terribly difficult to get away from your image . . .'

A few years later, he explained what he thought the customer saw. 'I wouldn't like to sell the car just on nostalgia. In fact it's a very functional car and competes very well with modern sports cars. But what it has got is character. Really, the mass-produced car has helped our popularity. Most modern cars today are a little bit tedious, a little too similar. Back in the 1930s there was a very wide range of cars, of bodywork, types of seating and so on. You could spend £100 on a Ford or a Morris – or £17,000 on a Bugatti Royale. In those days a manufacturer hoped a customer would be interested in his car. Since the war there's been a subtle change. Now it seems as if the manufacturer is often telling the customer what kind of car he wants. So it's better for us being an individual type of car. The sort of person who buys a Morgan is likely to be individually minded – as well as being able to cope with the limitations of running a two-seater with not all that much room for luggage. The Morgan owner by and large is an enthusiast,' he concludes; 'we won't have to tell him where the gearshift is . . .'

But Peter Morgan vigorously denies that he is a Luddite, and said as much to *Motor Industry Management* in the late 1980s. 'I certainly don't say you mustn't make changes. That's nonsense. If owners had had their way we'd still have the radiator sitting out at the front. But I've never wanted to change for the sake of changing . . . I don't think I could be making cars now if I truly lived in the past. But the balance

has to be just right for the Morgan car to continue successfully. Even with cars built in such small numbers you have
to have reliability, ensure that running costs are not too high,
and that the finish is first class. People have to see something
for what they're paying.'

Softening the blow of the commercial failure of the Plus 4
Plus, the unexpected bonus of winning the 2-litre class at Le
Mans in 1962, with Chris Lawrence and Richard Shepherd-
Barron's Plus 4, did exactly what the competition successes
had done fifty years earlier and told people that, whatever the
Morgan looked like, it was a serious performer. That also led
to the series of Lawrence-tuned Super Sports and Competition variants over coming years, which sold in small numbers
but did no harm at all in rebuilding the image. In the end it
was the combination of unobtrusively moving with the times
while outwardly retaining its individuality that kept Morgan
in business in the crisis days of the early 1960s, and arguably
has done so ever since.

Beyond design, Morgan's bigger crisis then was about
world markets. Even while the Plus 4 Plus was failing, Peter
Morgan's other necessity, of reshaping the market, was being
forced upon him. He knew he was losing America, he had
seen it happening with his own eyes. He was visiting
California at just about the time when the recession started
in the aircraft industry, which triggered the broader decline.

In 1979 Peter Morgan told *Old Motor* magazine how close
that had brought the company to disaster. 'We found, that
from about 1950, when we introduced the Plus 4, the demand
steadily tailed off in Europe and the UK, both for the new car
and the 4/4. So we found that more and more we were going
to America. It was virtually our only market eventually;
about 85 per cent of our production was going there. We
didn't worry too much at the time, but in 1960 I happened to
be in California when I became aware of a recession. My
agent in Los Angeles, who'd been good for up to three cars a
week, said, "I've got to stop taking them". Which he did for
eleven months, in fact – I just managed to ferry them along to
the eastern states and they took a few. It was no fault of the
cars; sports cars were just not selling. MG and Triumph had
auction sales to get rid of theirs. We were really in a bad state.

'On my way home I remember saying to my wife, "we must expand. I do not like having all my eggs in one basket". I looked around and found interest, particularly in Europe. France got better, we appointed two new agents in Germany, and that helped a lot. Then in about 1965 we heard about American safety and clean-air regulations, so that came into the picture. By 1968 we had to pull out of the States. The Rover was not in America at that time because they hadn't passed their detox test, and Ford had never tried to sell their European cars in the USA, so their engine didn't conform either.'

According to comments from Peter Morgan in an article in *Motoring News* in 1967, headed 'Problems in America', he was at that time, 'reasonably confident that the rules can be complied with in time. He is very much aware of his dependence on major manufactuurers and relies upon them to solve the main problem of exhaust emissions. Steering column collapsibility can also be arranged with the help of AC-Delco, dual braking with the help of Girling and so on. In fact Mr Morgan asked for nine months grace to make his cars comply and was given two years extension, so obviously there is an enthusiast in the right department.' In the end, it was not enough time to solve the problem in itself, but by now that was not such a disaster either: 'Luckily our American sales had been tailing off, and I can only say that on 1 January 1968 [the date when the first wave of clean-air regulations came into force] I didn't need the US market. Then others came along – France, Holland, Sweden – and the home market began to pick up as well . . .' Once again, Morgan had survived.

Peter Morgan's account of that period brings to light two more of his achievements of the 1950s and 1960s, both involving great escapes from potentially disastrous positions. Losing the 4/4 in 1950, with the loss of the 1267cc Standard engine, and replacing it with the bigger, more potent, more expensive Plus 4, had taken away a less powerful and more affordable type of car that Morgan would have preferred still to have in its range. In 1955, again through Peter's negotiations for an engine supply, they found an answer, with the return of the 4/4 – the Series II. It used the Plus 4 chassis powered by an 1172cc Ford 100E side-valve engine, in a lower, lighter body, which meant that, in spite of only having 36bhp, the new car still had ample performance.

Price was very important to Morgan, and Peter was always keen to keep prices low. That same 1967 *Motoring News* article revealed Peter's thoughts on the market: 'Until the Sprite came along in 1958, the Morgan was the cheapest sports car on the British market, and this is one advantage that has been lost and may not be regained. It really is a tall order to take BMC on at their own business, but, at some time in the future Mr Morgan would like to offer a really cheap sports car without sacrificing too much in the way of performance. Aesthetically, Peter Morgan says, he would argue with anyone who criticised the shape. He likes it, customers like it, and that's the way it stays.' And the shape did stay, but the idea of a much cheaper model never materialised, as the 4/4 continued to be the entry point to the Morgan range.

When Peter acquired rights to the Ford engine in February 1954 he had done a good deal. The engine would be available to Morgan at £66 a unit, which was a remarkable £53 less than the Standard engine, and planned savings on other components would add up to another £16–17, so Morgan had hopes of being able to offer the smaller Ford-engined car at almost £100 less than the existing model.

The Ford association was on going, even when a specific engine was not, and over the next few years that saw Morgan's smaller car closely reflecting the progress in Ford's mid-sized, four-cylinder production engines. In 1961 the 4/4 Series III adopted the excellent 997cc overhead-valve 105E unit recently launched in the new Anglia; in 1961 the Series IV gained the 1340cc 109E Classic engine; in 1963 the Series V brought the 1498cc 116E Cortina type; and in 1968 there was the start of a new 4/4 family, the 4/4 1600, first with all-new Ford Kent-type engines, very briefly during 1981 with Fiat twin-cam power alongside the Fords, then returning to Fords only, with the new CVH engine, and eventually, come 1993, the 1800cc Ford Zetec engine.

The roots of all those things had been forming while HFS was still alive, but the biggest change for Morgan since the original four-wheeler of the mid-1930s – and arguably Peter Morgan's most far reaching achievement of all – came in the late 1960s, long after HFS had gone. It was what would become the Plus 8.

The three starting points for it were another takeover bid, another termination of engine supplies, and a desire to get back into the American market then denied Morgan. This time, the takeover bid was from Rover and the lost engine was the four-cylinder Triumph TR unit. That was not lost because of any falling out with Triumph but because the TR4 was to be replaced in 1967 with the TR5, whose new six-cylinder unit would be too long to fit into the Morgan's four-cylinder engine compartment.

Triumph actually tried to overcome the problem and keep the association with Morgan alive by offering the V8 that later went into the Triumph Stag. At the time of Morgan's need, that engine was still a prototype, so Peter declined the offer. It was possibly one of Morgan's luckiest escapes. For one thing, the all-new single-overhead-camshaft engine did not reach production until 1970 – delayed first by Triumph building a four-cylinder derivative of the engine for Saab, then by Triumph-parent Leyland's merger with Rover in 1967, and finally by mechanical problems. It never did fully overcome the latter, and in spite of the production version turning out at 3 litres instead of the planned 2.5, with fuel injection rather than carburettors to improve low-speed flexibility, it was never particularly powerful but always dreadfully unreliable. In character, it was not really a Morgan kind of engine anyway, but the V8 that Peter Morgan found in its place could hardly have been better for Morgan's purposes. And it came from Rover.

In the mid-1960s, under the inspired direction of then chairman, later life president, Spencer Wilks, the engineering skills of his nephews, the cousins Peter Wilks and Spencer ('Spen') King, and the styling flair of David Bache, Rover was fast shedding its staid, 'auntie' image and creating a new generation of imaginative and commercially successful saloon cars, typified by the SD1 2000 family.

It was a Peter Wilks initiative to approach Morgan, in around 1966 or 1967, with a view to a partnership to build the sports car that Rover did not have in its portfolio, much as Sir John Black had done a decade and a half earlier while looking for a sporty Triumph. Peter Morgan resisted the offer, and no further approaches were made after Rover merged with Leyland early in 1967, but Rover (who had planned a mid-engined V8-powered sports car of their own for the early 1970s but saw it rejected by Leyland management after Sir William Lyons pointed out that it would be an unnecessary threat to stablemate Jaguar) did extend the offer of a new engine for Morgan. At the time, the engine deal was still a secret, and still to be properly finalised, but in Peter Morgan's words, 'in 1966 when Rover introduced the V8 engine, the suggestion was made, but I said that I wanted the engine but not to join up'. Thus the scene was set for one of the longest running of all Morgan lines, three wheels or four, the Plus 8.

The full story of the Rover engine and the Plus 8's development is told in Chapter 6, but the production model was unveiled at the Earl's Court Motor Show in 1968 to very favourable reviews. And, replacing the Triumph-engined Plus 4, it completely revitalised Morgan's image. No one objected any longer to the fact that the styling, aside from the whole car being slightly bigger and noticeably more muscular, was 'traditional' Morgan; all that mattered now was that the Plus 8 was the most powerful and the fastest Morgan to date, offering massive acceleration for the money, and a character unique among cars of this level of performance. In other words, the Plus 8 was a brand new Morgan, but one rooted firmly in the classic Morgan tradition. And again, that included not only the looks but also the familiar, craftsmen-based build methods.

The birth of the Plus 8, with another new major engine supplier, again put Morgan's relationship with the broader specialist industry into perspective. Peter recalls, 'We didn't have many organised contacts but we tended to bump into each other at circuits and so on. I did have occasional words with Ken Richardson, of Triumph. He was always very nice to me but he was bit off about Morgan because we always did have the edge and people would always be going up to him and saying, "why is the Morgan so much quicker than the TR?". He used to get quite annoyed by that, because at one time they did get close to matching our performance but as soon as they started putting in winding windows and making it much more sophisticated, up went the weight and, of course, away we went again. They had the best engine tuners but we had lightness.'

There was no formal association of specialist manufacturers in those days, but they had contacts, as Peter explains. 'The one thing we did have was the small manufacturers' group in the SMMT [the Society of Motor Manufacturers and Traders]. I remember Jem Marsh from Marcos was on it, Colin Chapman who never used to turn up, but Lotus were on it, Bob Walklett from Ginetta and so on.' Peter was not a big Lotus fan at the time: 'Latterly I found them a nuisance, because they got the small manufacturers such a bad name. They took Girling for a ride twice over, over payments, and unfortunately it reflected on all of us. It didn't do any good for the small manufacturers. Chapman was really only interested in his racing cars. As far as production cars go, I think he was a disaster really – he didn't want to do them really . . .'

With the halo of the Plus 8, it was no longer a fashion crime to be seen in a Morgan, as Eric Dymock hinted in the *Guardian* in May 1969. 'With-it young things,' he wrote, 'have floppy clothes, beads and nimble but fragile plastic sports cars. The without-it wear a suit, enjoy the country, and own a Morgan, with which, if they have a mind and the necessary skill and determination, they can blow almost anything else off the road.' Like the Mini, the Morgan, and especially the Plus 8, became a fashion icon. Mick Jagger bought one, as did Brigitte Bardot, who ordered hers at the Paris Motor Show. When Jagger and Marianne Faithfull went to court for cannabis possession in May 1969 they arrived in Jagger's yellow Morgan, but were smuggled out of the back door in a Mercedes saloon. Peter Sellers was another high-profile Morgan owner as well as famously a Mini man; so were the photographer David Bailey and the actress Samantha Eggar, the Shah of Persia, King Juan Carlos of Spain and King Hassan of Morocco, among others. And like everyone else, they all had to wait for their cars to be built.

Only one part of the thinking behind the Plus 8 did not go according to plan. Peter Morgan had intended that it should take Morgan back into America after the recent exclusion of its four-cylinder models under the new emissions regulations. That would rely on Rover certifying the engine for their own planned model programme in the USA, but the exercise did not turn out to be as straightforward as it should have been.

In spite of having been an American design in the first place, the Rover engine took longer than expected to be homologated for the USA, and it was not until 1970 that the Plus 8 gained approval under American safety and clean air legislation, and not until 1971 that it went on sale in the USA – and then only briefly. Rover went to the US market with an Americanised version of the 3500 saloon, using the same V8 engine, but America did not like it at all, and Rover pulled out. As Peter Morgan said, 'The car was Americanised on the advice of the US importer, and of course when it came out the Americans didn't want it. It was just too tarted up, and the Chevy which had the same styling was a lot cheaper. I think it's absolutely true, and history proves it, that when the Americans buy a car from elsewhere they do so because it's got character. You won't make better ordinary cars for America than Americans do themselves.'

The Americans loved the Plus 8 because it *did* have character, and it was anything but ordinary, but almost as soon as they'd welcomed it they waved it goodbye, because by 1972 it had been outlawed again. Morgan could have applied for certification in their own right, but the procedures were so complicated and the number of cars involved so small that it did not make sense to do so. It was therefore left to specialist importers, led by Bill Fink of Isis Imports in San Francisco, eventually to produce propane-powered, even turbocharged versions of the Plus 8, to sell under the less stringent personal import regulations to those few Americans who really could not survive without a Plus 8 and who had the money to pay for such a high-priced, specially modified version.

Because of Peter Morgan's timely broadening of markets, it did not do Morgan as much harm as it once would have, and by the 1970s the biggest problem was keeping up with demand. By 1970, Morgan, with a workforce of around a hundred and twenty, was building nine or ten cars a week, of which three or four were Plus 8s, and of which a far more comfortable 45 per cent, rather than the 85 of the old days, were exported.

In this happy position, the restructuring of Morgan into a new limited company (as part of a redistribution of capital shares among members of the family) was completed, and yet more space was added at Pickersleigh Road, when Morgan bought the piece of neighbouring land to the right of the main gates and with it several new buildings, including the ones put there by Morgan's tenants during the Second World War. The latest expansion involved the biggest investment Morgan had made in more than thirty years, but significantly, even after all the ups and downs of the previous decade, and the launch of the Plus 8, it was yet again financed entirely out of reserves, with no borrowing.

Under the commonsense management of Peter Morgan, and resisting inappropriate investment and expansion on the back of short-term booms, the company was continuing to enjoy long-term stability and prosperity, even when other parts of the industry were struggling, and Britain was going through a major crisis. In 1972 unemployment passed one million and the pound was floated, to stop its slide. It did not stop huge falls on the stock market early in 1973, or halt counter-inflation legislation. There were petrol shortages, too, in 1973, and huge oil price increases following problems and conflicts in the Middle East. Foreign imports outsold British-made cars for the first time late in 1973, and Rover parent British Leyland Motors Corporation was seeking government aid. In the middle of 1974, inflation hit a record 16 per cent, the *FT* index hit rock bottom, and earlier in the year Britain had endured industrial unrest and the three-day week. The local newspaper reported that Morgan was coping with the latter 'by putting all its staff on the machines when they do have power, on Monday, Tuesday and Wednesday. On other days the firm does manual work on the body shells and interiors. Where Morgans are feeling the pinch is in deliveries of engines. Production could be badly affected if current restrictions are maintained for any length of time.'

By 1975, inflation had hit 25 per cent and unemployment was the highest for thirty-five years, but even then Morgan's philosophy was allowing the company largely to rise above the economic problems of the outside world. Production had been slowed to around six cars a week, but Morgan was not laying off staff. Peter Morgan told *Autocar* in April that year, 'I think the current situation is summed up by the word inflation. This makes life very difficult for all firms, although I don't know whether it's more difficult for small firms or large ones – unless, of course, you're government sponsored and none of us want that. As a group we (the small manufacturers) mean more to the big suppliers like Lucas, GKN and Smiths than we do as individuals. We have a very good relationship but things could change if too many small firms dropped out.

'Demand for our cars is very satisfying,' he went on. 'We've got a good spread of markets except America where we're not sending any cars at the moment. This is because Rover have pulled out and we depended on their service agents for engine spares for the eight-cylinder. Unfortunately this has resulted in Morgans having something of a rarity value in the USA. We are in most of the advanced motoring countries like Germany and Japan. Germany is a terrific, growing market. To sell Morgans we need two things, a certain amount of affluence, because the Morgan is at least a second car, and a reasonably developed road system. The good roads don't have to be everywhere; just around the cities will do.

'In Germany, although our prices are going up, the value of the mark relative to the pound is going up faster. Despite delivery delays – people in Germany were waiting for up to two years – the market is still strong. However, one must not be complacent, because a market can go wrong overnight. We try to insure ourselves against that by having a good spread. The other problem is cost. Ten years ago I would not have wanted to sell a car in America, or anywhere else, for more than £1,500; now it would have to be more than double that and the more you go up the market the more the market contracts. Traditionally the Morgan is an economical-to-buy motor car. We save by having few people at the top, but on the shop floor it is labour-intensive; we need a lot of people to build it in the traditional way.'

Of the future, in spite of the difficulties of the present, Peter Morgan was generally optimistic. 'I think the opportunities are quite considerable. It all depends on the government not being too difficult or awkward with the smaller manufacturers. There is no evidence of there not being more contraction in the world of the volume-produced car. They will become less available, more expensive and less susceptible to change because of the cost of changing them. To this you must add the fact that people will always want something different.

'I can see a continuing demand for our cars all over the world. I would like to go back into the USA, even despite the bumper tests and the costs of meeting the emissions requirements, because they were the country which kept the Morgan flag flying during a very difficult period. The problem I feel we would have if we did double production would be that we would have to soften the suspension because the majority of the general public would want it that way. However, the existing system has its advantages; you don't have to modify it when you go motor racing and when the roads do become like billiard tables it will be perfect, the best of the lot.'

It was all there again: the tradition, the independence, the adaptability, the optimism, even the oblique reference to competition improving the breed. Far from making it more vulnerable, Morgan's insistence on doing things its own way was keeping it alive. While industries all around it were being crippled by strikes and redundancies, Morgan, in spite of a strong union presence, had never had a single experience of either. While others lived on credit, Morgan managed comfortably on their own resources, to the extent that Peter Morgan was once able to tell a reporter, 'we had an overdraft facility in the 1960s but we never used it'.

What has he enjoyed most about his life with Morgan? 'I've enjoyed most of it, but Le Mans was a wonderful time, and I loved it when the Eight came out – there have been quite a lot of ups, really. General achievements by people in motor sport around what the car can do – that's always pleased me a lot and still does. And I like the atmosphere here. I can't say that I've enjoyed wage negotiations or things like that but it's all part of the job. Remember as well that we had an effect on Longbridge in the days when they were suffering from all kinds of strikes. They actually did drag us out here, because they openly said to my people, "you never support us in anything, this time you'll damned well come out". It was about a two-day strike and most of them did come out but one or two didn't, and I remember one, who's still here now, who still came in in spite of the union people being at the gates and they let me in with a smile. It was quite friendly but very unnecessary, and I think they regretted doing it – but of course it was none of our making. The other thing I'm very proud of is that I've never had to make anybody redundant and I think that's quite an achievement.'

And the hardest parts? There is no hesitation here. 'It was when father died. It was very sad.' He pauses. 'Then the general worry. I don't get it now, it's a funny thing. When I got to retirement age I stopped worrying, because all of a sudden I'd got through to the seventy-fifth year of the firm and I thought "bloody hell, you made it! It doesn't matter what happens now, you've made it for your time!" That was a lovely feeling, and luckily it's been with me ever since. I sleep wonderfully now; I don't worry like I used to – I used to worry like crazy . . .'

Would he like to see yet another generation of Morgan in some even further off future? 'I'd like to see them do their own thing. I'd love the car to go on. I think the longer the car goes on the better so far as I'm concerned. It deserves to go on, for a few more years anyway. Heaven knows what transportation will be in the future . . .'

Whatever it is, it is a fair bet that Morgan will be there for some time yet. The winter of 1979 brought new petrol shortages, rubbish strikes and, by March, the collapse of James Callaghan's Labour government. May brought Margaret Thatcher as Prime Minister, but no immediate relief from the crisis. In 1985, unemployment reached new records, the miners' strike dragged to a close and the pound hit rock bottom against the dollar, at just about one for one. Morgan continued to rise above all of it, and in 1985 Charles Morgan joined his father. The third generation was beginning.

6 The Cars

T HROUGHOUT MORGAN'S HISTORY, whatever the business strategy, the thing that ultimately has had to make the business work is the one thing that Morgan actually sells – the cars. Staying small and independent has been desirable, but selling the product has always been an absolute necessity. In most companies (including those far beyond the motor industry), staying in business usually means keeping up with current trends and continually striving for growth. Both those require continuous investment and an ability to anticipate fashions and economic trends, with all the attendant risks. With its product as with its organisation, Morgan has ploughed its own furrow, and found a philosophy that might not work for everybody but does work for Morgan.

In an industry obsessed with high volume and ever-shorter product launch cycles, demanding massive preproduction investment and on-going marketing risk, Morgan has always worked on the principle of never having built a car that it could not sell and never having sold a car that it could not build. Morgan has always listened to customers – they have almost made a religion of it – and continuously changed and improved their cars where there was good reason to do so. But only then. Only once, in the early 1960s with the Plus 4 Plus, did they try to change the product purely for reasons of fashion, and that was the one change the market has totally rejected. For the rest, Morgan have built the cars they understand best, whether they had one seat or two, two speeds or three, three wheels or four, one cylinder or two, four cylinders or eight.

In 1918, with the end of the First World War, Morgan issued an advertisement, in French and Spanish as well as in English, reflecting some of the company's many overseas markets. Reminding the post-war world that Morgan still existed, it also more or less amounted to a mission statement for the three-wheeler Runabout. Unusually, it did not attempt to describe the mechanical make-up of the car in any great detail, but instead described the philosophy of the Morgan as Morgan saw it; that philosophy saw the three-wheelers through their entire production life, from 1910 to 1952, and by extension defined the early four-wheelers, with elements surviving even into the current generation. This, in a nutshell, was what originally made a Morgan.

The English text of the 1918 advertisement reads, 'The Morgan Runabout has been before the public for eight years, having been introduced at Olympia in 1910, and during that time it has proved its efficiency and reliability in all the most important public trials. It has a great advantage therefore over untried and unsuccessful machines. It is designed to meet the needs of those who require something cheaper and simpler than a car, but more comfortable than a motor cycle. To this end particular attention has been paid to the simplicity of construction, easy accessibility of all parts, lightness and strength. The price is fixed to suit the man of moderate means, but quality has not been sacrificed to cheapness. Every part is standardised, and as an illustrated price list is given with each machine, renewals can be made cheaply and without delay.

'Our intention in designing the Morgan Runabout has not been to copy in miniature the design of a car. Many so called cycle cars are small cars with all the parts and necessary complications of a car; lightness and cheapness are obtained by diminishing the size of the working parts, in other words their strength and durability; others again use a belt drive, which is certainly light and simple but they can hardly claim to have proved their reliability in severe road tests. We claim for the Morgan simplicity and strength, obtained by novel construction. That durability is not sacrificed to lightness is proved by the reliability of our car in the most severe public tests, and the good opinions of private owners expressed in the most gratifying terms.'

The first Runabout, as HFS would christen it, had a single seat, and the simplest possible mechanical construction clothed in vestigial bodywork. The single wheel was at the back and the two steering wheels at the front. On the prototype, they flanked an air-cooled 7hp vee-twin Peugeot motor cycle engine, the same engine HFS had bought with the intention of building a motor cycle before opting for something different.

The central element of his three-wheeler chassis was a single, large diameter tube running from the rear of the engine, in line with the crankshaft, to the rear of the car. A clutch, with metal-to-metal linings and controlled by a pedal on the foot-boards, was mounted on the engine's flywheel at the front of the tube. The propeller shaft passed through the tube, to a cast and machined bevel-gear housing at its rear end, which was the only really complex piece of foundrywork and machining on the whole vehicle, and almost the only part which had needed outside help. The tubes joining the bevel box were pinned and brazed in, the remainder of the chassis joints used lugs and brazing, as in contemporary bicycle and motor cycle practice. At the front of the large tube was the centre of an X-shaped frame, the four points of which supported longitudinal tubes, in turn supporting the forward frame which carried the engine, and also the upper and lower transverse tubes which carried the pillars for the sliding pillar suspension.

The lighter lower tubes ran the whole length of the car, from alongside the bevel-gear housing to forward of the front crossmembers, where they offered a mounting place for the number plate. Typifying the economical thinking behind the Runabout, as well as providing chassis stiffness, they supported the floor and doubled as exhaust pipes. The upper tubes swept down to meet the lower ones quite near the front of the car, acting principally as supports for the top of the X-shaped engine and suspension frame. The petrol and oil tank sat just behind the engine, above the driver's feet.

Aside from the three-wheel configuration, the transmission was where the Runabout differed principally from the Système Panhard. It was a simple affair, by open chain from the transverse bevel-box output shaft to the single rear wheel. There were in fact two chains, one on either side of the wheel, each driving through different sized sprockets to give different gear ratios. A simple lever and linkage, operating on sliding dog-clutches, engaged one or other of the drives while disengaging the other, giving a two-speed transmission. There was a neutral position, with both dogs disengaged, but there was no reverse gear, because the Runabout was so light that the driver could simply dismount, pick up the rear end and turn it around by hand. The rear wheel also included the braking system, a mechanically operated band brake on either side with both foot and hand controls; there would not be any front brakes on production models until they were offered as an option in the early 1920s. The throttle and ignition advance were controlled by levers. On tiller-steered cars they were on the side of the body, close to the seat; when the Runabout gained a steering wheel, they moved there.

It seems the steel chassis tubing for the prototype Runabout may have been obtained from Repton School and it was built up into its finished form by local metal worker Thomas Jones, incorporating the bevel box and front sliding axles which were cast and machined by J Smith and Co. of Derby. Those sliding-pillar front axles were one of the cleverest features of a simple but deceptively clever design and they were destined to become a Morgan trademark for many years to come, even into the twenty-first century. Here, HFS Morgan had apparently been inspired by a similar front suspension layout on a French light car, the Sizaire-Naudin, at a time when fully independent suspension was still a rarity even on far more exotic and expensive machinery.

The Morgan sliding-pillar system was, and is, extremely simple, and works just as its name suggests. Each front wheel (and later its brakes) was carried on a stub axle attached to the chassis via a collar which could slide up and down a vertical (or almost vertical) pillar. Unlike the Sizaire-Naudin's axles, which were controlled by a transverse leaf spring, Morgan's were controlled by coil springs around the pillars, with bump springs above and rebound springs below the axle carrier. Although a quick glance suggests something resembling an upper and lower link system, the 'links' are a fixed part of the chassis; the only things that actually move are the axles, the springs in compression or extension, and the steering links as the axles rise and fall.

Its biggest problem was that the bronze bushes in the sliding stub axles needed regular lubrication, and even then were prone to fairly rapid wear, although they were readily replaceable. The other problem is a geometric one, and because the sliding pillar suspension has survived to this day it has defined the ride characteristics of Morgans ever since. Basically, Morgan springing is extremely firm, because although the sliding-pillar system means there are no camber changes relative to the chassis, body- and chassis-roll during cornering cause the wheels to lean at the same angle as the chassis.

That was not a major problem with narrow tyres any more than it was on a motor cycle, but in later years, with wider tyres, it was necessary to minimise the roll effect, and that could only be done by keeping the springing rock hard. The result is excellent grip on smooth surfaces, but a rough, nervous ride on anything less than that. It has often been said that in a Morgan you do not feel so many bumps, because if you are going quickly enough you hit the first one, clear the second one and just touch down on the third. Then there is the most famous Morgan ride-and-handling joke of all – that if you run over a coin you can tell which side up it is – heads or tails. Nonetheless, that front suspension layout has survived on every production Morgan, three wheels or four, one cylinder, two, four or eight, right up to the launch of the Aero 8 in February 2000, and even after that it continues on the 4/4, Plus 4 and Plus 8 models.

Some early design features did not survive quite so long. On HFS's first car, steering was by a tiller to the right-hand side of the single seat, but he soon offered wheel steering, which was already more conventional. Rear suspension was by swinging arms, pivoting on the bevel box at their forward end, carrying the rear wheel in forks at the back, and controlled by quarter elliptic springs, fixed at their front ends to a crossmember on the bevel box and at the rear to the swinging arm forks. In the early days, there were no additional dampers, front or rear; those only arrived when the cars grew a little heavier and capable of carrying more than one person. The single seat of the prototype sat directly on top of the bevel box, and the bodywork, once fitted, was confined to simple mudguards and some covering over the chassis tubes.

The engine was completely exposed to the cooling air, and even when it was water-cooled it sat out in the open, ahead of the radiator. Only the first prototype had the vee-twin Peugeot engine. For the first Olympia Show appearance in 1910, there were single-seaters with both single- and twin-cylinder power, both air-cooled, both courtesy of JAP. They used Bosch magneto ignition and JAP carburettors. Their cylinder dimensions were identical, at 85.5x85.0mm bore and stroke, to give capacities of 490cc for the single and 980cc for the twin, with horsepower ratings of 4 and 8hp respectively.

Londoner JA Prestwich had started building complete motor cycles with his own copies of De Dion-type engines in around 1904, but in 1908 he introduced his first JAP 'propri-etary' engines, including some with pushrod overhead valves. The engines were intended originally for motor cycle use, or in the case of the vee-twins, for motor cycle and sidecar combinations. The main attraction to HFS, beyond their convenient size and power, was that they were readily available off the shelf, which made them just as attractive to him as they were to the motor cycle industry. They would be around for the lifetime of the twin-cylinder Morgan Run-abouts, too, with JAP keeping their independence, and a fine reputation, until they were taken over by Villiers in 1945.

The essentials of HFS's front-engined tubular chassis layout, save for the change to a three-speed gearbox, the addition of front wheel brakes, water cooling and the usual run of on going reinforcements and refinements, did not change until the introduction of the more conventionally car-like, four-cylinder Morgan F-type three-wheeler in 1933, with its Z-section pressed-steel frame and engine behind the radiator. From the beginning, as well, and even into the twenty-first-century Aero 8, body construction has used metal panels, either steel or aluminium, over a wooden (usually ash) frame. That method of construction allows most of the flexibility of the traditional Morgan chassis to be soaked up in a way that would not be possible with all-metal unit construction (although chassis flexibility will not be a problem with the hugely stiff Aero 8). Most importantly it allows Morgans, even today, to be built by traditional coachbuilding methods, without the need to invest in expensive mass-production press tooling.

Arguably the most important move HFS Morgan ever made – more important even than building his first car; possibly more important than the change, decades later, from three wheels to four – was the early change from one seat to two. With the first single-seater three-wheeler, as HFS later admitted, his only real intention had been to build a runabout, with a small 'r', for his own use. In introducing the two-seater in 1911 after he had built barely a dozen of his single-seat machines when there did prove to be a small market, HFS acknowledged a demand for the Morgan Runabout (with a capital R). That was where he committed himself to becoming a manufacturer.

Mechanically, there was little difference between the one- and two-seat Morgan Runabouts. All the essentials of torque-tube frame, front engine, bevel-box and chain rear drive, swinging-arm rear and, of course, sliding-pillar front suspension survived unchanged, but on top of it all HFS placed a more substantial body with side-by-side seating, straddling the centre tube. And because the two-seater Runabout was now meant for social and practical use (and for sale) as well as for sporting exploits, it was now slightly better equipped against the elements.

The two-seater prototype which appeared in August 1911 carried the same registration as the original single-seater, CJ 743, a number that would float between significant cars for much of Morgan's early history. In its original form it had an air-cooled 8hp JAP vee-twin engine, minimal bodywork comprising little more than the seat shell, foot-boards and low side-boards, but no mudguards, engine cover, or cover over the forward petrol tank. Initially, it also retained tiller steering, but as HFS made further cars during 1911 he changed to wheel steering. That had a direct action which gave less than one turn of the wheel from one lock to the other, making it heavy at low speeds, but with the advantage of being extremely quick and accurate at higher speeds, and it brought the Runabout into line with what was now almost universal practice.

The performance of the twin-cylinder two-seater was quite well sorted out before its first public appearance, and HFS lent one of the first to the motor cycle journalist (and later Morgan racer) W Gordon McMinnies, resulting in that first ever two-seater Runabout test (outlined in Chapter 3) which appeared in *Motor Cycling* magazine in September 1911, written by McMinnies under the pen name 'Platinum'.

As well as praising the Runabout's performance and hillclimbing abilities, McMinnies wrote about the development that was going to turn the Morgan into a commercial success, its newfound two-seat practicality. Before McMinnies drove the JAP-engined machine (inevitably registered CJ 743), HFS Morgan had used it in the ACU club championship trials based at Banbury, in Oxfordshire, completing 160 miles without a stop. When McMinnies collected the car, HFS himself drove him, in the pitch dark, from Banbury to Moreton-in-Marsh, on the way back to Malvern Link, to instruct him 'in the art of three-wheeling'. As 'Platinum' reported, 'The road was strange, but even then I could tell that the speed was high, as the water was streaming from my eyes. We reached Moreton in safety, and then I was left by my preceptor to drive the machine all by myself. I found no difficulty whatever in this, and arrived at a relative's house a few miles distant non-stop. On the next day, according to instructions, I oiled up the front springs, the chains (of which there are two), and suggested to the avuncular one that he might like a spin. As he drives a 15hp car, his impressions of my £90 two-seater may be of interest to other motorists. He admitted the speed and hill-climbing properties of the machine, but noticed the vibration when travelling fast or when climbing all out on the low gear. He also noticed that one collected a good deal of dust, owing to the machine being built so low. Otherwise, I think I am right in saying that he was much impressed.'

'Platinum' drove the 80-odd miles back to London alone, making light of various steep ascents and engaging in a running battle with a much larger car, which the Morgan eventually overtook and pulled away from. The following day in London he drove with a passenger, getting lost in Bond Street and having to climb out and turn the Runabout around by lifting the tail, as there was no reverse gear, to the amusement of passers-by. Later in the week, he took another long run, this time accompanied by a photographer with all his equipment, the magazine pictures showing McMinnies in the car with his suitcase perched on a carrier above the rear wheel.

McMinnies concluded this very first published test of a two-seater Morgan by reporting, 'We then delivered the machine over to its makers and, needless to relate, were most reluctant to part with it. I feel convinced that when a few more side-carists get to know of the existence of this little three-wheeler, and when they have had time to give the machine a trial, they will fall in love with it as much as I have done . . .'

There could hardly have been a better endorsement, or a better timed one, in such a respected magazine just weeks before the two-seater Runabout's public debut, at the 1911 Olympia Motor Cycle Show in November. One year on from Morgan's first, and only partly successful appearance at the show, the new format caused a sensation.

Motor Cycling reported, 'The interest displayed in the Morgan Runabouts was phenomenal. As all our readers know, these machines have competed with unqualified success in all the big trials of the last eighteen months, gaining a reputation of which the makers may be justly proud.' Just as important as the reference to the competition successes was this year's cartoon, now showing the two-seater model with the caption, 'The Morgan Magnet attracts all young couples by its double seating accommodation'. By the end of the show, HFS Morgan was almost swamped by orders.

His first reaction was to try to find another company to manufacture the Runabout in volume but he failed to do so; that failure almost certainly laid the foundations for all Morgan's future development as a manufacturer. Realising now that if he was to have a car for sale at all he must build it himself, HFS settled down to the long-term process of satisfying orders while continually improving the product. At the same time, he still managed to find time to prove the Runabout in trials and, very soon, races.

He was also now faced with growing competition as the cyclecar movement began to take off. The pioneers had all appeared at much the same time as Morgan's first experimental Runabout, around 1909 and 1910, and on both sides of the Channel, in England and France. In the next few years, as the motor sport authorities struggled to place the new kind of vehicle in the appropriate class, HFS and his father, HG, would have a prolific running correspondence with the car and motor cycle magazines about what exactly constituted a cyclecar and the relative merits of three or four wheels, but it is fair to say that most people would recognise a cyclecar if they saw one.

The cyclecars followed in the wheeltracks of earlier attempts at making cheaper and simpler transport for a wider market than the expensive, full-sized, 'conventional' car. Those included quadricyles like the early De Dion, which resembled two motor cycles joined by cross tubes, and the tricars – like HFS Morgan's Eagle. The quadricycles and tricars went out of fashion as they grew heavier and more expensive, removing their advantages over the ever improving light cars of the early years of the century. The best of the cyclecars in effect reinvented them, offering cheapness, light weight for ample performance, and simplicity – plus tax advantages for being at the low end of the sliding scale which depended on rated horsepower. And three-wheelers, like the Morgan, had the further advantage of a flat-rate tax irrespective of horsepower, with the proviso that to qualify for such rates a vehicle had to weigh less than 8cwt.

It was not, however, the established car (or even motor cycle) manufacturers who began to build cyclecars but enthusiasts and inventors like HFS Morgan. In Britain his earliest rivals were GN, and in France Bédélia, both of whose first offerings, like Morgan's, coincidentally used Peugeot vee-twin motor cycle engines.

The GN took its name from the initials of the two engineers who started the company, Ronald Godfrey and Archibald Frazer-Nash. Together they built a number of prototypes and in 1910, the same year as HFS Morgan showed his first Runabout, they launched their belt-drive, vee-twin-powered four-wheeler – with the emphasis, like Morgan's, on sporty performance. Both their production set-up and their early designs were even more basic than Morgan's. The first GNs were built in the stables of Frazer-Nash's family home in Hendon, north London, before they moved to small workshops nearby, and because the company had virtually no machinery the first GNs had wooden chassis and crude cable-and-bobbin steering. At first they offered either Peugeot or JAP engines, but in 1911 they went down a road that Morgan, in spite of later thoughts, always managed to resist, making their own engines – vee twins with some Peugeot components and later with their own over-head-inlet-valve cylinder heads.

The risk paid off for GN: they maintained their reputation and did well commercially, although that did not come until later. While Morgan's output had increased to nearly twenty cars a week before the First World War, GN were only making a tenth of that at best. Their boom years came after the war, after they were taken over by the British Grégoire company in 1919. Adopting the same formula of light weight and sporty performance, but now with a steel chassis and chain drive, GN were employing five hundred people and building as many as two hundred and twenty cars a month that year, and again like Morgan had a licence arrangement in France (in GN's case with Salmson). Unlike Morgan's, their success did not last; by 1921, after a receiver had been appointed, the company was taken over and started to build larger touring cars, until production stopped early in 1923 with the manu-facturing side showing a loss of almost £85,000. In the same year, Morgan built 2,300 three-wheelers, although demand was already being hit by the availability of the low-priced Austin Seven, launched in 1922.

The Morgan's main French rival, the Bédélia, was another product of almost exactly the same time, and it was frequently credited with founding the whole cyclecar genre – it is said that the sight of a Bédélia in Paris in 1910 prompted WG McMinnies to suggest the idea of *The Cyclecar* magazine to his publisher.

The Bédélia was created by Robert Bourbeau and Henri Devaux, and took its name from the initial letters of their surnames. Bourbeau was the designer, Devaux the financial backer. In 1909, Bourbeau, then an eighteen-year-old engineering student, built his very weird prototype. It looked like a low-slung oblong box with four wheels, powered by the Peugeot vee-twin motor cycle engine, and carrying two people, one behind the other, on rudimentary canvas seats, with the driver right at the back, behind the passenger. Mechanically it was even cruder than the spidery GN, and way behind the relative sophistication of the Morgan. Like the GN it had a wooden frame, and cable-and-bobbin steering, but on the Bédélia the front axle simply pivoted around its centre point, suspended on a single, vertical coil spring. It had a two-speed drive by extraordinarily long side belt to the rear wheels, it was little heavier than the Morgan, at about 425lb, and in 1910, with just 10,000 francs of capital from Devaux to set up Bourbeau et Devaux in Paris, it went into production, to sell at about 1,200 francs.

Despite building a fine reputation for speed and reliability, Bédélia (advertising itself as 'the largest producers of cyclecars in the world') did not have Morgan's staying power. During the First World War, Bédélia continued to build their cars, many of them to be used as field ambulances, each carrying a single casualty on a horizontal stretcher ahead of the driver, directly above the petrol tank, below which was the hot engine . . . Bourbeau and Devaux sold the company to a former distributor in 1920 and as the cyclecar era began to wane the cars became slightly more conventional, with side-by-side seating and three-speed transmissions. But while Morgan forged on, the Bédélia was finally laid to rest in 1925.

Both the Morgan and the Bédélia were among the most successful and best of a large and very mixed bunch of cars. By the time *The Cyclecar* magazine was launched, in 1912, it listed more than thirty makes available in Britain alone. Barely six months later there were more than a hundred models on the British market, the vast majority of them powered, like the Morgans, by proprietary engines, mostly of motor cycle origin. So many companies sprang up for exactly the reasons that HFS Morgan had recognised – that a simply designed, lightweight car needed very little by way of manufacturing machinery, and therefore little investment capital, certainly compared with the cost of breaking into the mainstream motor industry at this time. Not all of the new companies, however, could match Morgan's designs, his competition success, or his balance of marketing and cost-management skills. Consequently, most of them were very short-lived. Although those that survived enjoyed a brief spell of pre- and post-war success before the Austin Seven effect and the coming of other '£100 cars' kicked in, nonetheless the cyclecar boom was short-lived. Morgan, however, built a comfortable niche before the war, improved their financial position during it, and learned to adapt after it, without losing sight of their principles.

In the eyes of the law, you might have expected the definition of a cyclecar to be quite specific, because of the tax advantages that went with satisfying it, but in reality it was vague, and the cyclecar was in effect lumped together for tax purposes with the motor cycle and sidecar. For tax purposes there was the rule about weighing less than 8cwt (and early Morgans could weigh less than half that), but otherwise the only broadly accepted (and strictly unofficial) definition was that a cyclecar had fewer than four cylinders and something like belt or chain or friction transmission rather than a conventional gearbox. In 1911, HFS Morgan suggested how he saw the definition, and in doing so underlined how he saw his own design. 'The RAC limitation for cycle car chassis weight', he said, 'might well be lowered, say, to 4cwt. The cycle car is not and cannot take the place of the car; it is the friendly rival of the side-car combination. Economy of running and speed are essential, and for these lightness is indispensable.'

Establishing a pattern that still holds good to this day, and which gives the lie to the theory that Morgans are frozen in time, HFS began to modify and improve his early cars on a virtually continuous basis; with no expensive fixed tooling he could do this, without the disruption or cost of changing the fundamentals. Most of the on-going improvements were minor but real, including an early change from the harsh metal-to-metal to a leather-faced clutch, which was more forgiving as long as it was properly looked after and skilfully used. In pre-First World War motoring terms, the driving skills needed for a Morgan were not considered unusual, because every car had its own idiosyncracies and Morgan's were no greater than anyone else's. An article in *The Automobile* in 1984 put the experience into a more modern perspective, without losing track of the original expectations.

'A drive in a two-speed Morgan [it said of a late 1920s Aero, with water-cooled vee twin and front wheel brakes] is naturally quite an experience. Having started the engine (remember that the starting handle fits into the side of the car and works through the bevels, so the assistance of a valve lifter is necessary and its lever is screwed to the bodywork) you lower yourself into the driving seat to the accompaniment of the peculiar booming rhythm of the V-twin. To the uninitiated the control layout is utterly puzzling; in fact it combines standard car controls with the contemporary motor cycle's lever throttle and hand gear change. There are clutch and brake pedals in the conventional positions, the footbrake in this case operating an external contracting band brake on the rear wheel. A large lever to the driver's left operates the front brakes, while to the right is the gear lever. On the steering wheel are several controls: a long throttle lever, an air control (only needed when starting), and a single lever to control the magneto advance and retard.

'Morgan bodywork is very narrow, and worn, so to speak, tight under the arms. Nevertheless there is a surprising amount of legroom in the Aero, which also has more space around the pedals than the slimmer Super Aero and Super Sports machines. The clutch has little travel and can be fierce – appropriate applications of oil, grease, Fuller's Earth and similar substances to the fabric lining being one of the subtler points of maintenance. Once under way, the torque engine allows an early change into high gear, the car pulling strongly from low speeds. The steering appears very heavy to the unaccustomed driver; there is a reduction box in the column but the steering wheel moves less than a turn from lock to lock, and you adapt to using the wheel like a motorcycle's handlebars.' The earliest cars, of course, did not have the reduction gear ...

'Fortunately, perhaps, there are few distractions on the dashboard, but the oil drip-feed indicator has to be watched to ensure that the engine is getting a supply of lubricant for its total loss system, and adjusted to match the car's speed from time to time. Three-speed cars have automatic dry-sump oiling, so this particular complication is avoided.

'The level of performance often surprises newcomers to Morgans, and the sensation of speed is heightened because the car is so small, makes a variety of delightful noises and carries its occupants so close to the road. In fact an overhead-valve Aero's maximum speed is about 75mph. It is, above all, the effortlessness of its cruising and hill-climbing that makes the Morgan so attractive. The standard ratios leave the two-speeder rather undergeared in top; substitution of a 30-tooth rear-wheel sprocket gives a longer-legged top gear at the expense of interchangeability of the drive chains – an aid to maintenance. The ride is firm and the Morgan's three tracks seem to find every pothole; this is accentuated on cars like mine which, unlike some later models, have no shock absorbers fitted. Cornering, however, is outstanding, as anyone who has watched Morgans racing – some cars nowadays developing over 100bhp – will realise. Braking is not the Morgan's strong point but, as with all early cars and motor-cycles, one's driving technique evolves to compensate for this.

'The Morgan three-wheeler,' the article concluded, 'offers a unique kind of motoring – a car with something of the character of a motorcycle or aircraft . . .'

That short description (its language not dissimilar from an article of the 1920s) is as good as any extended road test in giving the flavour of all early Morgan three-wheelers rather than the details of any one in particular, and the last sentence hints at the same feelings as one of the best known and most evocative descriptions of driving an early Morgan, written by well-known American enthusiast Larry W Ayers, about a 1922 Aero. 'When you drove it at night,' he wrote, 'you saw the twinkling of the exposed rocker gear, sparks from the exhaust pipes, and oil spots appeared on the windscreen. On a bumpy road it felt like tearing across a grassy air strip. The name Aero aptly described this Morgan model. I've always felt it unfortunate that the (vee-) twin engined Morgans faded from the scene, for it was in this model that one had the feeling of being propelled along in a sidecar motorcycle.'

However HFS Morgan improved his design, he tried to do it without losing those essentials of simplicity, light weight and sparkling performance. He even kept the same characteristics in mind around 1913 or 1914, when he built, just as a family runabout (originally with a small 'r'), the prototype four-seater in which he and wife Ruth were pictured with his sister Dorothy and Ruth's brother Geoffrey Day, outside Stoke Lacy rectory, probably just before the outbreak of the war. And he devised a hood for the production Runabout which could be erected while the car was on the move.

At the 1912 Motor Cycle Show, held as usual at London's Olympia, Morgan exhibited a number of two-seaters and again did extremely well. As the motor cycle press reported, 'the business transacted on the first three days of the Show was sufficient to allow Mr HFS Morgan to announce that he had sold his output for 1913. On his stand were two notices of his recent hour record, surmounted by a wreath of laurel.' That event was also commemorated by the cover picture of the second issue of *The Cyclecar* showing HFS in his single-seater at Brooklands, with his top-hatted father looking on, and with the headline 'Nearly Sixty Miles in One Hour'.

In 1913, the existing models gained useful space in the redesigned tail, for luggage and tools, while two additions to the range spanned just about the entire spectrum. The Commercial had a box-like body capable of carrying reasonable loads on an otherwise standard chassis, while the Grand Prix, with longer chassis, lower seating position and over-head-valve JAP engines, was the first catalogued competition model. It was named after McMinnies' performance in the French Cyclecar Grand Prix.

The Grand Prix model marked one significant departure. Up to this point, all Morgans except the first Peugeot-engined prototype had been fitted with air-cooled JAP engines; now Morgan started to offer different makes as options. There was nothing wrong with the JAP engines, or with Morgan's relationship with their manufacturer, JA Prestwich of London, but HFS was keen to compare the performance of other alternatives, even to try water-cooling, initially as an answer to overheating on cars tuned for long-distance, high-speed work, such as some of the Brooklands runs. And just as importantly, on the commercial front HFS was already concerned by the risks of being dependent on a single engine supplier.

All the JAP engines used in the two-speed Morgan three-wheelers right up to 1932 were either 50- or 60-degree vee-twins, with big capacities for only two cylinders, and an ability to rev to something like 4,000 to 4,500rpm, plenty of slogging power, if not the smoothest mechanical balance. All the 60-degree JAP vee-twins had the same cylinder bore of 85.7mm so an 85.0mm stroke gave a capacity of 981cc while the longer 95.0mm stroke gave 1096cc. The early side-valve types were used in both air-cooled and water-cooled formats, the 60-degree overhead-valve ones were all water-cooled. The other type of JAP engine was the 50-degree vee-twin, air-cooled with overhead valves and bore and stroke dimensions of either 85.5x95.0mm for a capacity of 980cc, or 80.0x99.0mm for 995cc. The compression ratios ranged from a lowly (but for the day not unusually lowly) 4.75:1 for the early side-valvers to 5.75:1 on later two-speeders, giving power outputs between 25 and 42bhp. The 60-degree three-speed engines had compression ratios of either 5.0 or 7.0:1 and from 23 to just over 39bhp. The high-performance 50-degree twins, running much higher 6.6 and even 10.0:1 compression – with special fuel mixtures, and in the case of the 995cc JTOR engine capable of revving to 5500rpm – gave between 45 and 57bhp, which was enough to make the lightweight sporting Morgan very fast indeed for its day.

As well as the JAP engines, the two-cylinder Morgans used three other British makes of vee-twin, all essentially motor cycle types and all with their own followings. The vast majority, apart from odd interlopers, comprised air-cooled and water-cooled 57-degree overhead-valve Anzani vee-twins of 1078 or 1500cc, offering from 40 to 48bhp, air- or water-cooled, side- and overhead-valve 60-degree Blackburne vee-twins of 1096cc giving from 35 to 40bhp, and air- and water-cooled, side- and overhead-valve 982cc 50-degree Matchless vee-twins, good for between 27 and 42bhp. Morgan also used both air- and water-cooled MAG vee-twins made by Motosacoche Acacias Genève, in Switzerland, with overhead-inlet, side-exhaust valves, capacities of either 993 or 1093cc and unspecified power outputs but not quite such a sporty character as the higher revving British twins. When the engine was of the water-cooled type, it still sat well out in front in the airstream, but it had a radiator mounted behind it, just about over the driver's feet, and in the sporty versions with the handsome and distinctively shaped radiator cowl, usually with either a tall filler, a flying stork, or a personalised mascot.

Choice of engines apart, most of the changes in the first few years were more about offering a variety of body styles than changing obviously sound engineering. The distinctive 'coal scuttle' front engine cover had appeared by 1911 and recognisable derivatives of the shape would survive on Family models into the late 1930s. But there were also competition cars with exposed engines and 'torpedo' petrol tanks, the water-cooled cars with that shapely radiator cowl behind the engine, and even before the war there was a huge variety of body shapes and levels of weather protection on offer – all, as the advertisements said for many years, with 'Prices from 85 Guineas'.

The standard Runabout wheelbase in the early days was 75 inches and front track was typically a fraction under 4 feet, but the racing cars built for the French Cycle Car Grand Prix in 1913 brought both a stretched wheelbase and a slightly lower seating position. Those went into limited production soon after in the sporty Grand Prix model, with an all-up weight of just 500lb, and a price tag of £106 in 1915, before the outbreak of war stopped play.

It was also around the onset of the war that HFS started experimenting with four wheels, but his first venture came to nothing and it would be twenty years before the theme was revived. HG Morgan, that most unusual churchman, was a great supporter of three wheels versus four and often wrote to the press to argue the case. In 1911 he wrote to *Cycling*, 'I notice that Mr J Denew writes to you that he objects to tri-cars because for some time he rode a tricycle. It is quite a natural prejudice. I have also ridden tricycles, and my experience was not altogether pleasurable; my last pitched me into a ditch for venturing to take a corner at about eight miles an hour, and I exchanged it for a bicycle. But has Mr Denew ridden a modern tri-car? I venture to think he will find it a very difficult experience. Not long ago I was asked by the inventor of one of these machines [no prizes for guessing who that might have been] to come for a spin and see how it took corners. Remembering my tricycle experience I went all trembling and returned reassured. I felt as safe as in my own motorcar . . .'

In more serious vein he wrote again to *The Motor Cycle* in 1912. 'Theory,' he said, 'is not of much use in dealing with a practical question which must be decided by practical tests. Of course, anyone who has driven both a three-wheeler and a four-wheeler (and the best of each kind) is entitled to give his opinion – which will differ from the opinions of some other riders. But for those who have not that practical experience, the following facts may be more useful than theories: (1) A three-wheeler won very easily the only cycle car race yet held, at a speed of about 59mph. The three-wheeler was, in fact, "first, and the rest nowhere". (2) At this speed the three-wheeler was absolutely steady, whereas the only four-wheeler which approached it "snaked" badly and finally turned turtle. (3) No four-wheeler has, as yet, got through an official long distance reliability trial, open to both three- and four-wheelers, whereas a three-wheeler has been consistently successful in these trials. (4) So far no three-wheeler with single front steering wheel has entered for any official trial. I may add that I was all in favour of four wheels until I was converted by experience.'

But if HFS Morgan's conversion back to four wheels had to wait, four seats were on offer much earlier, in what became the Family model. Following that four-seater prototype of 1912 or 1913, Morgan was in a position to build production four-seaters by 1915, but was prevented from doing so by the war, which meant that the four-seater was only built in small numbers until it was launched properly, as the Family, in 1919. Names like Standard and De Luxe denoted the levels of equipment on offer, Sporting spoke for itself, while it has been said that the Standard Popular model introduced at the Olympia Show in 1921 (at £150 complete) was a play on the word 'poplar', because the frame used black poplar timber, although it is more likely that Morgan merely wanted to emphasise 'the economical motorist's ideal'. The other end of the spectrum was the Aero, a sporty model between the Standard models and the Grand Prix. Its origins dated back to 1916 when Morgan built a car combining elements of Sporting and Grand Prix designs, with low seats, curved wings, running boards but no windscreen or hood, and a water-cooled MAG vee-twin. Only a few were built because of the war, but the Aero proper, officially announced at the 1919 Motor Cycle Show although not really in full production until a year later, was not dissimilar, save for now having the distinctive tapering tail and individual aero-screen windscreens for driver and passenger.

Through the 1920s, as described in Chapter 3, HFS was obliged to cut prices in an attempt to compete with the Austin Seven and other rivals, but he also added value and improved performance with steady development. Help from outside came with the introduction of the new Motor Car Taxation Act in January 1921, based on the RAC horsepower 'Treasury Rating'. That left the Morgan untouched on the £4 'sidecar' rate but would mean an £8 levy for the Austin Seven when it came along, and one survey suggested that the Morgan also offered a fuel cost saving of up to £2 a year compared to a typical light car. Three tyres wore more quickly than four, but not quickly enough to take away an overall cost saving, and the smaller three-wheeler was cheaper to garage. Over a year's running, taking into account petrol, oil, tyres and insurance, the independent survey suggested that a Rover cost £68 15s 5d, a Jowett £65 18s 0d, and an Austin Seven £65 14s 0d. The Morgan's annual running costs were only £54 12s 3d, representing a substantial saving for the Morgan owner of almost £1 a month, which in the early 1920s was a considerable sum of money.

On the equipment side, electric lighting had been on offer for the Morgan owner since just after the war, followed by electric starting some years later, originally offered as a £10 optional extra. And to make life easier, also just after the war Morgan devised a useful modification comprising a hinged tail section, giving much better access to the rear wheel and drive chains, helping with regular maintenance. That rear-end layout was improved again about 1920 with a new rear fork design which made it possible for the first time to remove the rear wheel without first having to remove the chains – most useful when it came to repairing rear wheel punctures, for instance. At around the same time, the gear sizes were rejigged so that both sides could use similar length chains, making them interchangeable, to even out wear.

There were smaller improvements more or less continuously, many of them the result of lessons learned in trials and other competitions, many of them – like larger bearings, a redesigned gearshift mechanism, better lubrication seals and upgraded front hubs – to improve durability. There were also changes to improve overall performance, the most important of the early ones being to make the Morgan stop more effectively, first with a larger rear brake drum, and from 1922 with the option of small cable-operated front brakes, which were originally seen as being for emergency use only.

All the time, body styles evolved subtly, the reliability of fixings and fittings was improved and maintenance needs were generally simplified or reduced. The option of balloon tyres offered a bit more ride comfort, but essentially the design fundamentals were little changed from HFS's first production models, and the formula was still working because the level of orders at Olympia in 1924 was the highest yet.

By 1926, that level of orders was much harder to come by. Now it was product improvements (electric lighting was standard across the range by now, with electric starting as an option) as well as price reductions that were helping to prop Morgan sales up against the effects of both the Seven and the Depression. Morgan advertising, too, was now just as likely to shout about practicality and economy as it was about competition exploits. Nor was it afraid to point out that the Morgan had been there first. In March that year an advertisement headed 'The Pioneer and Still the Best' ran 'The first three-wheeled car, the forerunner of the economy light car and still miles ahead of any – the Morgan Runabout. The Morgan – whichever model you choose – will "get you there" with the same speed, the same satisfaction, greater reliability, and far less cost than any other car. In fact it offers you all the advantages of a car at a fraction of the cost. To buy, from £95. To run, 50 miles on a gallon of "juice". Tax only £4. Double the price and the petrol consumption, treble the tax, and you have the average light car figures. Buy a Morgan and pass such cars on the road. Simple, dependable, wonderful on hills, sporty, sturdy and easily managed, no wonder the first favourite for economy and value is, as ever, the Morgan.'

In June, featuring a picture of a family on the beach in their Family model, another advertisement suggested, ' "Make it a Morgan Holiday". Why stay at home and envy your friends who get out every holiday, every weekend? You can get away to the seaside too – as inexpensively, as comfortably, as surely, as satisfactorily – by Morgan. The Morgan Runabout costs much less than a car, yet gives the same performance. Its tax is only £4, its petrol consumption 50mpg, its speed 60mph, there are only three tyres to maintain, and the Morgan is easy to handle, easy to understand . . .'

At the same time, they were still promoting competition success, regularly publishing Morgan's results from the major production car trials and also outright performance achievements, boasting at the end of 1926, 'The World's Fastest Three-Wheeler. World's Records – 1 kilo, 104.6mph; 1 Hour, 91.48mph; 100 Miles, 91.54mph.' And those were still genuinely impressive numbers, but by now the emphasis on fun and economy was just as important, with snippets like, 'Cheap to Buy, Cheap to Run, Easily Housed'; or 'All England's at your feet when you own a Morgan!'; and, 'Cheap as a motor cycle combination, but comfortable as a car'. There was a version for everyone, 'There's a Morgan for the Sportsman and a Morgan for the Family Man too – both providing the speed of an expensive car with the running costs of a motorcycle combination. Wherever your tastes lie, therefore, you will do well to get full particulars of the Morgan, for nowhere else will you find efficiency and economy so well combined in one vehicle. Write now for the Book of the Morgan.' And people still did.

Many of the changes, like the lowered M-type chassis with underslung rear springs for the 1927 Racer model, and a revised chassis for the Standard model in 1928, just before it was discontinued at the time of the Olympia Show, were not particularly easy to see, but geared steering from 1929 was very easy to feel, especially at low speeds, and was welcomed by virtually everybody. There was also a new performance model in the Super Sports Aero, with the lower chassis, shock absorbers all round, a hinged tail and tuned JAP engine. Olympia 1929 brought another round of changes, with more room in the Family models and a new rear chassis layout for the sporty two-seaters, with internally expanding drum brakes rather than the older band brakes, underslung rear quarter elliptic springs and a new pivot point for the rear forks, allowing a slightly shorter wheelbase. 1930 brought the first sight of the biggest change in basic design since the adoption of two seats, with the switch to three gears and the addition of reverse. This was not the first time Morgans had had more than two gears, only the first time in standard production form. In 1912 there was the option, mainly for competitions, of an additional reduction gearbox, mounted behind the clutch between engine and bevel box, and offering a 50 per cent reduction in propeller shaft speed before the final drive, which with the two normal chain and sprocket options gave a total of four forward speeds. It was rather complicated to use, however, and engaging the highest or lowest ratios involved moving two levers at once, one for the chains, one for the reduction box. It also cost £10 as an option, which was a substantial extra outlay in 1912. It caused a small controversy when one competitor used it in his trials Runabout and was accused of running a non-standard machine. The ever-ready HG quickly wrote to the press in his defence, pointing out that it was a modification readily available to anyone.

The same type of four-speed option was offered again shortly after the war, by which time the price had gone up to £20, and in 1923 there were experiments with a four-speed constant-mesh gearbox, also offering reverse gear, which was fitted in place of the normal bevel box, necessitating other modifications to the frame. It was never offered in production, or even as an option. By the late 1920s, when a two-speed chain transmission probably sounded archaic to the Austin Seven generation, there were other 'after-market' modifications on offer for the Morgan, including several reverse gear conversions, and a three-speed gearbox from the London company FH Hambling, similar to that used by several regular Morgan racing owners.

When Morgan finally offered their own version, final drive was still by chain, but now just one chain, as the compact three-speed and reverse gearbox took the place of the original bevel box, cross shaft, dog-clutches and twin chain-and-sprocket layout. Into production by 1931, it undoubtedly made the Morgan slightly more refined and more conventionally car like, possibly gave it a bit more flexibility, and certainly made it easier to back up or turn around, but it did not please everybody. Reporting its launch in October 1931, *Motor Cycle* reported, 'To state that the Morgan Motor Company have designed a new chassis for 1932 would be quite unfair to the amazingly simple design which has characterised this most successful three-wheeler from its earliest days. The essential features of the three-tube construction are unchanged, but so far as engine and transmission are concerned, the design has been brought so much up to date that it is difficult to regard the machine as a whole as anything but new. Those who know and love the old two-speed Morgans will still be able to obtain this type unaltered from the 1931 design, at very modest prices, but the main range for the future will include a three-speed and reverse gear box with a single driving chain, and a redesigned engine which is available in all the usual types.'

The change coincided with the change from 50-degree to 60-degree 1096cc JAP engines which were supposed to be much smoother running, and the range on offer now comprised the Family model, with air-cooled side-valve engine for £95, the Family with water-cooled side-valve twin for £100, the water-cooled side-valve Aero at £115 or 10–40hp water-cooled overhead-valve Aero at £125, the water-cooled side-valve Sports Family at £120, 10–40hp water-cooled overhead-valve Sports Family at £130, and the very quick Super Sports with specially tuned overhead-valve vee-twin at £145. All of them now had Lucas electric lights and starters, a speedometer and windscreen wiper. The Family could be had as a two-seater, in which case the rear seats were replaced by a luggage locker with space for more luggage on top of the tail. The cheaper two-speed models were now listed at £75 or £80 for air- or water-cooled side-valve Family models respectively, and £95 or £110 for the side-valve or 10–40hp overhead-valve water-cooled Aeros – savings of up to £20 over the three-speeders.

Unfortunately, to the two-speed purists the change took away much of the original character. They saw the three-speed Morgan as more of a touring car than a sports car in the old tradition of sidecar competitions and Brooklands record runs, but by the end of 1932, the sporty simplicity of the two-speed Morgan was a thing of the past, still available to special order but no longer in the normal catalogue.

The next big change was undoubtedly even more of a shock to the early Morgan purists. So far, evolutionary changes apart, Morgan had always at least stood for the same kind of elegantly clever tubular chassis and the familiar, thumping motor cycle-type vee-twin engines, in bodies quite distinct from more conventional cars. In 1933, Morgan changed all those things in one fell swoop, with the introduction of the F-type three-wheeler.

The F-type was really the first completely new Morgan design since the first day, and the F, depending on how you looked at it, could equally stand for four cylinders, or for Ford, the engine supplier. But there was more to the break with tradition than that, as the F-type moved much closer to 'conventional' 1930s motor engineering. After almost a quarter of a century, the original tubular chassis design was finally replaced by something more in line with current practice, in pressed steel. Although it waved goodbye to one long-running piece of Morgan design, it shepherded in another, because essentially the same Z-section side members as were introduced on the F-type survive into the year 2000. They survive on every model except the new Aero 8, after a production life of more than sixty-five years which makes even the original tube chassis look ephemeral. And, of course, the sliding-pillar suspension spans both those chassis . . .

The prototype for the F-type followed unsuccessful attempts to fit a small four-cylinder side-valved Coventry-Climax engine into a modified two-speed tubular chassis, when Morgan knew that even to hang on to the fast-shrinking market they were now seeing, they had to offer something more than the old vee-twins. The Z-section chassis was clever enough in its own way. It was easy to make, with no expensive tooling and no particularly specialised machinery. By some typical lateral thinking HFS made it perform more than one function, in the same way he had with the early tubular chassis' lower side-members-cum-exhaust-pipes. The central backbone was retained, now flanked by pressed-steel side members. The F-type's traditionally built (if not traditionally shaped) metal-panelled, ash-framed body sat directly on the top of the Z while the floorboards sat between the bottom part on each side of the car, the latter forming flanges which pointed inwards. For the first time, the engine was moved back behind the front suspension frame, and behind the radiator, to the 'conventional', longitudinal location for a four-cylinder engine in a 1930s car. The three-speed gearbox, however, stayed where it had been on the last twin-cylinder, tubular-framed cars – at the back – where the old bevel box used to be. Final drive, as with the three-speed, twin-cylinder cars was by a single chain, and the rear suspension, like the front, was much as it had always been, with a swinging arm controlled by quarter elliptic springs.

When the car first appeared in public, at the 1933 Olympia Show, it still had the 750cc Coventry-Climax engine, but that would change before production started. The production F-type started life with a mildly modified version of the 933cc side-valve Ford 8hp engine, two seats, and the distinctive barrel-shaped tail and rear-mounted spare wheel which were soon adopted by the twin-cylinder models. The 8hp-rated engine gave an actual output of about 24bhp, which was good enough for a top speed of 65mph and a comfortable cruising speed of 60mph, while still offering 40mpg – and still qualifying for the £4 tax rate thanks to maintaining the light weight philosophy. It also introduced coupled brakes on all three wheels, operated by a single pedal, with the handbrake operating just on the rear wheel. And it still looked like a Morgan.

Although the move towards competing with more conventional four-cylinder, four-wheel cars was an obvious one given the alarming decline in sales, Morgan did not present the new four-cylinder cars as a replacement for the two-cylinder models, only as an extension of the range, in the words of *The Light Car & Cyclecar* magazine, 'an addition to the range and a worthy addition which will undoubtedly prove immensely popular with hundreds of people who have wanted a four-cylinder model bearing the name of Morgan and who welcome the newcomer with open arms.'

Morgan advertised the welcome newcomer in November 1933, just prior to its appearance at Olympia – 'Introducing a New Four Cylinder Morgan Model'. It read, 'After several years of experimental work, the Morgan Motor Co Ltd are able to introduce to the public an entirely new departure in three-wheelers, the "Morgan" Three-Wheeler Model F, fitted with a powerful four-cylinder water-cooled engine . . .' It was priced at £120, 'fully equipped with electric lighting and starting set, wiper and all-weather equipment, tools and fitments.' Plus, of course, £4 tax.

It was not a bad car, and Morgan soon added a slightly more powerful 1172cc Ford side-valve 10hp model for only £7 10s more than the 8hp one; not long after, they were offering four seats as well as the original two. Although HFS Morgan initiated that aggressive programme of price cuts, none of it was enough to halt the decline in three-wheeler sales through the mid- to late 1930s. In 1934, already way down from their peak years, Morgan sold 659 three-wheelers, in 1935 it was down to 286, and in 1937 to only 137 cars, but now there was another Morgan alternative. Finally, in 1936, more than twenty years after HFS had first toyed with the idea, and three years after the first four-cylinder car, Morgan launched a production four-wheeler.

However reluctant HFS Morgan was to accept it, the day of the three-wheeler was coming to an end; the four-wheeler was a necessary step for Morgan to take if it was to survive very much longer as a car builder. If it was a hard step for HFS to take philosophically, it was a relatively straightforward one mechanically, given the layout of the three-wheeled, four-cylinder, Z-framed F-type which had already done most of the job for him. Slightly perversely, one of the problems Morgan faced in trying to make a four-wheel car based on the twin-cylinders' tubular chassis was that the chassis was actually too stiff – the exact opposite of the problem most cars are faced with today, but a corollary of

3

Morgan keeping faith with the sliding-pillar front and swinging-arm plus leaf-spring rear suspensions, which only worked properly if the springing was stiff enough to keep wheel travel, and therefore geometrical changes, to a minimum. With three wheels and a near-rigid chassis and suspension it worked, but with four wheels it did not, because four wheels could not cope with rough ground as well as three could. The Z-section pressed-steel chassis of the F-type three-wheeler, on the other hand, was relatively soft, and so offered some of the flexibility that Morgan needed but which the familiar suspension system alone could not offer. It was also a fairly straightforward operation to replace the single rear wheel with a conventional axle and two wheels.

In 1934, therefore, Morgan built another four-wheel prototype; this time it would lead to something. Forward of the seats it was essentially a standard F-type chassis, although the front track was made slightly narrower because HFS reasoned it did not need to be as wide for comparable stability with four wheels. Further back, there was a mid-mounted gearbox and a fairly ordinary rear axle mounted on quarter elliptic springs attached to the outside of the Z-section rear chassis members. The car kept the usual 933cc Ford 8hp four-cylinder side-valve engine, and bodywork based on the F-type's, and it was registered WP 7490. What did not work was the rear suspension, and soon HFS replaced it with a new layout using semi-elliptic underslung springs inside chassis rails which had been moved slightly further apart.

Peter Morgan has suggested that his father may have conceived the layout after looking at the similar rear suspension of his older sister Sylvia's Hillman Aero Minx, but whatever HFS's inspiration the new layout worked better than the old and the Morgan four-wheeler moved a step nearer production. In a reversal of the four-cylinder, three-wheeler gestation, the engine was changed from Ford to Coventry-Climax and, as described later, the Ford-engined prototype was given to the young Peter Morgan to use while he was learning to drive, while its registration number was transferred to the Coventry-Climax-engined prototype once it was ready for testing.

Much of that testing was done on the same trials routes and hills that had been used for years by the three-wheelers and it was also tested at Brooklands, where journalist Gregor Grant, then editor of *The Light Car & Cyclecar*, later founder of *Autosport* magazine, was allowed a brief test drive. A third prototype was then built, which had revised bodywork, including running-boards for the first time, but in this case a Ford engine again, the new 1172cc 10hp which was just appearing in the F-type. Finally, the Climax-engined car was given another revised body and the design was almost there.

Most appropriately, it made its first public appearance, and its last step on the way to production, in the 1935 London–Exeter Trial, driven by HFS, with Peter as co-driver. The trial, as had become traditional, started on Boxing Day, and the Morgans were entered in a class specially created for drivers who had competed in the first running of the trial, twenty-five years earlier – which HFS had, in the first outing with his original production three-wheeler. The Morgans were the only entrants in the 1935 class to win a first-class award and in doing so they had proved that the new car worked.

It went into production in March 1936 with a long-stroke, 1122cc Coventry-Climax engine with overhead inlet and side exhaust valves – the long stroke reflecting the fact that the British tax system was still based on the anachronistic RAC rating system which was in turn principally based on the cylinder bore size. The Climax engine was therefore rated just inside the 10hp class, and taxed accordingly, 15s below the 10–11hp class. Its actual power output was about 34bhp, which gave the 1740lb two-seater a top speed of about 70mph, with lively acceleration. The car was given the new model designation 4-4, for four wheels and four cylinders, changed post-war (for no special reason) to 4/4.

At first Morgan relied more on its competition outings than conventional advertising to promote it, but prior to its appearance at the Olympia Show in October 1936 it was advertised in the press as 'Entirely New! The Morgan "4-4" High Performance Ten – A Leader of the Smart Set.' The copy capitalised on Morgan's past glories: 'The New Morgan high-performance Ten embodies much of the experience gained in the design and construction of our racing three-wheelers. The illustration shows the smart and distinctive appearance, and it will undoubtedly appeal to many motorists who prize a lively performer, stability and ease of control. The driving position is low and comfortable. Luggage space is provided behind the squab, which also accommodates the hood when lowered. Two spare wheels are carried. Specification includes four-cylinder water-cooled 1122cc engine, overhead inlet valves, three-bearing crankshaft, independent front wheel suspension, four-speed gearbox, Girling brakes, Stevenson jacking system, 12-volt 5-lamp lighting set, attractive facia board with generous equipment. Also two spare wheels with tyres. Colour is British racing green. May we send you full particulars and specification?'

The price was listed as £185 complete, and although four-wheeler sales started quite slowly, they reached 130 in 1937 which was now virtually level with the fast declining three-wheelers, which sold just 137 cars in the same year. And even that number of sales offered the possibility of a profit, because the evolution of the four-wheeled 4-4 from the three-wheeled F-type had cost very little. By 1937, Morgan could also offer a four-seater roadster version of the four-wheeler, and in 1938 added a more luxurious Drophead Coupé style, with wider body, folding rather than removable hood, deeper doors with sliding windows rather than lift-off sidescreens, and a generally heavier, 'tourer' look than the purely sporting roadsters.

In 1938, with Coventry-Climax engine supplies threatened by the financial problems of Climax's owner, Triumph, Morgan entered into the arrangement with the Standard Motor Company for the supply of a modified Standard 10 engine for the 4-4. Introduced in 1938, it had a capacity of 1267cc and produced almost 39bhp, both figures just a little bit ahead of the Climax fours, and giving appropriately improved performance, while the 4-4 also now switched from the four-speed Meadowes to four-speed Moss gearboxes

In 1939, before the outbreak of the Second World War, Morgan sold 263 cars in all, of which only 29 were three-wheelers, while the 4-4's tally of 234 that year was its best to date and brought the total number of 4-4s sold since launch to 883 cars. With figures like those, it is more than likely that, however reluctant HFS was to do it, the three-wheeler would have to have been dropped and all efforts concentrated on the four-wheelers, but he would be spared the decision for at least a while longer, as the war began.

This time war halted car production in Britain completely, and presented Morgan and the remainder of the industry with far bigger problems than it had experienced after the First World War in getting back into production. It did, however, give a small breathing space for the three-wheelers, and deepened the relationship between Morgan and Standard, who had taken wartime production space at Pickersleigh Road and who would soon resume their engine supplies to Morgan. Ironically, the fact that the three-wheeler had survived would briefly prove to be a bonus for Morgan, as it had a new appeal for a market that, for some time to come, would be short of cash, petrol and new cars of any description, in equal measure.

Morgan delivered their first post-war cars in March 1946, which, due to continuing shortages of materials, were essentially built up from parts that could be scavenged from old stock. Amazingly, but perhaps unavoidably given the circumstances, the first consignments of post-war cars included a handful of Matchless-engined, tubular chassis vee-twin three-wheelers of the old school. That meant what was in essence the original 1910 design had survived through thirty-six years, two world wars and two quite different later generations of Morgan, the F-type three-wheeler and the four-wheeler 4-4. Admittedly, they only amounted to a dozen Super Sports models, and most of them were exported (as almost all Britain's new car production had to be under government regulations), in this case to Australia, but it was a remarkable survival story. That, however, was the end of the road for the original design, and the F-type three-wheeler only survived a few years longer. Once the market began to settle down again, three-wheeler sales, having clung on for years, finally evaporated for good. The last F4 was built in March 1952 with the last F Super in July, and that was the last Morgan three-wheeler of all.

The four-wheelers, however, were going from strength to strength. After the war the 4/4 was reintroduced with Standard engines now the standard offering, so to speak, and the car was soon doing well enough to prompt Standard's moves towards a takeover of Morgan – a move that was rejected, as described in Chapter 5. The continuing reliance on Standard engines combined with the demise of the old 1267cc supply following the merger of Standard and Triumph led directly to the introduction of the Plus 4 at the Earl's Court Motor Show in 1950, replacing the first generation 4/4.

The Plus 4 used the Z-section chassis, lengthened by 4 inches with the body and tracks widened by a couple of inches but otherwise virtually unchanged. It adopted the larger, 2088cc Standard Vanguard engine and the heavier Moss gearbox used by later 4/4s (mounted separately from the engine and connected by a torque tube), and like the 4/4 it was offered with two- and four-seater roadster and Drop-head Coupé body options. The substantial gain in power, up from 39 to 68bhp, more than offset the increase in weight, and the Plus 4 added another level of performance – albeit with a rather higher price tag. Morgan advertising introduced it as, 'The New 2-litre Morgan Plus 4 – A small car with a large engine and a wonderful all round performance.'

In September 1951 *Motor* magazine tested the Plus 4 and introduced it in just the way Morgan needed to see: 'Costing rather more than preceding models coming from the factory at Malvern, but also performing very much better than its predecessors, the latest "Plus Four" Morgan proved on a recent 1900-mile 11-day road test that the "fastest at the price" claim of its manufacturers remains very fully justified.

'Sporting two-seater cars, built to a price limit which keeps them within reach of a large and reasonably youthful public, are an established part of Britain's range of car types. Emphasis on performance at a moderate price means that, inevitably, touring car luxury and carrying capacity are sacrificed to a greater or lesser extent. But, given acceptance of this bartering of spaciousness for speed, the open two-seater Morgan is a car which can give immense pleasure to the right sort of owner.'

The 'right sort of owner' was one who understood the Morgan tradition. There was no arguing with the perform-ance aspect: the *Motor* test recorded a mean maximum speed of 85mph, and a 0–50mph time (a more common yardstick in the early 1950s than today's 0–60) of under ten seconds.

Other strengths noted were its acceleration and its hillclimbing abilities A different aspect of Morgan tradition, however, was about to become an issue. The Plus 4 had what were by now considered the classic Morgan four-wheeler lines, and what were generally accepted as the universal lines of the open sports car. The look included long, sweeping, separate wings, running-boards, the long louvred bonnet, rakish windscreen and cut-down doors, and it was echoed by rivals from the MG Midgets to the SS Jaguars. But for most of the industry that look was about to change and give way to the first steps to modern, all-enveloping shapes.

The 1948 London Motor Show at Earl's Court was the first post-war British motor show as the industry started to get back to normal and introduce its first genuinely new models as opposed to dressed-up, pre-war carry-overs. It saw the launch in Britain of a new generation of smoother shapes, echoing what was now coming out of America, and to a lesser extent the rest of Europe. On the family car side, it saw the launch of Alec Issigonis's superb little Morris Minor, and on the sports car front it saw the super-sleek, 120mph Jaguar XK120. That was the cue for (most) other sports car makers to follow suit, and within a few years MG had moved from the Morgan-like T-series Midgets to the all-enveloping MGA shape, and Triumph had launched the similarly 'modern' TR series. Suddenly, the Morgan was not just one of the sports car crowd, it was the odd shape out.

Morgan, however, were about to make another far-reaching policy decision, and although the next few years would see some token modernism in the form of first a sloping radiator and then the elegantly cowled shape which still survives today, and a gradual move from stand-alone to partly faired-in headlamp cowls, the essential flowing outline would not be tampered with. In November 1949 Morgan took what might now be seen as a mild dig at the modernists with one line in an advertisment for the reborn 4/4 which read, 'untouched by exaggerated styling and retaining all that is best in true British sportsmanship and character'. By 1954 they were claiming a new look of their own, but without going over the top: 'A new sloping radiator shell, faired headlamps, restyled wings and streamlined tail/petrol tank unit, give a new look to the 1954 Morgan two-seater . . .' But that was as far as their claims to new age styling ever went, and soon they were content to concentrate again on performance and price.

As well as the mildly updated looks in 1954, Morgan could justifiably talk about considerably uprated power, as the Plus 4 adopted the new TR2 engine, giving another big jump, to 90bhp. They greeted its launch at Earl's Court in October as, 'The immaculate Morgan Plus 4 sports two-seater powered by the TR2 engine – a car in the exclusive 100mph class.' It claimed a place among the 'select number of production cars capable of 100mph', with steering, suspension, chassis and transmission to cope with the 'extra power of the TR2 unit'.

As usual, it was a very keenly priced way of buying so much performance, substantially undercutting Jaguar prices and offering much better performance than the real Triumph TR2 for less money even than that mass-production model. That had always been part of Morgan's success as a specialist, small-volume manufacturer, but the company was about to enter the life-threatening phase of the 1950s and 1960s, where style became more important to the market than content; the Morgan, perhaps for the first time in its life, started to be seen as old-fashioned and therefore, no matter that the performance figures suggested otherwise, inferior.

Sales in the UK and Europe began to fall quite dramatically as sports car buyers abandoned Morgan for the arguably more superficial qualities of their more attractive rivals, and although Morgans could still hold their own in competition, they were struggling in the marketplace. Ironically, one market in which Morgan's fortunes were on the up-turn was America; the pioneer of new styling trends, it was perhaps the last country one might have expected to stand by the time-warp looks of the Morgans.

But in America in the late 1950s, Morgan's popularity began to grow; what had now become their individuality made them, perversely, fashionable. The company, with Peter Morgan very much in the forefront, began to hit America with the story of all Morgan's attributes, from competition success, to heritage, to value for money. Early in 1955 Morgan stated their presence in the American motoring magazines: 'The New and Greater Morgan Sports for 1955 is Here! And with the very latest TR2 Engine calibrated and tuned by Morgan for over 90hp Guaranteed to out-perform any and every other Stock Sports Car in the world selling under $2000 in the 2 litre class. This fabulous new 1955 Morgan is fast becoming the most talked of sports car on the road today. Already it has won many events leaving in its wake much larger and more expensive machines with their owners blinking at its startling performance.' It listed a string of 2-litre race wins, including the prestigious Sebring 12-Hour Race, and ended with a 'Special Note – The new Super Morgan requires less extras for competition work than any other car. In fact, Morgans can be entered for almost anything just as they are purchased.'

This was a big selling point in mid-Fifties America, and especially on the West Coast where a huge slice of European car imports was heading. After the war, American service-men returning from Europe had taken home with them a love for both small European (especially British) sports cars, and for European-type circuit racing, as distinct from the oval track racing more usually favoured in America before then. After the war, too, there were literally hundreds of almost ready-made racing venues, in abandoned or accessible war-time air bases. Amateur motor racing became one of America's great weekend pastimes, and, in the old tradition, Morgan won races on Sunday and sold cars on Monday.

For Americans who preferred not to race but still wanted a sports car distinct from the common herd, they advertised craftsmanship, pedigree and personality. They talked, too, of 'hand-built cars since 1911', 'honesty of design', of 'startling performance and positive control'. Advertisements further claimed a top speed for the TR2-engined Plus 4 of 104mph, with 0–60mph in just over ten seconds (impressive for 1955) and 35mpg – with 'four distinctive body styles to suit your individual needs' – and prices from $2,595 for the two-seater Sports to $2,750 for the four-seater Coupé. They also adver-tised *image*, in an advertisement which featured a Plus 4, and a smiling man in Gatsby-like white linen suit with an Alsatian dog. 'Designed and engineered,' the copy read, 'for those who demand the finest . . . Morgan Plus 4, "last of the real classics"

First in All Else.' Even by 1955, tradition had become a selling point. And as ever, the Plus 4 was not standing still, with the switch to TR3 power in 1956, the welcome improvement of Girling disc brakes and knock-on wire wheels in 1959, and the Triumph TR4 engine from 1962 until 1969 – the end of the beginning.

In Europe, meanwhile, Morgan's efforts to revitalise flagging sales in the mid-1950s took a different tack, with the introduction of a lower-priced range in 1955, bringing the reintroduction of the 4/4, as the Series 2. 'Best performance in its class!' was the selling point. 'For the enthusiast with a limited budget – seeking the elegance of line and the superb roadholding offered by Morgan but requiring a power unit capable of inexpensive development after purchase.' The power unit they referred to was the Ford 10hp side-valve engine and its unit gearbox, the first time Morgan had used such a layout as opposed to the old separate gearbox and torque tube arrangement. This was a very shrewd move; in Britain the late 1950s were very much the era of the cheap and cheerful Ford-engined special, the sort of build-it-yourself sports car using off-the-shelf chassis and body parts, and, significantly for the Morgan owner who wanted 'inexpensive development after purchase', a time when there was a vast range of bolt-on tuning equipment for even the most mundane of Ford engines.

Alongside the Plus 4, the second generation 4/4 opened up a new market, and it helped keep Morgan alive. This was the start of a long-running sequence of smaller, less expensive Morgans, which survive alongside the bigger-engined models even today. Using the Plus 4 chassis and a lower, lighter body, the first version was powered by the 1172cc Ford 100E side-valve engine, and even with only 36bhp it was light enough to have a respectable, Morgan-like performance at a price which kept it competitive against newer, lower-priced, mass-produced models.

Over the next few years it kept pace with the changes in Ford's mid-sized four-cylinder production engines, with the new Anglia's 997cc overhead-valve 105E unit in the 4/4 Series III from 1960, the 1340cc 109E Classic engine in the Series IV from 1961 and the 1498cc 116E Cortina type in the Series V

Left: in 1990 Ludovic Lindsay and Bill Wykeham took their 1961 Plus 4 to the Carrera Panamericana classic re-run, won their class, and finished the 2000-mile, seven-day marathon sixth overall

Below: Charles getting the 4/4 all crossed up for a brochure shot, shortly after he had joined the company in 1985

Above: following another family tradition. Where Ruth used to compete with HFS in trials, Charles's second wife Jane, who he married in 1990, joined him on the 1992 Tour de France

Right: in the old days, the wooden frames were fitted to the chassis and panelled on the car, the streamlined system has panelled bodies fitted complete

Above: a starting point for the Aero 8. The first aluminium-honeycomb chassised Plus 8 racer, at Silverstone in 1996, with John Burbidge (now chief of the mechanical development department) on the left, repair shop man Mark Baldwin in the middle, and Danny Monk (now with Bill Wykeham) on the right

Above: the second and third generations, Charles with his father Peter, and Peter's great creation, the Plus 8

Left: the third generation and perhaps the fourth generation? Charles some years ago with his son Xan, sixteen in 2000 and, with his two younger sisters, Kate and Harriet, part of the Morgan succession?

Above: the Plus 4, and the wood and leather interior of the earlier type Plus 4 four-seater

Right: as part of his graduate project at Imperial College, Charles's nephew Lawrence Price (his sister Jill's son) did wind tunnel work in 1995 which led to the 1996 race car

Below: classic Morgan lines, the still handsome 4/4 in the 1990s

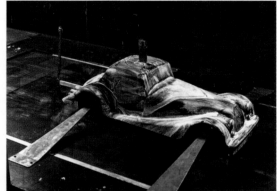

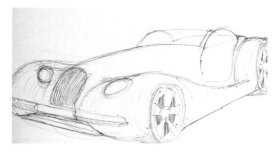

Top and Left: steps towards the Aero 8's distinctive, and controversial, styling. **Above,** Charles doctoring a picture of the long-tailed race car mock-up in 1998, and also in 1998, **left,** a much more finished concept sketch

Left: the previous generation chassis, with its Z-frame, sliding pillars and cart-sprung rear axle, all of which the Aero 8 replaces with new thinking

Bottom: the Plus 8 race chassis in the winter of 1997, with a long-tailed body which reduced drag to 0.44Cd, but which was never actually raced

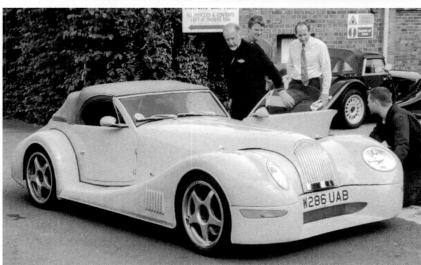

Above: the first completely new Morgan in more than
sixty years, and the doorway to the company's future –
the third example of the Aero 8, with hand-formed
aluminium body, and now nearing its final shape

from 1963. A new 4/4 family, the 4/4 1600, was launched in 1968, with Ford's all-new Kent engines, and apart from fewer than a hundred 4/4s built with 1.6-litre Fiat twin-cam engines between 1981 and 1985, Ford power has been the order of the day for the 4/4 ever since, with the new CVH engine from 1982, the EFI from 1991 to 1993, and eventually, come 1993 when it became the 4/4 1800, the 1.8-litre Ford Zetec engine – which still powers it.

The brief interlude of the Fiat-engined 4/4s in the 1980s reveals something about the affection for Morgan in the higher echelons of the mainstream industry. Why Morgan had to find an alternative to the Ford powertrain in the early 1980s was not strictly about engines, rather gearboxes. Ford's small cars from which Morgan's parts were sourced were moving to a transverse, front-engined design and supplies of the older gearbox that Morgan used were no longer available. The Fiat engine and five-speed Abarth manual gearbox were a viable alternative, but it seems that one customer on the waiting list for a 4/4 was a senior Ford executive who was disturbed by the sight of a Fiat-powered Morgan on the company's Motor Show stand. He therefore started an initiative at Ford to adapt the new front-drive CVH engine to mate with the older rear-drive Cortina gearbox, via a modified Capri gearbox and a Morgan-designed flywheel (later replaced by the Sierra's five-speed gearbox). Ford themselves did the conversion, including the necessary minor modifications to the chassis and engine mountings, and the Ford-engined Morgan was saved.

The short and rather unhappy story of the Plus 4 Plus, Morgan's brief, early 1960s attempt at reversing its sales slump by trying to look like everybody else, is told in Chapter 5. In a nutshell, putting a curvaceous glass fibre body on a Plus 4 chassis may have worked well mechanically but it was a disaster commercially, and its failure taught Morgan a lesson it has been in no hurry to repeat – do not lose the look. By the time the next major product change was forced on Morgan, that was no longer an issue.

The birth of the Plus 8 marked another chapter in the long story of Morgan's never-ending search for the right engine at the right time. It was also something of a watershed in the Morgan styling dilemma. The 1960s had not been the best of times for Morgan commercially, and it was one of the few times in the company's history when the traditional shape of the cars was more hindrance than help. The early 1960s were obsessed with fashion, youth and the future, a period when the Morgan shape was considered archaic rather than iconic and unfortunately the fashion for retro themes was still some way off. On the other hand, the recent experience of the Plus 4 Plus had shown the market did not want a Morgan that was not Morgan-shaped, either. So Morgan did what they usually do and went their own way, against the tide.

In the early to mid-1960s, Morgan sales were at a very low ebb, with the collapse of the US market removing even that usually dependable safety net. There was also the problem of impending American emissions and safety regulations, and the unfortunate end of the line for the TR engines. Peter Morgan's search for a replacement power unit and some new markets is further described in Chapter 5, but the outcome was one of the best and most enduring cars Morgan ever built, the Plus 8.

The real story of the Plus 8 is the story of its engine, of how Morgan squeezed it into their traditional chassis, and came up with an instant performance car classic. The engine which became the Rover V8 is still in production, still powering the Land Rover, Range Rover and Discovery, still powering the Plus 8 and a number of other specialist sports cars, including Morgan rivals from the likes of TVR and Marcos, but more than thirty years ago, when Rover first came into contact with it, in theory it was already obsolete.

Originally, it was a Buick engine and Rover found it virtually by chance. For some years they had been experimenting with bigger and more powerful but also light and compact engines of their own, and had tried various configurations of V4, V6, their own unconventional V8, even gas turbine power, but by the early 1960s they were still looking for the answer. And they found it in a boat yard in Wisconsin.

Their saviour was William Martin-Hurst, an engineer who had joined Rover in 1960 from the aircraft industry as production director, and soon became managing director. In

1963 he was visiting Carl Keikhaffer, the boss of boat- and marine-engine builders Mercury Marine, in their experimental department at Fond du Lac, Wisconsin. He had first made contact when he had tried to sell Keikhaffer a Rover- built gas turbine engine for use in Mercury's sports boats; this time he was working on a plan to sell them marine versions of the Land Rover diesel engine for use in fishing boats for the Far East market.

In the Mercury experimental shop, Martin-Hurst saw an engine with which he was not familiar but which looked very interesting for Rover's purposes. It was a compact, light alloy V8 that appeared to be neither much longer nor much heavier than the four-cylinder engine Rover was trying to supplant. More interesting even than that was what Keikhaffer now told Martin-Hurst – that the 3.5-litre engine had come from a Buick Special compact, and that General Motors had recently taken it out of production.

Even in 1963, it was quite an old engine. Its design had started as long ago as 1950 and it had first run in 1952. It had gone into production after further gestation in 1960, in General Motors' range of compacts, and had been used with minor specification differences in the Buick Special, the Pontiac Tempest and the Oldsmobile F85 Cutlass. By 1963 GM had built three quarters of a million examples of the engine before deciding to take it out of production. There was nothing wrong with the engine itself, only the economics of building it, and now GM had a better alternative.

Back in the early 1950s, the Buick engine was designed with all-aluminium construction because the compact car programme needed an engine that was powerful but light, and at the time aluminium was the only answer, if an expensive one. Then, within a few years of launching the alloy V8 into production, GM, in parallel with Ford, developed new techniques for casting thin-wall cast-iron blocks that were almost as light as the alloy ones, easier to make because they did not need separate cylinder liners, and very much cheaper. So GM started to build cast-iron engines of very similar design to the alloy V8, and the original was retired.

As soon as he saw it Martin-Hurst believed that it was virtually the ideal engine for Rover's purposes, and to help convince him Carl Keikhaffer had the engine from his workshop crated up and air-freighted to England for Rover to examine. It turned out to be as promising as Martin-Hurst had believed, and physically it was only half an inch longer and 12lb heavier than their 2-litre, four-cylinder engine, but with almost twice the capacity, the potential for almost twice the power, and the smoothness of eight cylinders rather than four. It was also more compact, more powerful and lighter than Rover's 3-litre in-line six. All they needed now was permission to use it.

William Martin-Hurst carried out the negotiations, returning to the USA during the New York Motor Show and, after some difficulty making contact, spoke to Buick vice-president Ed Rollert over breakfast in his hotel. Rollert then put Martin-Hurst in touch with GM's international branch and eventually, early in 1964, they agreed to negotiate a licence for Rover to manufacture the engine, and to make available all the drawings and whatever tooling had not already been scrapped. It is said that one reason why the negotiations were so long and drawn out was because GM couldn't understand why Rover wanted to take on an engine that they themselves already considered totally obsolete.

GM quickly supplied a small batch of complete engines for Rover to experiment with while it was completing the tooling and other preparations for making its own version, and Rover worked on fitting it into their own car. At first Peter Wilks, the technical director, did not believe it would fit into the Rover 2000, but Martin-Hurst gave the project to the competition department who squeezed it in with remarkably few problems. Meanwhile, early in 1965, the Rover and GM managements agreed commercial terms, and even those were apparently very favourable to Rover.

Before launching it into production, Rover 'Europeanised' the engine, to suit European regulations, driving patterns and, not least, production volumes, in a £3 million pre-production programme which had the help of Buick's chief engine designer Joe Turley, who was soon to retire and who was seconded to Rover as part of the deal. Rover changed the manufacturing process to take advantage of more efficient assembly solutions developed since the engine had been designed, but they changed very little of the basic design. And although the engine has subsequently been made in considerably larger capacity versions and producing very high power outputs in tuned forms (not least in racing Morgans) it has always been both strong and reliable.

Aside from its alloy construction, the engine is quite simple and conventional – a 90-degree V8 with five-bearing crankshaft and a single central camshaft operating two valves per cylinder through pushrods and hydraulic valve followers (the valve followers being the only part of the engine that was not now British built). Rover also changed the American Rochester carburettor for British SUs and the AC-Delco ignition for Lucas, did their own exhaust plumbing and set the engine up for European tastes, to be a bit more free-revving and over a wider rev range – a bit more sporty, in other words. It went into production in mid-1967, and onto the road in October in the big P5B saloon, where the 'B' stood for Buick. As fitted in that car, the 3.5 V8 produced a commendable 160bhp, which was almost 40bhp more than the best of Rover's old straight sixes from an engine weighing around 200lb less and using less fuel.

The Morgan connection was already taking shape, first as a Rover takeover bid, subsequently as an engine supply arrangement. In an echo of the relationship between Standard and Morgan many years earlier, Rover would originally have liked to have built a sports car of their own, and when they could not do it in the short term they went Morgan hunting. But now, all of this was also distorted by the fact that in March 1967 Rover had become part of British Leyland, and BL already had their own sports car brands in MG and the one who supplied Morgan's engines at the time – Triumph. Triumph persevered with its own ultimately underachieving V8 engine (the one Morgan rejected as a TR replacement) for the Stag but eventually adopted the Rover V8 for the short-lived and largely unloved TR8 in the late 1970s. It was more successful putting the engine into an uprated MGB GT in August 1973 to create the B-V8, but not by much. The MG used a 137bhp version of the engine, significantly less power than it had had in Rover's stately saloon, and BL hoped to sell most of what they could make to America, but that did not work out. The B-V8 was not a bad car but its timing was disastrous. It ran straight into the energy crisis with its fuel shortages and general antipathy to gas-guzzling, big-engined cars, and into other sporty cars like the V6-engined Ford Capri, that offered everything the B could offer for less money. Even launching the TR8 as what amounted to an in-house rival was symptomatic of the muddled thinking that was rife within BL at the time, and unfortunately that also killed what might have been the best sports car bet of all the options open to Leyland at the time, which could have come from Rover themselves.

Before the takeover, but with the V8 deal in place, Rover designed a mid-engined three-seater sports coupé code-named P6BS, which had an angular and rather unlovely body but dynamically was apparently very promising, with De Dion rear suspension for a comfortable ride combined with excellent roadholding. That and a fastback saloon were supposed to go into production with Alvis badges, another famous old sporting marque now owned by Rover, but neither went beyond the prototype stage once BL took over. Undercutting the E-type, the mid-engined sports car would have been a threat to Jaguar, and a rival, too, for the planned V8-engined Triumph Stag.

The putative Morgan takeover also evaporated at the time of the merger, but by then Morgan and Rover had done a deal for the supply of V8 engines to succeed the old Triumph fours; GM were happy to see the engine returning to the US domestic market in Morgan numbers where they might not perhaps have been so keen to see a Rover sports car invasion in competition with their own sporting models. At this point, almost ten years after his father had died and nearly twenty years before his son would join the company, Peter Morgan was the only member of the Morgan family involved with the everyday running of the company, so the Plus 8 was really his car, just as the three-wheelers were his father's and the Aero 8 would come to be Charles's thirty years or so later.

Peter Morgan's right-hand man in developing the Plus 8 was Maurice Owen, an engineer who first arrived at his office one day in 1963 asking if he wanted any engine installation jobs doing – or, as Peter says, 'in his own words, "any shoe-horn jobs?"'. Peter had nothing to offer him at the time, but contacted him again in 1966 when the Rover deal was in the offing and asked him to join him.

Because Rover had such a limited supply of engines before it started its own production properly, Morgan actually built the Plus 8 prototype around a Buick engine modified to something close to Rover's specification, but with American inlet manifolds which meant it had small bonnet bulges (which production cars would not need), to make space for the British carburettors. In November 1998, Peter described the development of the Plus 8's timetable: 'Before Peter Wilks from Rover came to see me in 1965, he asked whether Morgans would like to join forces with Rover and whether we would like to use their new ex-Buick V8 engine. An American by the name of Bruce McWilliams had discussed the idea with William Martin-Hurst who was a close friend, and it was Bruce McWilliams who helped Martin-Hurst obtain permission from GM to use the engine. He also had interests in importing British cars for the US market and in view of the success of the Plus 4 with the Triumph TR engine he apparently saw the potential of a Morgan 8 with the Rover-Buick engine.

'I turned down the offer to join up with Rover but Peter Wilks agreed that we could still have the engine. That led to a meeting with his assistant, Vic Rogers, who was most helpful throughout the whole project. Right from the beginning I knew that it would be quite difficult to develop the car, although I did have time to do a number of drawings. We also needed a development engineer, of course, which is where Maurice Owen came in – and he remained in the picture for a long time afterwards. The first difficulty we were confronted with was obtaining an engine, but we got around that by contacting a friend of Maurice's, Alan MacKechnie, who had done work on the Buick V8 for his racing cars. And he happened to have a spare engine, which Maurice acquired. That duly went to Rover who carried out some minor modifications to bring it in line with their specification and then it came to us. It wasn't long before we had a prototype built and running, but we still had problems with the supply of engines. Although I did not know it at the time, I'm almost certain now that the reason was that since British Leyland, who already owned Triumph, had taken over Rover, they didn't want Morgan to introduce an eight where Triumph were still using a six.

'I think the truth of that was virtually confirmed when Harry Webster, who'd been a friend of mine since the days with Standard Triumph as engine supplier, asked me to meet up with him. He tried to interest me in Triumph's forthcoming engines, the four-cylinder that went first into a Saab and the V8 that they designed for the Triumph Stag. I told him our prototype was virtually complete and that we wouldn't want to change engines now in view of the amount of development we had already undertaken.

'But I was still unable to get a firm answer from Rover about their engine and I was told I should contact George Farmer – Rover's representative in the British Leyland organisation, who later became Sir George. The meeting with him presented us with a complete bombshell when he announced, "You can't have the engine until we receive permission from General Motors for you to use it". So I asked him who had to apply for the permission, them or us, and he said that they would. I subsequently found out that they had asked for permission to use the engine in both Triumphs and Morgans.

'I immediately contacted a Morgan owner in Canada, Dave Elcomb, who had raced a Plus 4 and who worked for General Motors. Rover then received an early reply saying that GM had no objections to Morgans using the engine, but they didn't make any mention of Triumph using it, and the legal position was that General Motors had an "embargo" against the engine being used anywhere else for five years. Our prototype, however, was running in the summer of 1967, and more and more time was going by, still with no word about the engine.

'In desperation I telephoned Harry Webster and asked him if he could arrange a meeting with Sir Donald Stokes, head of British Leyland and subsequently Lord Stokes. A few days later he returned my call and said that he and George Turnbull, who was managing director of the Austin Morris division and also knighted later, would come and check the car over so that they could give us a yes or a no. So Harry

Webster and George Turnbull took the prototype Plus 8 for a run around Malvern, they both came back impressed, and accordingly they gave us the official nod to go ahead ... so long as Morgan continued to build cars "roughly in the same style".' Which in effect meant not in a style which would conflict with any future, 'modern' sports car from BL.

The Plus 8 prototype had used an only mildly modified Plus 4 chassis, but that made things a tight squeeze, so the production car would have a slightly longer and wider frame to accommodate the engine more comfortably, but it would still have the familiar architecture of Z-section pressed-steel ladder, live rear axle on semi-elliptic springs and, of course, sliding-pillar front suspension. And it would look exactly like a Morgan, with a slightly larger version of the usual hand-panelled, ash-framed body.

The first 'production' cars were completed in time for the London Motor Show, and for testing by the motoring press, in September 1968. Not surprisingly, it created a bit of a sensation, with its original 151bhp in only 1900lb of car not only following the ancient Morgan dictum of maximum power to weight but also giving performance figures that even Morgan regulars were not used to. Those included a maximum speed of almost 125mph (ultimately limited by aerodynamics) and 0–60mph in only 6.7 seconds – reflecting the fact that the Plus 8 had 55 per cent more power and 60 per cent more torque than its smaller stablemate but weighed less than 5 per cent more. By any standards, this was a very fast sports car for 1968, faster accelerating even than an E-type Jaguar, if not so quick at the top end. And not only that – all of a sudden people were no longer worried by the old-fashioned looks; with performance like this, the anachronism had become part of the appeal.

The Plus 8 was competitively priced – not only was it faster accelerating than an E-type, but at £1,478 as launched it was also around £640 cheaper – and it began to sell well almost immediately. In the early days the waiting list was quoted as about two months, which was much the same as the build time, but it soon started to grow.

The Plus 8 also evolved, unobtrusively but firmly. The engine specification moved in parallel with Rover's own changes, and emissions requirements, which was sometimes good, sometimes bad. When Rover introduced their SD1-specification V8 in 1976, Morgan adopted it too, its 155bhp clawing back some of the performance that earlier versions had lost to legislation. Unfortunately, it was legislation that thwarted the Plus 8's planned career as an official Morgan model in America – but you could eventually buy a 'federalized' version, so long as you did not mind it guzzling propane instead of gasoline. Not that that created an inferior breed, because in the version built by Bill Fink's Isis Imports in San Francisco, propane plus a turbocharger gave an estimated 225bhp at the flywheel and some 240lb ft of torque, which in the 1970s were figures Morgan themselves would have loved.

In 1979, Peter Morgan talked about how the changes between launch and SD1 had affected their version of the engine, and Morgan performance. 'One of my worries now, and a big worry, is that the Plus 8 I brought out in 1968 was a more lively and faster car than the Plus 8 I've been building until very recently. I mean it's a disgraceful performance really, for a 3.5-litre engine; that engine is so inefficient – they've done nothing to it. If only Peter Wilks had not died, it might be quite a good engine by now. It used to have 10.5:1 compression then it went right down to 8.5 and now it's 9.35:1. I maintain that for my type of sports car I must give performance. I'm not trying to make just a nice little open car for shopping or anything like that. I still want to make a sports car, which has a sporting performance. The thing about making a sports car is that you're either going to get it through light build or through engine power. There's nothing mysterious about it . . .'

To Morgan, there never had been. In 1977 they added new manifolds to increase output again, to 162bhp and 198lb ft of torque, and by 1992 the standard specification included a capacity of 3.9 litres (that had been increased mainly to compensate for what had been lost to emissions controls), with 190bhp and 235lb ft of torque. Further developments followed, many of them through Morgan's involvement in racing with the Plus 8, including changes to the valve gear to allow more revs, bigger valves and better breathing to take advantage of higher engine speeds, and Lucas electronic ignition to give better control. From 1982 Morgan replaced the original SU carburettors with a Stromberg type with automatic choke control, to satisfy new European emissions legislation, and by 1983 they could offer an optional high-performance version of the engine producing 200bhp and 220lb ft of torque, which was more in line with Peter Morgan's views on what the engine should have been delivering. The transmission changed significantly, too, in 1972 from the original four-speed Moss gearbox to an all-syncromesh Rover four-speed, and changing again in 1983 to a five-speed unit.

In the meantime, largely reflecting the evolution of ever-wider, lower-profile tyres, the Plus 8 body and tracks grew wider by degrees, the handsome alloy wheels went through several styling variations (while the optional wire wheels were strengthened) , and trim and equipment levels were more or less continuously improved. Nowadays, the standard power options are 3.9 litres with 190bhp and 225lb ft of torque, or 4.6 litres with 194bhp and 260lb ft of torque, which keeps most customers happy.

In September 1997, other moves were afoot: the whole range – 4/4, Plus 4 and Plus 8 models – was updated, with the emphasis on safety and comfort features, and improved manufacturing methods – in Morgan's own style. The market's expectations of safety levels had moved on considerably in the 1990s, and although Morgans might be anachronistic that did not exempt them from modern legislation. So the company invested heavily in research and development into passive restraint systems in particular, and in 1997 introduced the option of full-sized driver and passenger airbags, anti-submarining seats and an internal stainless steel, side-impact protection hoop. The airbag installation was achieved without having to lose the traditional walnut veneered dashboard, and the effectiveness of the systems was proved by a comprehensive crash-testing programme at MIRA, the Motor Industry Research Association, of which Morgan is a member.

Driver and passenger comfort were improved, by changing the hood line and lengthening the cockpit and the doors by 2 inches, to give more leg room, easier access and more luggage space. A rake-adjustable steering column was added for a more adjustable driving position, the minor switches and stalks were improved, a bigger glovebox fitted when the passenger airbag option was not, security improved by a new engine immobiliser and bad-weather visibility improved by an electrically heated windscreen.

As described in Chapter 1, Morgan adopted new manufacturing technology in the form of superplastic aluminium forming for the largest and most complex body panels – the front wings. This was a major investment but it improved both efficiency and quality. At the same time they 'streamlined' the assembly process to improve output to two cars a day and rising, and they continued looking at other options.

The Plus 4 came back into the range in 1985, after an absence of sixteen years since the last of the Triumph TR4-engined cars, to bridge the gap between 4/4 and Plus 8. At first, slightly confusingly, you could have your Plus 4 in either 4/4 or the larger Plus 8 size, and with two seats or four, but by 1992 it only came Plus 8-sized, with a slightly narrower front chassis and 4/4-type suspension – sliding pillar, of course. It was originally offered with 2-litre twin-cam Fiat power but the problems of dealing with an overseas supplier and eventually a repeat of the earlier scenario with a change to gearbox specification led Morgan to adopt Rover power for the Plus 4, as well as for the Plus 8. From 1988 it used the 2-litre twin-cam sixteen-valve M16 engine with the same five-speed gearbox used in the Plus 8, and from 1992 it adopted the more powerful 2-litre T16 Rover four, which gave an excellent performance boost.

In July 1999 another of Morgan's lost models made a comeback with the relaunch of the four-seater version of the 4/4. From the door hinges back, the body was all new and, instead of the rear bench seat of the older four-seaters, this one has individual bucket seats in the back as well as in the front. They are set much lower for a more comfortable ride and to allow a lower hood line, and the doors are longer for easier access – while the front seat-belt mounts have been moved to the middle of the car, also to give unobstructed access to the rear seats, with their own three-point belts. The four-seater adopted all Morgan's new safety features, including the option of airbags, to receive European Whole Vehicle Type Approval, and although it might not be the prettiest Morgan in the world it does revive another important market niche. It would not be long, however, before it was eclipsed by a very different newcomer.

The launch of the Aero 8 at the Geneva Show in February 2000 brought Morgan into the twenty-first century in a style that HFS Morgan would very likely have approved of, with a mixture of innovative design, a continuation of all the fundamental Morgan philosophies, and with the family influence still very much in evidence. It also provided quite a shock for the cynics who are still convinced that Morgan is frozen in time.

In his 1960 article in *The Motor* entitled 'The Quiet Man', reminiscing on Morgan WG McMinnies looked at the future: 'Peter Morgan is managing director, and when he is not rallying successfully he lives comfortably with his wife and family in a long, pleasant country house, looking across the Severn Vale from the Wych Cutting on Malvern Hills. He has two daughters and a son. I wonder if this boy will carry on the great tradition, and if he does, what the AD 2000 model will be like.' The answer is that Charles *did* carry on the Morgan tradition, and even McMinnies would immediately have recognised the 'AD 2000' model as a Morgan – if under the skin a quite different Morgan.

One link with HFS has finally gone: the Aero 8 is the first-ever Morgan production car to forsake the sliding-pillar front suspension, not to mention leaf-spring rear suspension of one kind or another. The long-serving 'second generation' Z-section chassis has gone, too, in favour of something altogether more modern and high-tech. There is also a new engine supplier and a controversial new shape, but it is a Morgan shape rather than a sop to modern fashion, and underneath it all there are still the trusted formulae of high power-to-weight ratio and essentially hand-built production.

The Aero 8 follows another Morgan tradition in that it has competition connections even before it goes on sale, because the design programme had its roots in the late 1990s works GT2 racing programme, run with what was nominally a Plus

8 but which, engine supplier apart, was in reality more like a prototype for the Aero 8.

The production car development project was managed almost entirely in-house from Pickersleigh Road, while using outside facilities wherever appropriate, from the automotive engineering department of Birmingham University, to the full-size wind tunnel at the Motor Industry Research Association in Warwickshire, to engine supplier BMW's secure test track facility at Miramas in the south of France – as well as much disguised road testing. The project spanned some four years and was the biggest development programme Morgan has ever undertaken, but again leaving Morgan's independence intact and, amazingly as ever, signed off with its bank balance still in the black.

As Charles Morgan explains the thinking behind the car, 'The objective of the development programme was to recreate the position we held in 1968 when we launched the Plus 8. At that time the Plus 8 was the car with just about the most flexible performance you could buy, due to the combination of its light weight and large capacity engine. We believe we have achieved this again with the Aero 8 through our dedication to weight saving and its development as an aluminium intensive vehicle.'

The use of aluminium in the Aero 8's chassis construction is the first fundamental departure from the old design, replacing the simple and notoriously flexible Z-section steel ladder-type chassis with a massively strong, rigid – and far more complex – aluminium structure, made from bonded and rivetted extruded sections and sheets.

That follows on from the lead of the GT2 race car which competed in the 1997 FIA GT Championship, but the first steps towards the aluminium chassis rather than the old steel one came even earlier than that, right at the end of 1994 in preparation for the 1995 season, on Charles's blue Plus 8 racer. First time out, in dry practice before a wet race at Silverstone, the first aluminium-chassised car took ten seconds off the previous best V8 Morgan times on the same circuit. It was six seconds a lap faster even in the wet. Charles had first sketched ideas for a chassis like this in 1992, with Chris Lawrence – the same man who had co-driven the class-winning Plus 4 at Le Mans in 1962, and who became technical director of the Aero 8 project.

The 1995 chassis was really an original Z-section chassis with sheet-aluminium reinforcement, and the new elements used adhesively bonded aluminium honeycomb sheet, produced by aluminium specialists CIBA-Geigy of Cambridge. Tests at MIRA showed it to be almost twice as stiff as the standard production offering, and a much better platform for a completely revised suspension layout. Developed by touring car racing specialists Andy Rouse Engineering, it used double wishbones and coil springs at the front, plus trailing arms and coils at the back, all with telescopic dampers and anti-roll bars (and not a sliding pillar or a leaf spring in sight). That was tested on the road, for around 10,000 miles, with a more or less standard 3.5-litre Rover V8, mainly to prove that it worked in principle. From there, with the help of suspension expert Roddy Harvey-Bailey, Morgan created a racing version with wishbone suspension on the rear as well as on the front, which was again tested on the road before having the front suspension revised again and then making its Silverstone race debut.

By 1997, Morgan had developed an even more extreme GT2 racer, which used an all-aluminium chassis rather than the earlier hybrid, and was in effect the last link to the Aero 8 programme. Powered by a full-race version of the Rover V8, developing around 400bhp, it was competitive in chassis terms but with its only mildly modified Plus 8 shape it was left for dead aerodynamically, which made it only a limited success at the top of the racing tree.

In 1998, though, it led to the first prototype of the new road car, and the beginning of a dedicated road car programme, led by Charles Morgan and Chris Lawrence. Their objective was to combine the excellent ride and handling characteristics offered by a softened and refined version of the aluminium chassis and all-coil-and-wishbone suspension with a more aerodynamic, but still classically Morgan shape and class-leading performance.

The production chassis had to be more sophisticated in many respects than the race car chassis, to be economically buildable in Morgan volumes and to pass all current legislation and crash tests worldwide. It also had to combine maximum strength with minimum weight, and to be durable and easy to maintain.

The initial development was carried out by Jim Randle, a highly respected former Jaguar engineering boss, using the resources of Birmingham University, but, as Morgan point out, that was only the beginning: 'The design started with Charles speaking to Jim Randle about a honeycomb box-shaped chassis, but that was not deemed stiff enough. The guys at Birmingham under Jim designed a basic tub, onto which Chris Lawrence added the front demountable section past the bulkhead, and the rear suspension, to make the race car. Jim Randle wanted to design the supension etc, too, but we felt we should do much more work in house to make it a Morgan Morgan.

'The racer relied heavily on the roll-over bar for torsional rigidity, which wasn't what was intended, so we stiffened the tub here with many design changes using Chris's expertise. And it was a natural progression to make the car into a road car, especially when Charles realised what a cracking chassis package it was . . .'

The design finalised, Morgan became the first European car maker to use new materials produced by Alcan in Nachterstedt, Germany. These advanced aluminium alloy materials were designed for automotive use but before Morgan adopted them they had only been used in one vehicle before this – General Motors' EV1 low-pollution electric car, built for California only. The latest Alcan material has the advantage over earlier types in that it already carries its final protective coating, which is rolled on during manufacturing. Crucially that allows more secure bonding, and, because the completed chassis does not have to undergo the earlier process where the coating was applied with heating, there is no risk of distortion after the chassis has been built. The assembly process with this material is also quicker and less expensive.

The Aero 8 chassis is built from Alcan aluminium components bonded with a high-performance adhesive produced by Gurritt Essex, gaining further strength from riveting with specialised rivets produced by Bollhoff. The components are cut by laser and folded where necessary, much of the material cutting and all the chassis assembly process being done by specialist material handlers Radshape. Tool makers Survirn helped create the panel shapes in their original foam form, then digitised their dimensions to define tool cutter paths for the panel-making process. The engine bay uses aluminium extrusions, designed specifically to combine everyday rigidity with exceptional crash-test performance, and the new chassis had already passed the necessary European Whole Vehicle Type Approval crash tests before the car was unveiled in Geneva. Aluminium extrusions are also used in the suspension and braking systems, and Morgan describe the Aero 8 as 'the world's first all-aluminium coachbuilt car', qualifying for Charles's description as an 'aluminium intensive vehicle'.

The suspension was as big a departure from Morgan tradition as the chassis, and again it is said to be a unique design. The front suspension uses lower wishbones with very long upper cantilever arms operating inboard coil spring/ damper units, with racing specification Eibach springs and Koni dampers. The rear has long wishbones with fully floating coil spring/damper units operated by the upper cantilever, and according to Morgan the layout means the geometry remains consistent over a wide range of suspension travel (not something Morgans have really had before) so there is no need for the usual anti-roll bars. To keep unsprung weight to an absolute minimum, the wheels are the lightest available OZ Racing five-spoke magnesium design, 18 inches in diameter, 9 inches wide and with racing style centre-lock hubs and peg drives. Those carry 225/40ZR18 Dunlop SP Sport 9000 tyres with a touch of their own technology, featuring a foam-filled, run-flat capability and with a pressure sensing system with audible and visible low pressure warnings for the driver. That is not only a safety feature but means the Aero 8 does not need a spare, thus saving weight and space.

The engine is the highly respected all-alloy 4.4-litre BMW V8, from the German manufacturer's 5- and 7-series saloons, specially modified for Morgan's purposes; under the terms of the agreement with BMW, it carries Morgan rather than BMW badges on its cam covers. Not that BMW wanted in any way to distance themselves from this car – exactly the opposite applied – and BMW were closely involved in the Aero 8 development programme virtually from the outset.

Thoughts of a new engine began at the same time as the rest of the project, in the late 1990s. At that time, Morgan believed that they would have to find a replacement for the Plus 8-type Rover V8 quite soon, because they anticipated the old Buick-derived engine would finally be forced out of production soon after 2000 by new 'Euro 3' emissions regulations. (As it transpires, the engine – and therefore the Plus 8 – will live for the moment but it will eventually go.)

Charles Morgan first made contact with BMW at the 1996 Geneva Show four years before the show in which the Aero 8 was unveiled. Interestingly, BMW were not the only potential engine supplier to whom Morgan spoke at the outset of the project, nor even the only German one. Audi's excellent V8 was also a possibility, and Audi admit that they would also have been very pleased to have powered the Aero 8, not least because Morgans are almost a cult sports car in Germany. Other options were ruled out by size, weight, certification requirements, and the level of co-operation on offer, so it was BMW who won out, and they became far more than just a supplier. As Morgan say, 'we purchased in effect an installation package, including their engineers, test facilities, Bosch ECU development and the relevant EU sign-off. They, of course, had to be happy with the installation ...' Clearly they were, but Morgan were also happy with BMW: 'They offered a terrific package and delivered much more ... and at the time they hadn't given the engine to anyone else, which was also good.'

BMW seconded two engineers to Morgan for two years, including engine installation specialist Gunther Ranzinger, while Thomas Moessner from Robert Bosch developed the unique-to-Morgan engine management alongside Morgan's electronics specialist David Goodwin, with Derek Jones running the CAD (Computer Aided Design) programme and Chris Lawrence in overall charge of engineering. As Morgan describe it, 'the targets were: 1000kg vehicle weight; an unstressed, large capacity V8 with loads of torque; 50/50 weight distribution; aerodynamic stability at speed; quieter and easier to live with than the Plus 8; coachbuilt construction; aluminium technology; and full European type approval with the requirement later for USA approval'. They add, 'we benchmarked all aspects, against Porsche Boxsters, Mazdas, MGs, TVRs, even Ferraris – including things like hood fit, interior noise at 70mph and so on, to equal or beat the best'. At Miramas the Aero 8 has recorded better than 1g lateral cornering force, on road tyres, leading one senior BMW man to comment that here was a car finally worthy of his engine.

It is interesting to compare the design philosophy of the Aero 8 with that of BMW's own Z8, a front-engined, rear-drive V8-powered two-seater sports car which, like the Aero 8, is aimed at individualists, and like the Aero 8 has echoes of its maker's previous designs; in the case of the Z8, it evokes the styling of the beautiful 507, designed by Albrecht Graf von Goertz. With 286bhp and 322lb ft of torque, the Morgan is some way behind the Z8's 400bhp and 369lb ft – but it weighs 1000kg compared to the Z8's 1585kg – for a power-to-weight ratio of 286bhp/tonne compared to the BMW's 252, and torque-to-weight of 322lb ft/tonne (said to be the best of any production car in the world) versus 233. That in a nutshell is the advantage of Morgan's age-old philosophy of light weight being just as important as a big power output. Morgan claim a 160mph maximum versus the Z8's limited 155, and 0–62mph in 'under five seconds' as against 4.7. As the Aero 8 would be launched with a price tag of £49,950 compared to £86,650 for a Z8, Morgan could be quite pleased with their own interpretation of the sports car theme while BMW could be equally proud of theirs.

Charles Morgan describes the Aero 8 as 'the world's first all-aluminium coachbuilt car'. The production chassis had to be economically viable in Morgan volumes, while satisfying all current legislation. It had to give maximum strength with minimum weight and be durable and easy to maintain. It was a very different proposition from developing the last 'new' Morgan, the Plus 8, launched as it was thirty yeas ago.

The whole Aero project spanned four years and is the biggest development programme Morgan has ever undertaken. Importantly, however, it leaves Morgan's independence intact. 'In the past our developments have all been an evolution of an existing demand,' Charles Morgan says. 'The Aero 8 has been an all-new project from the word go, including an engine specially developed for the car. The last time Morgan had one of those was from Standard in the 1930s! We now have to work to such fine parameters for type approval, emissions and noise, that the two launches, Plus 8 and Aero 8, can't be compared. The new car only has sixteen parts in common with the old one – nothing beyond the hinges and latches for bonnet and doors. The use of CAD, electronic data transfer and so on allowed maximum speed in the design and allowed us to engineer the car from the start for production – rather than work out how to build it after we've designed it. We have had a very professional development group, which started with a set of objectives and worked to develop the car to a proper timetable and cost base. We also used resources from all over the factory, which in the long-term has meant total buy-in from the factory floor. The factory as a whole is genuinely proud of this car . . .'

The body is very much in the coachbuilt Morgan tradition, but with a little help from modern technology. The Aero 8 uses the familiar construction of metal panels over an ash frame, and for this car aluminium is the standard body material. Most panels are still hand-shaped, but as they have been for several years now the largest and most complex panels on the car, the sweeping front wings, now with the even more controversially faired-in headlamps, are preformed. Like the older cars' wings, they are made by Superform, in Worcester, using superplastic aluminium forming. There is no actual plastic involved, however; 'plastic' here refers to the malleable state of the aluminium sheet before it is shaped. As Morgan explain the process, 'the aluminium is heated by electrical induction and then gently blown over a male mould using air pressure. Lots of it. The alloy folds and flows to a stress-free panel in perfect complex shapes, yet once it is cold, it forms a tough and heavy gauge component which is also very light in weight.'

The body design process has also come a little way since HFS chalked outlines on the wall and took measurements with a piece of string or a stretched-out handkerchief. Morgan began to adopt computer technology in the late 1980s, starting, some people would be surprised to hear, with CAD for prototype parts and machine-shop tooling, followed by computerised stock control, leading to computerised production planning and accounting systems, mainly run at desktop levels.

The Aero 8 body shape was designed in-house, using CATIA-CAD software, following guidelines mainly laid down by Charles Morgan, but with a 'styling committee' which also included Mark Aston, Tim Whitworth and sales and marketing manager Matthew Parkin. Charles (like his father) firmly believes in the lesson learned with the Plus 4 Plus almost forty years ago – that anyone who wants a Morgan is also likely to want a car that is Morgan shaped, and anyone who does not like the Morgan shape would not buy it no matter what was underneath. So the Aero 8 is very Morgan, but its shape was by far the most controversial subject for most people at its launch.

Charles Morgan was particularly irritated by one description, by Andrew English of the *Daily Telegraph*. English was positive and complimentary about the technology of the Aero 8 but far from convinced by the looks. 'It's also stupendously ugly,' he wrote. 'To me it looks like a car that hit a telegraph pole head on. The squinting headlamps just look, well, dreadful, as if the company couldn't decide whether to place them in the wings or next to the radiator shell, and the rear panels look as though they've been cold chiselled off a 1950s Triumph TR2, which was not exactly a high point in British car design. The aluminium alloy and plastics coachwork might be hand crafted in the time-honoured Morgan way, but on the show car the panels fit where they touch and the shut lines are pretty wavy. After staring at the beautiful naked chassis and engine which had been on display all day, the final appearance of the Aero 8 was a bit too much to swallow in one go. My initial reaction was to ask if customers would be able to specify their Aero 8s without the body. Morgan staff looked slightly pained. It's been signed off by the directors, which means Charles likes it and criticism is futile.

'In the few hours that remained after the unveiling, I walked past the Morgan stand many times. After a while the

Aero 8's appearance ceased to shock and even looked quite mean and moody, but those cross-eyed headlamps still looked awful, reminding me of Clarence the lion in Daktari.' After the show English spoke to a well-known British designer working at the highest level for a major foreign manufacturer and says 'he refused to talk about the Morgan, "Not because I'm worried about the reaction to my comments but because it makes me so angry that they have wasted such an important opportunity".'

Andrew English alluded to another, favourable bit of Morgan tradition, the flexibility of the manufacturing process, 'There's still time to fix it, of course. The chassis design was done on a computer, but being handbuilt means there are no expensive press tools to alter. A change to the headlamps would be the main thing, moving them one way or the other. It would never make the Aero 8 a pretty car of course, but it would gain a tough mien like the 1997 endurance racers that provided its inspiration.'

He concluded, 'Or perhaps Charles Morgan is keen to go down in history as the man who gave the world its first strabismic sports car.' Charles Morgan was not amused.

Writing in his Motormouth column, also in the *Daily Telegraph*, Mike Rutherford was no more convinced than Andrew English. He wrote about Citroen's 'advanced design chief', but said, 'Clearly, nobody at the Morgan Motor Company has such a fancy job title, and it shows: many people considered the new Aero 8 a design disaster. "It looks like it's been punched in the face", quipped one cruel and influential industry onlooker.'

But inevitably, there were others who thought the Aero 8 was more than just a cross-eyed beast. The British weekly *Auto Express* said, 'The UK's most traditional sports car maker has blasted into the spotlight this week with a new, sophisticated 160mph challenger. Morgan is embracing the 21st century with the Aero 8, powered by a 4.4-litre BMW V8. The ultra-light roadster is said to combine state-of-the-art technology with Morgan's traditional hand-built craftsmanship to create a machine with supercar performance and classic looks. The sports car uses an aluminium chassis similar in concept to that of the Lotus Elise. But instead of a plastic body, it has Morgan's legendary hand-crafted alloy panels and ash frame. Inside, the Aero 8 is the most luxurious Morgan ever and, despite traditional wood and leather, options such as satellite navigation will be available . . .' Also previewing the launch, rival weekly *Autocar* said, 'An outrageous mix of aerodynamic and retro styling, high-tech construction and BMW V8 power should make Morgan's £50,000 Aero 8 one of the stars of this week's Geneva Motor Show', and after the event they enthused, 'the company has blown out of the water all thoughts of it being static and old fashioned. This miracle has been performed by a car that uses scarcely a dozen parts from its predecessors – just hinges and bonnet latches and doors. The £50,000 Aero 8 is a BMW V8-powered supercar. It is not only the most technologically advanced model Morgan has ever made, but is arguably one of the most advanced production cars unveiled at this year's Geneva Motor Show. That might be hard to believe at first glance because, despite the swoopy new bodywork, the Aero 8 retains an unashamedly pre-war demeanour. However, underneath the new wind tunnel-honed body lies an ultra-stiff aluminium alloy chassis produced by Alcan in Germany, specifically developed for high-tech automotive applications . . . Despite its outrageous performance, the Aero 8 is probably the most user friendly car Morgan has built. If you've got the readies, it might just be the easiest to get your hands on, too . . .'

It was only easier to get your hands on, in the first instance, if you were already on the waiting list (currently around four years) for one of the existing Morgans. Those customers would be invited to upgrade their order to the new model, but after twenty-eight days, that option closed and the queue reverted to normal. Morgan revealed that they had had more than fifty orders for the new car even before it was unveiled; within days of the Geneva launch that was up to one hundred and fifty, and within three weeks to twice that and climbing rapidly. The aim was to build up to two hundred Aero 8s a year, alongside the continuing Plus 8 and the various four-cylinder models, and to aim for a waiting list of no more than two years.

Soon after the launch, Morgan revealed how happy they were with the way things had gone. 'We've been confident about this project from the word go. We realise the responsibility we have with a new Morgan design. The fact that it has been developed here instead of some agency somewhere, and designed by Morgan people, has meant we've had a very tight rein on the project. Few other manufacturers could have done it so quickly and cost effectively. The reaction has been astonishing. Of the three hundred and twenty orders to date [three weeks after launch], two-thirds are from existing customers, and so far very few have seen the car first-hand. We know that it's a challenge to understand the shape, particularly for people who do not get "the Morgan thing", but we're finding that when people give it more than a passing glance, they come to love its individuality . . .'

Retaining that individuality, for both car and company, has been a religion with Morgan for ninety years, and as Morgan see it, it makes no sense to change it now.

7 Outside Looking In

F OR ONE OF THE world's smaller and more anachronistic car companies, Morgan has a remarkably high public awareness, but there's more to it than just recognising the cars. It's rather ironic that one of the most attention-grabbing things that has happened to Morgan in recent years had little to do with what you might expect most people to focus on – the product – and everything to do with what's usually kept quietly in the background – the business. But, for several years in the 1990s, if you mentioned Morgan, the reaction probably wouldn't be, 'Ah, sports cars', it would more likely be 'Ah, *Troubleshooter*'. And if you said '*Troubleshooter*', you were almost certain to hear, 'Ah, yes, Morgan'.

Troubleshooter was a series of television programmes screened by the BBC in 1990. In the series, flamboyant business expert Sir John Harvey-Jones set out to analyse the business strategies, and as he saw it the managerial errors, of a broad spectrum of companies, from a brewery to a pottery. Morgan was the subject of the last programme in the series, and it became the one that attracted by far the most attention, even notoriety.

At the centre of the programme's appeal was its jovial, larger-than-life presenter. Sir John Harvey-Jones was a for-mer chairman of chemicals giant ICI, and was credited with turning that company around from its problems of the mid-1980s. But his style was controversial, and his critics, Peter Morgan included, would point out that, in later years, not all his own management ventures would be as successful as his days at ICI. That said, his initial analysis of Morgan was not entirely surprising. To put it mildly, he was horrified by what he saw (and presented to the world) as a company frozen in time. Morgan people, naturally, did not agree, and the 'T' word became anathema at Malvern Link.

Harvey-Jones is a free thinker, certainly not bound by convention, even, to superficial appearances, bordering on the eccentric. He is a large, avuncular-looking man, with a ready smile, a neat moustache and long, rather unkempt hair, which, like his taste for wildly colourful ties, is slightly at odds with his thoroughly traditional business suits. From the way he describes himself in his autobiography, *Getting it Together* (written after the *Troubleshooter* series and in the wake of the celebrity it brought), he could have been the classic Morgan enthusiast, maybe even a Morgan owner. 'From my early boyhood,' he wrote, 'when I spent so much time living in my imagination and the world of the great adventure books of the 1920s, I have had a picture in my mind of the sort of person I wanted to be. A sort of *Boy's Own Paper* composite, archetypal British gentleman – simultaneously strong and compassionate, stiff-lipped yet emotional, courageous both physically and morally, doing incessantly to others as you would be done to yourself . . .' Surely a Morgan man?

But no, not exactly. Harvey-Jones is a complex character, with depths way beyond the *Boy's Own Paper* stuff. He was born in east London in 1924 but brought up until the age of six in India, where his father was tutor to a young maharajah. The family lived in classic late-days-of-the-Raj style: young John with his own pony, his father spending much of his time hunting big game – a happy, privileged life. The happiness came to an abrupt end, however, when he was sent back to prep school in England. There he was treated badly and missed his family – in spite of the fact that his relationship with his father, who had little time for either him or his mother, was a difficult one. Aged thirteen, he went from prep school to the Royal Naval College at Dartmouth, where he was far happier, then into the Navy and into the Second World War as a submarine commander, during which he built a distinguished career. After the war he became involved with Naval Intelligence. In 1956, because the Navy would not allow him to leave any other way, he resigned his commission – to help his wife look after their young daughter, who had developed polio – and joined ICI.

He started at ICI – *Troubleshooter*-style – by doing efficiency studies, and later managing a factory. In 1973 he was invited to join the board, and in 1982 he was elected chairman. By the time he left ICI, in 1987, he had turned the company round, from making small losses to making large profits, and, in doing so, made something of a name for himself as both business guru and highly visible pundit, for television as well as business audiences.

He has said, after the event, that his aim with the *Troubleshooter* series was not so much to assassinate other people's business methods and impose his own as to demonstrate that the world of small business (small, at least, by ICI's scale) could be 'interesting and attractive'. It seems that Morgan didn't expect anything like the public assassination that Harvey-Jones delivered. Charles Morgan, who already knew of Harvey-Jones through his television connections, has said that, 'The BBC approached us to take part and obviously we were happy to co-operate.'

But Harvey-Jones was not impressed by the Morgan philosophy. He arrived for his first visit to the factory by chauffeur-driven car, prompting the rather cynical observation from one long-time Morgan employee, 'You'd think that someone coming to tell a car company how to run its business would at least be able to drive a car himself.' The visit, having started on the wrong foot, was mostly downhill from there.

One of the most quoted passages from the programme is Harvey-Jones's opening exchange with Dave Day, the long-time foreman of the chassis shop. 'How long have you worked here?' he asked.

'Just over 30 years,' replied the foreman.

'And always on chassis?' he continued, smiling.

'Yes,' he was told.

'You must have seen a lot of changes in that time?'

'Not really, no,' came the reply, and Harvey-Jones's smile turned to a chuckle. When he was then told that quite a number of would-be owners die before their name gets to the top of the waiting list, his chuckle became full-blown laughter.

The timing of the programme is important. It was made between the end of 1989 and the beginning of 1990, and shown on 1 May 1990. In the Thatcherite days of yuppie wealth, that was a boom time for the motor industry, especially for anything that remotely smacked of classic cars or exclusivity, and the Morgan had elements of both. Morgan also had what was then frequently reported as the longest waiting list in the industry – quoted at the time as being between five and six years. Again, it was a product of the times, and Morgan weren't proud of it, but it was a function of the conspicuous consumption of the newly rich whiz kids, and speculation on the part of those who had seen the prices of out-of-the-ordinary, hard-to-get cars rocket. Cars themselves, especially cars in the Ferrari, Porsche and Jaguar supercar league, were being sold way above list price to people who didn't want to join the waiting lists and could afford not to. Some were actually bought to drive; many were bought, like art or antiques or fine wine, to lay down and appreciate.

Appreciate, that is, in the sense of value. For a while, cars listed at maybe £200,000, like the low-volume, super-high-performance Ferrari F40 or Porsche's rival, the 959, were on offer for about the £1 million mark. For genuine, older classics with the right name and a racing history, you could spend five times that. For some speculators, the car itself was of absolutely no consequence – it was only pieces of paper and rights to buy that actually changed hands. And the phenomenon affected Morgan more than most: to get on to the order list for a Ferrari or a Porsche demanded a substantial investment up front; to get on to Morgan's list, even though the ultimate values were nothing like so stratospheric, took little more than pocket money. To their credit, Morgan had refused to capitalise beyond taking more orders – notional orders in some cases, as it would turn out, in the light of the subsequent collapse in the market. A deposit of £250 (refundable) would reserve your new Morgan, and (then as now) you didn't have to pay the balance, let alone finalise the specification, or even confirm the model, until the actual build process started just a few weeks before delivery, albeit years after the order, if you waited. What's more, Morgan hadn't raised prices to take advantage of the soaring demand, because that was not their way.

Sir John Harvey-Jones was appalled by the whole scenario. Here was a man whose entire business philosophy was based on the belief that, if you were not going forwards, you were going backwards. He could not come to terms with the Morgan method of production at all. Looking at the hand-building process he said, 'Their pride seems to be in manu-facturing from the furthest-back state they can, starting with the most basic material. I'm surprised they don't start with the tree itself . . . they won't even use bloody power tools.' He was horrified by the arcaneness of the systems, from the way part-built cars were wheeled around the factory (just as they always had been) to the way the paperwork and planning were handled – in most cases literally with paper and pencil. He could not believe that the stores inventory system comprised, in effect, a man in brown overalls looking to see which bins were empty, which were full, and ordering accordingly. He could not believe that there were no computers, and no obvious forward-planning procedure. As he described it then, 'Basically it's a discussion between the foreman and the chap on the bench.' Especially, he could not believe Morgan had no estimate of how many cars they could sell on an open market.

'I have never,' he said, 'been anywhere where there is such total conservatism. The whole place is imbued with the fear of change.' And suggesting change, based on his own expert-ise and philosophies, was the object of the *Troubleshooter* exercise.

Harvey-Jones's suggestions to Morgan were that they should dramatically increase production, drastically reduce waiting lists, and – as a matter of urgency – increase prices to take advantage of a market that was clearly willing to pay for such a product. At that time, output was around 400 cars a year. He wanted to see that increased by 300 cars a year – preferably 400 – in other words, a doubling of production. He suggested that prices be raised from the order of £13,000–£20,000 towards £17,500–£27,000 – an increase of about

one-third which, he argued, would have no discernible effect
on demand. He believed that, if Morgan didn't do such things,
the company would slowly wither and die.

Not only did Morgan not agree with his opinions, they
were also genuinely saddened by much of what Harvey-Jones
had said. They argued that, while his ideas might be appropriate for some businesses, he had completely missed the
point of Morgan's traditions. The day after the programme,
Charles Morgan, speaking also for his father, told the *Daily
Telegraph* motoring correspondent, John Langley, 'Whatever
Sir John says, we are not in a rut. The average age of our
workforce is just 34 and we have already increased production by 10 per cent, from nine cars a week to ten. We are
actively looking at ways of reducing the five-year waiting list.
But you can't do that overnight with our sort of car.'

It is important to consider both sides of the picture –
Morgan's and the troubleshooter's – in the context of the car
market around 1989 and 1990, which was not a 'normal' time.
Just a few months before the programme was broadcast,
Professor Garel Rhys, the Society of Motor Manufacturers and
Traders, and professor of Motor Industry Economics at
Cardiff Business School, University of Wales, published a
paper in the series *Long Range Planning*, headed 'Smaller Car
Firms – Will They Survive?' Then, as now, Rhys was one of
the industry's most respected observers, and his introduction
to this particular paper read: 'Motor industry operations are
being increasingly conducted on a global scale. To world wide
sales is now being added a global production system, with
world output being dominated by a limited number of huge
producers. Economies of scale are significant in the industry,
so smaller firms are faced with the problem of finding a
survival strategy. This paper examines the success or otherwise the smaller firms have had in response to this state of
affairs, using the UK motor industry as an example.'

He looked at four categories of smaller manufacturers:
'London' taxis, quality cars, prestige cars and, Morgan's
specific group, sports cars. The quality car group, argued
Rhys, 'tries to convince customers that their product is
superior to that of the mass producer, even if this claim may
be difficult to substantiate. This class of "smaller" car firm

can still include firms which are "large" by the standards of most other industries.' And as an example he quoted the Rover Group, at the time Britain's largest engineering company in spite of its diminished stature as a car maker. 'The second group [prestige cars] directs its attention to the wealthiest members of society, and tries not to compete on price. However, cost-plus pricing is sometimes modified by the needs of the market because the number of very affluent and price insensitive customers varies from time to time, over a business cycle. So on occasions price does matter even for prestige cars, and real price cuts occur. There is a very limited number of firms like Fiat's subsidiary Ferrari or Rolls-Royce who seem to have a large supply of price insensitive customers. In the late 1970s and early 1980s firms like Lotus or Aston Martin demonstrated that they did not have such a clientele, or such strong waiting lists.' When Sir John Harvey-Jones went to Morgan just a couple of months after this paper was published and suggested they raised their prices because the market would not worry about the difference, he presumably hadn't read Rhys's analysis.

Of the sports car sector the report said, 'The third group consists of some well established firms, but a larger number of precariously under-capitalized ventures, the latter often catering for a lower income price conscious clientele who are very sensitive to the nature of the prevailing economic climate. Some of this group of firms have spacious, often well appointed "factories" but others have smaller "workshop"-type premises with minimum manufacturing functions. The bane of most small or new firms is a shortage of working capital which clearly puts the venture at risk should there be an interruption in the flow of sales . . .' Again, Morgan were perhaps more aware of that than Harvey-Jones.

Professor Rhys put the position of the smaller manufacturer into the context of wider industry trends, such as the mergers which were helping create them by the realignment of many once-famous names. In Britain immediately after the Second World War there were six major manufacturers: Austin, Morris (as part of the Nuffield group), Standard, Ford, Vauxhall and Rootes. Between them, they accounted for 88 per cent of UK production (led by Austin with 23 per cent and

Nuffield with 20 per cent). That still meant that the 'others', the smaller firms, between them accounted for a significant 12 per cent. By 1987, Ford and Vauxhall remained, Austin and the Nuffield marques had been agglomerated (via BMC and British Leyland) into the Rover Group, Rootes had metamorphosed through Chrysler and Talbot into Peugeot, and the then defunct Standard had been replaced in the 'big five' by Jaguar. Led by the Rover Group's 41 per cent share, these five manufacturers 99 per cent of Britain's cars, and the smaller manufacturers the remaining 1 per cent. What's more, that was a picture repeated in virtually every car-making country in the world.

Professor Rhys's paper also discussed economies of scale in the big manufacturers – including the need for any major plant to build more than 200,000 units a year to optimise output. For individual elements of the car, the minimum efficient scale was usually far greater: for example, a million units for engines, up to two million for panel pressings, and an expected output of five million units to justify research and development for a new model. In the mainstream industry the scales could be achieved by sharing components (especially engines, drivetrains and chassis components) between models and, increasingly, between marques.

For the smaller survivors there had to be different processes. The report went on, 'As well as charging premium prices for a differential product the small and medium sized firms attempt to minimize the cost disadvantages they have compared with larger firms, by not only producing a narrow range of vehicles, but also by producing the same basic model for a much longer period than is usual for the mass producer.' Rhys then looked at the 'added value' argument: 'The very small car firm, by buying in most of its costs, must, in effect, use cost-plus pricing systems. Furthermore, as the unit costs of the sub-optimum sized firm are higher than those incurred by a larger firm, the only way for the small firm to sell its product on a cost-plus basis would be by persuading customers that "quality" and "exclusiveness" are worth paying extra for.'

As an illustration of what could still save the small firm from extinction, he quoted an interesting example – Morgan. 'So the small producer selling in a price sensitive sector has found it difficult to compete on both quality and price with larger firms. Only if a specialist niche, or gap, in the market could be found would a firm be able to operate profitably while paying attention to quality details. A firm like Morgan selling a Ford-engined sports car has such a niche: by continuing to produce a largely unchanging *style* of product since the 1930s the firm became the only source of "traditional" metal bodied sports cars.'

That academic paper, by one of the industry's sharpest and best respected observers, included references to almost all the key points of the Morgan philosophy: the advantageous use of outside suppliers; the niche market and the long product life; the best (and longest term) use of relatively low-cost resources and a pricing strategy which didn't respond with knee jerks to short-term market fluctuations, such as those happening at precisely the time of the report and the *Troubleshooter* episode. In most respects, if you took the Morgan-specific case, it was a different viewpoint from Harvey-Jones's suggestions.

After the programme was broadcast and the blaze of publicity began, Charles, then marketing director, put the company's point of view again, in a letter to the following week's *Autocar & Motor* magazine. It reiterated, almost verbatim, the text of a press release issued by Morgan immediately before the programme appeared. The letter read, 'On 1 May the Morgan Motor Company was the subject of *Troubleshooter*, the BBC2 programme presented by Sir John Harvey-Jones. The programme discussed the company and ways in which we should increase production to reduce our waiting list.

'It was Sir John's view that we should double our production in a short timescale, paying for the investment that this would require by increasing the price of our car.

'We strongly disagree with this solution.

'The Morgan Company is indisputably successful, but we recognise the need to increase production to reduce our waiting list.

'To call for drastic change/action is to fundamentally misunderstand the ethos of our company and the very reason for its on-going success, where so many others have failed.

'The Morgan is a hand-built sports car; the degree of craftsmanship and skill which goes into its construction is what differentiates it from a mass-produced car. Our customers are enthusiasts buying a Morgan, not just a set of wheels.

'To bring radical change to our production methods would undoubtedly increase the numbers we produce, but at what cost? The loss of our integrity, our unique appeal and our future, we would say.

'We are proud that we build for the enthusiast and that we can still allow each owner to watch his/her car being built and can offer a degree of individual choice and specification far beyond that of many "luxury" car manufacturers.

'But beyond pride there is a very sound business strategy. Our car is not priced in the top market sector. Our customers are not just the rich, who are notoriously susceptible to fashion and change. Nor do we compete with a host of luxury cars. The enthusiast is a niche market – we are loyal to them and they are loyal to us.

'The Morgan Motor Company is a private company. We need profits to re-invest in its future, but we have no hungry and fickle shareholders forcing us to make money now, regardless of the future cost. Our predictions for 1990 (year end 31 May) are that it will have been another "exceptional" year, with pre-tax profits anticipated to be around £500,000.

'We are open to change and we are adopting new technology, but only when it enhances our product and only when its adoption makes sound business sense to a small, hand-crafted business.

'Sir John's opinions have been noted but his solutions are unworthy of us.'

That letter summed up pretty much in their entirety the principles that had served Morgan for more than eighty years; the only thing it didn't specifically mention being Charles's and Peter's fierce belief in the company's continuing independence.

The Morgan viewpoint was soon supported by others, notably the aforementioned Professor Garel Rhys. Two weeks later Rhys wrote in *Autocar & Motor*, 'I read with interest the letter from Charles Morgan in which he took issue with Sir

John Harvey-Jones' prognosis ... In general this would be sound advice, but I share Charles Morgan's view that this would not be the correct policy for the Malvern Link company.

'The main failure of Sir John's approach is to ignore the fact that Morgan is following a successful *long term* survival strategy. If one looks at a list of small firms from 1960, only Morgan and Bristol survive under the same ownership, or indeed at all.

'Even companies with such strong cachet as Ferrari or Rolls-Royce have found it prudent to seek the security of large groupings. Only Bristol, albeit in a different segment of the market, since its sale in 1960 by Bristol Aeroplane has displayed the same continuity and stability as Morgan. This was by duplicating a central tenet of the latter's policy of avoiding the temptation of "chasing the market" whenever temporary booms beckoned.

'The life of the small firm,' he went on, 'even those as "large" as Saab or Jaguar, has proved to be difficult throughout the history of the motor industry. If a small car company can find a successful survival strategy when most others fail, it should be wary of change for the sake of it.

'Small makers of sports cars survive, if they do survive, by making cars of exclusiveness born of small volumes at a price as near as possible to that charged by the mass producers.

'So Morgan sells in a price-sensitive sector and only by finding a niche in the market can it operate profitably while paying attention to quality details.

'The characteristics of a Morgan – both in terms of the product itself and its method of production – have not been duplicated by MGs or Triumphs in the past, by GTIs in the present, and probably not by Mazdas in the future. Yet the car appeals to sufficient customers for it to make a profit, year-in and year-out.

'Any major increase in price would, notwithstanding waiting lists, erode Morgan's customer base, especially as any doubling of volume would undermine its exclusivity.

'Sir John's strategy is often the correct one, and would have been appropriate to Jaguar in the late '50s and early '60s but could prove unfortunate if applied to Morgan. After all, there are always exceptions that prove the rule.'

That was very powerful support but, in the same issue, the correspondence columns heard from the Harvey-Jones's supporters, too, including John Morrison of London, who (under the heading 'Museum Mentality') wrote, 'It is understandable that Charles Morgan would wish to defend his family's stewardship of their company. But it is sad that he can only do so by misrepresenting Sir John Harvey-Jones's advice in *Troubleshooter*.

'Sir John clearly loved the Morgan car and repeatedly stressed that he did not wish to change its handcrafted nature. But he was understandably appalled at the sheer inefficiency of the production operation and the quite unneccessary use of human musclepower for the simplest operations.

'He did not say, as Charles Morgan alleges, that ". . . we should double our production in a short timescale . . ." He did say that Morgan should increase production *capacity*. This would allow it to expand output and increase profits in times of buoyant demand, but would not require it to keep output levels up at all costs.

'Charles Morgan recognises the need to cut the waiting list for Morgans but rejects the obvious solution of pricing his cars at levels which would come closer to balancing supply and demand – apparently because low prices attract a nicer class of clientele. That is not running a business, it is enjoying a hobby. It is also depriving Morgan's customers of the cars they want so much.

'Many British firms have shown they can produce a quality hand-crafted product tailored to their customers' needs, while at the same time running an efficient business profitably. It is a great pity that the Morgan family's only response to Sir John Harvey-Jones' eminently sensible suggestions has been to defend at all costs their management of an industrial museum.'

The Morgan-knocking, pro-Harvey-Jones lobby was also supported by RE Berry, of Hertfordshire, who wrote, 'I am not surprised that Charles Morgan seeks to justify his company's philosophies and methods through the pages of *Autocar & Motor*. In doing so he adds a further disservice to his company – the first being to take part in the series at all when a willingness to consider change was a prerequisite to inclusion.

'To demonstrate a total reluctance to change of any sort, regardless of merit, is to misunderstand the role of management in its most crucial form and, therefore, his presence in the business at all – apart from nepotism.

'That the workforce itself saw all too clearly the need for radical change was one of the programme's most powerful impressions.

'The Morgan Motor Company appears to survive despite its management. Its workforce as well as its customers deserve better, and Sir John pointed the way forward with great clarity and sympathy. To ignore him is to risk the business, and that would be a tragedy.'

A week later, with the controversy having been splashed all over the national papers, and having become a talking point in bars up and down the country, JR Johnson of West Sussex questioned what HFS Morgan might have thought of the whole thing. 'Charles Morgan's defence of the high standards set by his grandfather for the building of his company's cars is admirable. But many viewers who watched the programme on BBC2 will despair at the blinkered approach of the management and board of the Morgan Car Company to even the slightest modernisation in working practices.

'Peter and Charles Morgan have done a magnificent job in steering the company through the very difficult years which have followed the oil crisis. They have maintained the quality of their product where many other companies have failed. Within a narrow focus they have accurately judged the demand for their cars.

'Unfortunately, where they have failed, completely, is to capitalise on the skills and experience of themselves and their employees. Would Peter Morgan's father today:

1 Set up a factory where the workers used hand files?
2 Not have replaced the hand-operated sheet-bending machine before it became a museum-piece?
3 Attempt to build a car without the use of a jig?
4 Suffer his workers pushing part-completed cars around from one shed to the next with the complete engine and drivetrain in place?

5 Produce a car without attempting to plumb the depths of demand and be happy to sit back and rely on an "enthusiast" clientele?
6 Not want to do his "bit" for the country and increase production in order to better meet export demand?

'The Morgan Car Company must typify to many what is so right with British skills and industry and so dreadfully wrong with British management: it is easier to maintain the status quo than to take the risk of expansion.'

And finally, more than a month after the controversial programme had been shown, the view of a particularly interested party, Ross Herbert of Surrey, who (as a prospective owner) said, 'After reading Charles Morgan's letter concerning the *Troubleshooter* programme, I scanned subsequent 'Your View' pages expecting to see support expressed for his views. With the exception of the learned Professor Rhys, I found a stream of the worst yuppie sentiments borne from an increasingly material world.

'Of course a Morgan sports car is an anachronism and long may it continue to be so. As one of the waiting customers, I would be appalled if I thought radical changes were to affect the way Morgans are made.

'If you want a traditional English sports car at a reasonable price, then you should be prepared to wait for it. For those who can't, let them drive Mazdas!'

At which point the editor declared correspondence on the subject closed. But the story was far from over.

The *Troubleshooter* episode, as might be gathered from the above, brought Morgan into the public eye like nothing else had since its greatest competition successes. And although it upset some people at the heart of the company quite deeply, ultimately it showed how other people thought that Morgan's principles, not Harvey-Jones's, were right. Far from having the negative effect of making the world think less of the company and its cars, it created a burst of solidarity that saw several hundred additional orders over the next few months. It also saw Morgan pursuing some of Harvey-Jones's suggestions, but on their own terms. Production was increased, modestly rather than dramatically, from eight to ten cars a week by 1992. In the same period, in spite of the boom market collapsing all around Morgan, their pre-tax profits virtually doubled, from £488,000 in 1989 to £900,000 in 1992.

During that year, the BBC ran *Troubleshooter II*, in which Harvey-Jones previewed a new set of subjects by revisiting some of the companies he had analysed in 1990. But not Morgan, who declined the offer. As Peter Morgan explained, 'I didn't think we wanted any more of that sort of publicity. We didn't agree with his findings. Nothing is perfect; we do have some problems and I think he identified some of them. But his ideas were wrong and they proved to be wrong.' Some years later, in 1995, he added, 'If we had gone ahead and implemented Sir John's recommendations, we'd be in deep trouble. Such is the recession, we wouldn't have the demand.' Which, of course, is central to the philosophy that had kept the company alive through many previous crises – 'cautiously maintaining demand ahead of supply,' as one business writer put it, 'so good times cancel out the bad'.

Charles Morgan also confirmed that in this instance, discretion had been the better part of valour. 'We've not felt the recession at all', he told the press in 1995. 'All that's happened is that delivery times have come down a bit, from six years to perhaps four or five in Britain. We don't build cars on spec like other manufacturers. Every car is built to order. I don't think Harvey-Jones understood that.'

Harvey-Jones, for his part, said in 1992 that, whenever he was asked about *Troubleshooter*, of all the programmes in the original series, the one on Morgan was the one that he was asked about most frequently. But he also said that he felt his visit to Morgan had possibly been one of his greatest failures. Then, in March 2000, exactly a week after Morgan had launched its most significant new car in decades, the Aero 8, Harvey-Jones reappeared, in the first programme of another series of *Troubleshooter* – subtitled 'Change or Die'.

Looking as Falstaffian as ever, he recalled the problems from late 1989 to early 1990, when the Morgan company was building nine cars a week and had an 'eleven-year' waiting list. The return visit started with a brief look back at the first programme. Back then Harvey-Jones had described Derek

Day, the sales manager, as 'the non-sales manager' and suggested he would be better described as a rationer of cars; had said that production is always an area that you can do something about; that 'the layout of the factory is historic'; and concluded that, 'Any change will be difficult, so Morgan may as well go for radical changes – because you can only be shot once.'

Early in 2000, soon after Harvey-Jones had been back to Morgan, Charles talked about the aftermath of the first *Troubleshooter* programme. 'The Harvey-Jones experience was cataclysmic, because all those people who didn't want to change for various reasons – and don't forget there's a comfort factor here – were very upset.' Charles will always remember that he played a central role in making the first programme possible. 'They approached us, but I take full responsibility for going through with it. I thought it was going to be a programme about a successful family business in manufacturing. I didn't even know it was called *Trouble-shooter*. What's good about Harvey-Jones, or any consultant, is that they look at things from a completely objective viewpoint and give you a platform for insights of your own. They probably don't have the solutions themselves, and why should they? They're around for maybe a week – in Harvey-Jones's case a day. He didn't give us a lot of time. He's a bright bloke, but he didn't know everything there was to know about Morgan.

'One thing that annoyed us was that he never came except with the cameras. And it was a very tough time. It was so tough that I, as marketing director, had to put out an apology, saying we didn't think he was right, we didn't think the programme presented Morgan in a fair light. I did that simply because I felt (and still feel) that the producer of the original programme presented the company in a false light and didn't give credit to the initiatives that were already going on. The programme deliberately asked rhetorical questions, like the one to Dave Day, the chassis foreman, about seeing the changes over the years. But the suggestion that nothing had changed simply wasn't true; in reality we'd had about fifty parts changes even in the three months before the pro-gramme was made.'

Charles also had to face up to the effect it had on the workforce. 'Mainly they found it irritating,' he says now, 'but the support of the owners' clubs and the wider world was very important, and I think they were particularly pleased to hear people say, "OK, make the place more efficient, but don't, for God's sake, do what he says and throw everything out. We're happy for you to make money, but the philosophy is something we want to preserve." That provided a great incentive for me to sit down and think, You're right, but how do we do that without going the same way as the corner shop and gradually disappearing, while actually turning the company around to the best parts of modern systems?'

He was aware that with the company's new celebrity his every move was now being watched more closely than ever before, but he was also very gratified by the balance between support for Morgan and criticism of the troubleshooter. 'It reminded me that I work for a wonderful company. We must have had 30,000 letters, the vast majority saying he'd got it wrong, and I replied to every one of them. I've got them still, and some of them were marvellous. What meant more than anything was that people cared, and the reaction to the launch of the Aero 8, where we had more than 80,000 hits on the Internet site alone after the unveiling, suggests that they still do care, ten years on.'

Charles's father, Peter, had every right to be even more upset by the programme than Charles was, because the implication was that this was a regime he had allowed to survive far beyond what Harvey-Jones saw as its sell-by date. Charles knew his father was tougher than that and, anyway, he'd actually seen it all before. 'He wasn't as hurt as you might imagine, because he's a trooper. The BBC's *Wheelbase* programme came to the factory in 1967, not long before the launch of the Plus 8, and did a whole programme on Morgan. Their premise was "Morgan have lost the American market, so they will disappear. Emissions regulations will come in and they won't be able to survive." The impression was that that was the only reason they wanted to make the programme. The public relations man from Shell suspected the same. He had lunch with my father and said to him, "For God's sake, Peter, watch out for this programme. I know what the agenda is – The End of Morgan, that's the title."

'Of course people had been saying the same sort of thing about Morgan for ever, but in the end the programme was remembered for different reasons, because my father and Maurice Owen turned the message around very neatly. The Plus 8 was in development, and the final shot was the presenter against the backdrop of the Malvern Hills, saying, "But Morgan have something up their sleeves, and news of their death may be premature, because here is the new Morgan. It has a V8 engine, it weighs less than the existing Plus 4, and it is the future, we think, for the company." Which was the cue for Maurice to start the engine and drive away with growling exhausts and showers of dust. It was brilliant timing . . .'

Some thirty-three years after that neat piece of opportunism, and a decade after the first *Troubleshooter* episode, Morgan had the opportunity to resolve what might still have been seen by many people as unfinished business, when they agreed to have Sir John Harvey-Jones back. 'We discussed it,' says Charles, 'and we knew that things were very different. On the positive side, the first series did start people thinking again about manufacturing, and it was the precursor of all those programmes which make people within businesses think a bit harder by telling people on the outside what business actually is.

'This time we weren't asking Harvey-Jones for his advice, we were asking more for ratification of what we had achieved in the interim. Knowing his previous ambivalence to the company it was a nervous moment, of course, but in the event it was fine. Oddly, my father was less concerned about it than I was and our biggest concern was about whether or not to show him the new car, which still hadn't been seen by anyone outside of the development team. Sir John isn't really an aficionado of cars, or a connoisseur of sports cars, so we had to ask ourselves whether he would understand it or not. But of course we couldn't resist the opportunity of talking to an audience of nearly nine million people . . .'

It worked out very positively – far more positively, in fact, than some of the still highly cynical Troubleshooter's other return visits. Harvey-Jones prefaced his return by saying that Morgan had been so angry with him the first time around that it had taken him ten years to get back – and in the meantime Charles had become managing director. He was impressed by what had changed, especially within the production process, and even managed to be sanguine about what had not – notably the character of the product. The main changes he saw were a build sequence down from forty-eight days per car to seventeen, and only half the 'work-in-progress' taking up valuable space and materials. He noted that they were still pushing cars across the yard, but at least they weren't pushing them uphill any more, and he even ventured that the process was looking more like a production line. He was beaming when he found Dave Day, the chassis foreman whose response to the question about thirty years of changes had somehow summed up the first programme. He asked him the same thing again, and this time the answer was different. Dave had seen an awful lot of changes, and changes which made the whole process easier and more efficient – including laser cutting many bodywork blanks, superforming the wings, and may other new developments. Charles agreed that, in that respect, Harvey-Jones had been right from the start: the customer actually isn't worried that the panels are laser cut rather than hand cut; on the contrary, what the customer is interested in more than anything is the improved quality that such things can bring.

Harvey-Jones, obviously warming to the changes, smiled. 'I must say, there's a transformed feel about the place, and it's bloody good.' He noted that production had increased from 420 cars a year, when he was last there, to 580 cars a year already, and with plans to move up to 700 in the foreseeable future. Having seen the new car, and obviously been impressed by it in just the same way as *Wheelbase* had been impressed by the Plus 8 so many years before, he had one major concern: he could not see how they could fit in capacity for a completely new model. If it was a success, he reckoned, 'You'll have a tiger by the tail'. But his summing up this time suggested that he was more impressed by what had happened at Malvern Link than anyone might have expected him to be. 'I would not have believed,' he said, 'that Morgan would have had the ability, or the will, to change as completely as they have . . .'

Charles was not so surprised, because he had always insisted the changes were beginning anyway and, while he freely admits that Harvey-Jones got some things right the first time around, he still defends that. 'He was quite right that the company wasn't going anywhere. What he didn't give credit for, however, was the fact that I was there wanting to change things, and a lot of young people had joined the company. Even Dave Day, contrary to the famous "no changes" quote, was anything but a stick in the mud – in fact by the time Sir John came back he was deeply involved in the trial build programme for the Aero 8 chassis. Some exciting things were happening even when he was there in 1989, but they ignored all that. I admit, though, he did suddenly make me think, what's it all about? . . .'

That is a thought shared not only by Morgan people but also by observers throughout the industry, many of them quite cynical about Morgan's image, but most of them intrigued by the company's promised future – personified by the Aero 8. Andrew English, the *Daily Telegraph* motoring correspondent who memorably described the Aero 8 on its unveiling as looking like Clarence the cross-eyed lion and dubbing it 'the first strabismic sports car', knows that Morgan does not follow the usual rules. 'Of course Sir John Harvey-Jones was right,' he says, 'but he was also wrong. Because, while Morgan could have improved their production methods and made more cars, that misses the point. People buy Morgans as much for the craft and skills that made them as for their appearance and performance – although I'm pleased to note that nowadays it is gravity that helps the cars down the hill to the next production stage rather than men with muscled forearms and well-scraped boots.

'And what a fearless and valiant cove is the Morgan owner. On the track, an implacable foe, but once off they are firm friends who would lend their last spanner. On the road, Morgan owners are a constant source of wonder, as they hurtle, flies in their teeth and roaring in their ears, across countries and even continents. They seem transfixed by the flickering instruments, the bonnet louvres and the winged badge. For them the journey seems an end in itself. No, it's not a rational choice, the ash-framed sports car from Malvern, but it is an authentic one. As for the new Aero 8, I and several others have drooled over the chassis engineering, the obvious performance capability and admired the pride and skill that made it happen. I still think it's boss-eyed, but it wouldn't stop me owning one . . .'

In 1999, another *Telegraph* (and *Daily Express*) writer, Anthony Ffrench-Constant, took a new four-seater Morgan a very long way indeed to find the best view of the total eclipse for *Top Gear* magazine, but looking back on it he can see the complexities of the Morgan experience. 'It took just 15 of the 3,571, solar-eclipse-chasing miles of a round trip to Romania,' he says, 'to fall deeply in loathe with the Morgan 4/4's endearing eccentricities. The hood – in spite of requiring twenty minutes plus several Band Aids to remove – fits as snugly as any tarpaulin thrown over a haystack. So it tends to rain on the inside, and the cockpit air can be thicker with spray than the perfume section of a large department store. The three tiny wipers appear to have been constructed by those Vietnamese children who make helicopter gunships out of Coke cans for the tourists, and serve as much real purpose as the Austrian navy. At speed the car is so noisy that the fitting of a stereo constitutes optimism akin to a mouse crawling up an elephant's leg intent on rape. And over the average road surface the car endangers all but the most secure fillings with a ride like a frog in a sock. Furthermore, a toddler armed with a feather duster could break and enter in ten seconds flat, so even hasty trips to the gentleman's convenience must be accompanied by every scrap of luggage that can't be nailed down.

'However, in spite of the fact that assorted items of trim disintegrated like a flower arrangement in a thunderstorm, the Morgan proved mechanically unburstable and, mile upon mile, I found myself growing grudgingly fond of the damned thing. Like a favoured horse that you should have had destroyed years ago, but haven't quite the heart . . .'

Looking more closely at the company's business philosophy, Richard Feast, editor at large of the highly respected industry observer *Automotive World*, says, 'Personally, I can't see the attraction. Fortunately for Morgan, there are enough people who can. Morgan is a company in the balance. It is a

Mercedes-Benz or a Ferrari with a different scale and style. The reason: it has consistently offered products people want, at prices they can afford. Its cost base (including modest expectations by shareholders and minimal investment in product and plant until recently) and a full order book for as long as anyone can remember, mean it doesn't need to sell cars in millions. The Morgan owner gets no discount and has to pay in full before delivery. How many car makers are in that position today? As long as Morgan can keep demand ahead of supply – which favourably affects residual values – the mystique continues. But it probably had to step up the glacial pace of its evolution. Four-year waiting lists are nothing to be proud of. The issue presented an interesting business dilemma: how much change could the marque absorb? These are early days – the Aero 8 isn't on sale so far – but my guess is that the new model and the factory floor improvements will be good for a few more decades. I hope so. The world needs more eccentricities like Morgan.'

Jeff Daniels, engineer, technical writer, formerly project officer (cars) with the Consumer Association, and a regular columnist for *Motor Industry Management*, *European Automotive Design*, *Evo* magazine and *The Economist* Intelligence Unit's quarterly publications, balances the technical view with the commercial one: 'Retro styling, a cramped interior, rickshaw ride, noisy, hard to drive – it doesn't sound like a recipe for success. But try this instead: the last traditional sports car from the Great Days (whenever they were), still built in the same way as they always were by a team of dedicated craftsmen still working for the descendants of the company's founding father.

'Mix that with a deliberate policy of restricting output (and thus capital commitment) and letting the waiting list stretch to ludicrous lengths, at least by any normal industry standards. For as long as you can get away with it, abstain from spending money, or blurring the image with new or additional models. Then, if you're lucky (but only if you're lucky), people will come to revere you, despite the impressions of that opening sentence.

'Morgan proves it. Morgan has been lucky. Many of the people who aspire to Morgan ownership have never driven one, still less lived with one, but they hanker after a dose of yesteryear – of feeling like granddad when he was courting grandma in the 1930s. And there will always be enough of those people to keep the waiting list long. Probably. Either that or the Aero 8 will turn out to be a great car. Possibly . . .'

And finally, from a man who has known Morgans – the cars, the company and the people – for many years, Phil Llewellin, a motoring writer for newspapers and magazines too numerous to mention. 'After visiting Morgan for the first time, way back in the 1960s,' he says, 'I honed and polished all the cliches about a delightfully eccentric family business operating in a time-warp while 'Land of Hope and Glory' played in the background. But the olde-worlde image belies a very shrewd operation. For instance, Peter Morgan once told me, "We wouldn't be sitting here now, talking about the company's present and future" if he or his father had decided that a Morgan car should be powered by a Morgan engine. It would have been the automotive equivalent of "vanity publishing", so, of course, it never happened.

'There is a very small market for neo-classical sports cars, so the temptation to spend big money expanding the factory has been resisted. The legendary waiting list that goes out of sight when times are good comes down to a more realistic two or three years when potential customers decide that they can survive without a Morgan after all. However, in 2000, Morgan is on target to produce fourteen cars a week. And while that isn't a big number in itself, it does represent an increase of 50 per cent since my first pilgrimage to Malvern Link. As Peter Morgan commented, a few years ago, "We've made a profit every year since 1909, so we must be doing something right."'

That's one observation that any outsider, however sceptical, could hardly argue with.

8 The Third Generation: Back to the Future

TEN YEARS ON, Charles Morgan believes that while the infamous *Troubleshooter* episode was one of the lowest points of his time with the company, it was also a catalyst for change – but change in Morgan's way, not change in Harvey-Jones's way – and change that ultimately made the company stronger and better able to survive and grow.

'I think probably the worst thing of all was the occasional falling out that father and I had after the Harvey-Jones programme,' he says, 'mainly over whether I should ever have invited him in in the first place. Although the BBC approached us, they certainly wouldn't have come if I'd said no. I said yes, expecting a different treatment and I suppose my father's argument was "for God's sake, you'd worked in the media for ten years – how could you have landed us in that one?" My reaction was, "well was it all bad?": I suppose my father took a long time to come around to it but now, he would agree, it wasn't entirely negative for the company. In fact we learned a lot from it, as you do any time you invite someone else in.'

It was barely five years since Charles had arrived himself, and when he had, he was probably coming from an even less likely background for a motor manufacturer than his father had been when he joined the company from the army in the late 1940s.

Like HFS Morgan and Peter Morgan, Charles Peter Henry Morgan is an only son – in his case with two sisters, Sonia and Jill. He was born on 29 July 1951, not too long after his father had joined his grandfather at the Morgan Motor

Company Ltd. He went to The Elms preparatory school in Colwall, then, like his father, to Oundle, the Northampton- shire public school with a reputation for promoting engineer- ing subjects.

He was brought up, just as his father was, against the comfortable background of Morgan family life. He remem- bers his grandfather, HFS, very well. 'I would have been about eight when he died in 1959, but we saw him very often. He used to come and stay with us every week when we were living at Braeside on the side of the hills. I used to go and stay with him in Maidenhead, too, at Oakwood, a house built in the grounds of Cannon Hill. He was very good with children. He was a charismatic character who had models and trains to play with, and he was always on the go. He was a bit of a child himself in a way, so being with him was always interesting – like going to somebody's laboratory. The things he made really worked. There's something different about making soap boxes that don't work, but soap boxes that go very fast with minimum effort delight a child. I think that's why my appreciation of engineering is quite strong – even if my ability to achieve results myself is rather low.'

It was by no means a foregone conclusion that Charles would join the family firm once he was old enough to start job hunting. As it turned out, Oundle was a valuable experience, as it had been for his father, and as the combination of Crystal Palace Engineering College and the railways at Swindon had been for his grandfather. 'At Oundle every term you took off your school clothes, put on an overall and went to work under a foreman from the local area to learn about a trade – either foundry work or lathe operation or whatever. Sadly, nowadays all that's gone. Nowadays they're building imitation Lotus Sevens; what I learned was how to operate a lathe, how to work a foundry and how to smelt metal. I also learned what it's like to be the oily rag, the bloke who's shouted at and cuffed round the ear if he drops a bit of aluminium on the floor or that kind of thing. I did have that training.'

Peter Morgan knows that Charles is not a formally trained engineer in the sense that he is himself or his father was, but he thinks the basics Charles learned at Oundle were very important. 'He likes the idea of coachbuilding and so on, but he's never been a model maker, for instance, which is a shame. I love building models – virtually all the ones in the display cabinet in the entrance lobby are mine. But I've always said to Charles, "you won't be as good at doing a lot of things as people here are, but what you do want to be able to do is to talk to them intelligently about what you're doing. If you can't do that you're lost. Make sure you know a little bit about what the job is".'

These days, Charles knows quite a bit about that: 'I think the one thing that probably was instilled into me very early on was the engineering appreciation – not the engineering skills, sadly, but certainly the appreciation. Accompanying my father on a number of occasions, on trials, rallies, test drives or whatever – and seeing my grandfather put things together, for me and the other grandchildren, things like toys and models – all that had an influence too.'

That influence did not take him straight to Pickersleigh Road, however. From Oundle he went to Sussex University and studied for a BA honours degree in the History of Art, and from there he went to spend a year as a bookseller while he planned his future. 'Then I worked in the film industry, which isn't exactly engineering but it's certainly technical. I worked as a cameraman for ITN, and that also gave me an appreciation of electronics, because video came in while I was working in the industry. I suppose you could argue that I have a technical background. I've certainly handled some expensive and complicated kit, put it that way.'

He was aware, from an early age, of being surrounded by cars. 'When I was at university I had a Morgan, which was unusual, but I promptly lost my full licence because it was too much temptation for a student. The first thing I ever drove was a Trojan ride-on lawnmower, and my father had tinkered with that by adding some strategically placed concrete to improve the balance. I really learned to drive on an F-type three-wheeler. That was my grandmother's car, and it's still in the works. It was very good training because it had a completely crash gearbox, with no syncromesh at all. It also required a lot of thought when you were driving it, because the brakes weren't very good. But it went pretty well, and with one person in it you could get it up to about 70mph. It was a superb machine, and at sixteen I was quite young to be experiencing those sorts of thrills. But I loved it, of course.

'I was seventeen when I got my full licence, and I did a trial that year I think, but not very successfully as I remember it. After that I did quite a few trials with the Morgan team, which was really good fun. I think trials give you everything you need to know for other kinds of motor sport. You have the rallying aspect because you have to make certain checkpoints in certain times, so it may not be about ultimate speed but there's certainly the discipline of learning about average speed, and how to keep a good average up. Then you have to be able to cope with tiredness. And when you come to the hills themselves it is just as adrenalin-pumping as motor racing – I mean, those hills; you might only achieve a maximum of about 40mph but it still feels like 200. Then of course to get up the hills at all you're using the maximum performance of the car. You know what it's like: 8,000 revs and you're still going nowhere because it's in a hole.

'I haven't done a trial now for a long time, but I would love to do some again. I love things like the Land's End because it's almost like a secret event; nobody knows it's going on, because it all happens between about four o'clock in the morning and nine. You also get to see lovely roads that you'd never normally go on, and a lot of people in Morgans. I think trials are also seen by us as a bit of a test track, because if things don't fall off in a trial it tends to be quite a robust kind of car.'

Charles Morgan, as third generation head of the company, went on to have a considerable career in racing, but he is well aware of trials as part of his heritage. 'It's where the family came in as manufacturers. Trials were a very big thing. In my grandfather's day they were as important as major rallies are today. Pathé News would report on them, and they were tough – it was by no means certain that you'd finish. My grandfather definitely saw trials, combined with circuit work, as the only way to test the product properly. Very early on he combined the trials side with high speeds round a banked circuit, including his famous hour record at Brooklands in 1912.

'He also realised that competition was a very good way to gain publicity – at least when the newsreels were filming. But that started to die out in the 1920s when mass-produced cars came in and trials became more of an enthusiasts' area. Still, it was always good for business, because the bedrock support for Morgan depended a lot on the integrity the car had in competition, and still does. Even nowadays, in a series like the 750 Motor Club's Roadsports championship, you get somebody turning up in something like the latest Porsche GT3, thinking he'll walk it – and actually he's beaten by a Plus 8. It's very satisfying, and that's the heart of club motor racing.'

Putting the Plus 8's longevity into perspective, perhaps, that model had already been in production for seventeen years by the time Charles finally joined the family firm, in 1985. He arrived just before his thirty-fourth birthday and just after the birth of his son, Xan, in January 1985, to his first wife, Vivien Lipschitz, whom he married in 1979.

Charles's son is fifteen now, and Charles has two daughters, Harriet and Kate, by his current wife Jane, 'There's no way I would ever push them to come here just because they are next generation Morgan. It's certainly no foregone conclusion that you follow the family path. I think that for me to come to work for the company was a bit more of a struggle than, say, Matthew [Matthew Parkin, the current sales and marketing manager] getting to work for the company. I had to prove that I hadn't got the seat just because I'm family; I'd got it because I'd a lot to offer. I'm always aware of the danger that people will say you're where you are because of who you are, and I really don't want that, for me or for my children.

'I remember the questions I was always asked when I arrived. "You were an ITN cameraman; don't you find all this rather boring?" But it isn't; it's exactly the opposite. Even after ten years of ITN camera work I wasn't bored with that either, but the snag with television as a medium is that you get obsessed with a particular programme, then it goes out and that's it, finished. It's such an anti-climax. You get this extraordinary sense of "now what?" and with news it's probably even worse. You can actually risk your life for what's supposed to be a slot on News at Ten at maybe item fifteen, then they cut it down to one minute thirty-five, and you think, "why did I do that?". You come back and people say, "where have you been?" and you say, "I've been dodging bullets in Afghanistan, I nearly lost my life". That can get very hard and it's why some people in the business get cynical as they get older. I didn't want that to happen to me.'

There was a deeper reason for the timing behind Charles's change in direction. He really didn't want to die for the job. 'I went to Afghanistan, on the biggest trip I'd ever done and it was the worst trip I ever did. It was a wonderful eye opener. It was the toughest thing I'd ever done in my life, and to be honest I really didn't think that we'd get out of it – I seriously didn't. It puts business problems into perspective; you don't die doing this, but on the other hand it's just as important to get it right. So it was at that point that I came home, sat down and thought, "time to do something different . . .".'

Even given the enormity of that situation, Charles still insists that there was no family pressure on him at this point, from either his wife or his father. 'My first wife had virtually gone off to do her own thing by that time, anyway, and although we'd just had our son we were semi-separated. He was born almost immediately before I went to Afghanistan, so I wasn't really a very good dad at the time, was I? I went off for three months, and that made me think about things, too.

'Now my children are very much a part of things, and I think they're going through a very similar thing to what I went through. I have two daughters who I take to school in a four-seater Morgan every day, and my children have been to a lot of the GT races we've been involved in; they've been testing the new car. I picked Xan up for half-term recently in the prototype Aero 8, while the whole of his school stood and watched. It was great. As a fifteen-year-old kid you remember these sort of things. I always remember my father picking me up in the Plus 8 the year I left Oundle, and he spun the wheels all the way up the road. It's terrible to show off in front of your children, but I'm sure his father did the same kind of thing with him. It's probably why the Morgan family weren't always popular with the establishment.

But Charles knows that being in Malvern is a big part of why Morgan became the way Morgan is, and he knows his history. 'Malvern was a big tourist resort at the turn of the century. People didn't go to Spain; they tended to take holidays in the UK, and Malvern became a focus for a lot of odd motoring history. The very first car that was driven from France into England by the man who started the RAC was driven to Malvern. Daimler in particular, being in Coventry, came here to test cars, and that meant driving them to the tops of the hills. The big thing in 1900 was to get a car on to the top of the Beacon. The other thing was that there were several large bicycle manufacturers, Santler included, in Malvern, and of course the early cars tended to be made at bicycle premises, with very similar technologies. The early bicyclists really didn't like early motoring. Malvern was one of the first places to have the roads tarmacked, but the dirt roads were simply sprayed over with a thin film of tar on the dust. When the tar melted the bicycles just stuck. The other thing was the cars didn't so much frighten the horses and cattle as kick up the dust, and the dust wasn't just ordinary dust, it was horse manure dust – and we think we have emissions problems now.'

The company had its logistical problems when Charles arrived – notably not being able to build cars quickly enough to keep up with orders – but he soon identified what he saw as a bigger problem. 'Generally things weren't too bad, but I have to say, and I'm probably being a bit arrogant here, when I arrived I didn't think the quality was as good as it should have been, and I think we were suffering from that. We were getting a lot of letters of complaint saying "how come if I buy my Honda nothing ever rusts, but if I buy my Morgan you're still not zinc-plating my nuts and bolts"; that type of thing.

'My father had done thirty-five or forty years of sterling work, but by that time he wasn't, perhaps, quite as active as he would have been twenty years before. And the whole factory wasn't, perhaps, quite on top of the quality control situation. The first thing I did was zinc-plate all the nuts and bolts, then installed a new paint plant so the paint was much improved. We could paint the wings off the car, so we didn't have the ridiculous situation of corrosion coming from the inside of the wheelarch outwards. Of course, it added to costs – but that was the quality people wanted. In fact, I found out very quickly that people were quite prepared to pay extra if the quality was there.'

Charles had a good deal of discussion with his father on the real basics of the company – its size, its continuing independence, and its general directions into the future. And with his art history background and his media contacts, he had taken an interest in the marketing side of the company long before he actually came to join it full-time. When the Plus 8 was new, and Charles was only seventeen, he had suggested painting the cars for the London Motor Show orange, and he hit the spot. '1968 was when I said paint them orange, and it just so happened that almost everything was orange and yellow in 1968, so I'd just absolutely caught the Zeitgeist. It doesn't happen all the time.'

In July 1974, just before his twenty-third birthday, Charles was involved in a publicity stunt which bridged the whole history of Morgan to date – racing from London to Glasgow and back to London via a very circuitous route against the man who had scored one of Morgan's most famous victories in the company's early years, W Gordon McMinnies. McMinnies, who had written the very first Morgan Runabout test as 'Platinum', and who won the 1913 French Cyclecar Grand Prix for Morgan, was now eighty-eight and he took the train, impeccably turned out in suit and raincoat. Charles, living in Hampstead, with long hair, flared jeans and big 1970s collars, shared a Plus 8 (the well-known BUY 600M) with William Franklin. While McMinnies sped along at 100mph in the train, Charles told the press he had stuck strictly to speed limits, but in spite of the car's route adding up to just over 1,300 miles against the train's 1,200, and Charles finding time for both a bit of filming and a leisurely breakfast en route, the Morgan won. They finished the twenty-four-hour event at an average speed of around 57mph, and by the time they reached Bristol on the way back to London they were five hours ahead of the train. Petrol and oil for the car cost £30; McMinnies' seven-day first-class sleeper ticket cost £40. 'You can read, write, sleep or watch the countryside from the train,' he told reporters, 'but I have been on roads which are smoother and quieter than some of the tracks.' Charles did not say how comfortable twenty-four hours in a Plus 8 had been, but it was a nice meeting of the generations and very good publicity.

Charles also designed the factory sales brochures in the mid-1970s, and when he finally did arrive at Pickersleigh Road a decade later, there was more of that to come: 'My initial role was organising things like motor shows and publicity and that kind of thing. I joined as marketing manager, while Derek Day was the sales manager. I very quickly realised that the real dilemma was about production; it wasn't about the sales as such, and the best thing we could do was to improve the quality.

'I was very interested in what Maurice Owen was doing; we worked quite closely together on a couple of projects, like improving the performance of the fuel-injected car, for instance. We were determined it was going to be a lot more powerful than it had been. Maurice had been with the company for ages, but I think by this time he lacked an ear. You know he'd developed things like independent suspension for the rear, only to be told "forget it Maurice, put it back in the garage, it costs far too much".

'He needed a sympathetic ear. Part of the problem was that there was no pressure from the market to do things; almost the opposite. You know, "keep the sliding pillars to the very end", that kind of thinking. Maurice wasn't like that. He was an engineer like any other and he kept having new ideas. He also had ideas about building the car, and ways in which it could be built more efficiently. But Maurice was not good at dealing with the shop floor. He was a fine engineer, a very good race mechanic, and an extremely good man if you wanted an engine shoehorned into a car. He was the perfect person for that – but he didn't have the patience to convince the shop floor that his idea was a good one. In fact almost the opposite; they would literally dread Maurice coming in. Sadly, I think he was that old school of motor manufacturing really, where you had your development engineers or your race car team and then you had your production engineers – and the two never met, never even spoke to each other.

'That just doesn't work nowadays. I mean, look at BMW. What are BMW doing with their Formula One project? They are actually getting people from the 3-Series assembly lines to go and spend a day at Silverstone or wherever. What a bloody good idea in terms of motivation. There's absolutely nothing more motivating than motor sport.'

Charles is proving that theory today with the motor racing genesis of the Aero 8 – surely his defining project to date in the same way that the Plus 8 will always be associated with his father.

In the mid-1980s, Charles thinks that lack of motivation was another of the company's problems and that the situation with Maurice Owen summed it up. 'I think it affected the development of Morgans at the time. There may have been fascinating things going on in Maurice's workshops but absolutely none of it was ever seeing the light of day in production. He kept us in America through the workshops' fiddling about, and he did a lot of other things, but there's a lot more he could have been allowed to do.' It was the thorny old subject of Morgans and change: Charles wanted to start things off in new directions; his father was far more cautious, but when push came to shove Peter was still really in charge, even though, in theory, he was past retirement age. Oddly perhaps, Charles says, now, that there was very little pressure, either, from the suppliers wanting things to change, or even from the customers. 'Every year, or at least every couple of years, there would be new engine specs to be engineered into the cars. When I first joined, the emissions levels changed so often that we had a new model every couple of years just to keep up with legislation. I took on responsibility for type approval, and back then there were forty tests for every different model; it's fifty-three now but there were forty then. I did all the paperwork for that and kept it up to date. It's terribly expensive when you're only writing the costs off against a limited number of cars, but you don't do all the forty-odd tests in one hit. What you do is work out that over the next three months you have to do emissions, noise, radio suppression and so on. Then we would plan to do other tests in, say, six months' time. It was almost a full-time job, but I was combining it with the marketing by then, and already thinking that what I was really interested in was the production process. Then Harvey-Jones comes along, and more or less distils all my thoughts. He said, "it's all very well you beavering away, getting the car type-approved and being proud of getting it back into America, but you're not making enough of them, you're not making enough money, and you don't have an iota of a chance of getting a handle on the waiting list problem for the moment . . .".'

So John Harvey-Jones and *Troubleshooter*, for all the bad press and the cries of 'foul', actually did set some important wheels in motion at Morgan.

The years leading up to the programme had generally been good ones, as Charles readily admits. 'When I arrived in 1985 we had had problems in America, but they were nothing like the real problems we had had with America in the early 1960s. Back then my father, just because of the way the market was, had a situation where he was only building around four hundred cars a year, but three hundred of them were going to America, and that was too many. What happened then was a combination of circumstances. The dealers were slightly tricky and suddenly there was a huge recession in about 1962 or 1963, centred in the defence industry on the West Coast. We were very badly hit, with our market going from about three hundred cars to one hundred, virtually overnight. In spite of all the success, in spite of the class win at Le Mans, in spite of Lew Spencer winning every roadgoing sports car race in America in Baby Doll, it was collapsing around us. Father went out to try and revive the market and that was the start of his travelling as a spokesman for the marque.

'I think he did pretty well. He did well. He generated a lot of orders. He made great contacts through the clubs, appealing, really, on a direct basis. So the market didn't entirely disappear, but its collapse suddenly meant that we had to develop Germany, France, the European market in short, in a way that up to that time we'd never really done. As a result, the company became much more balanced and nowadays it isn't like, say, Jaguar where 75 or 80 per cent of production goes to America, so you have to listen all the time to American dealers.

'The American market is so big you almost have to have a separate organisation running it. Back then, we had officially-appointed dealers who were good: Fergus Fine Cars in New York, for instance, was managed by a nephew of Harry Ferguson, the tractor man – who was originally also Borgward's main dealer in America. Fergus were big business, the showroom was right in the middle of New York, but Morgan was big business to them, too. The same with René Pallandini; we had a big, big American following. I didn't go to California, but I went with my father to New York, and we went to Sardi's Restaurant, we were wined and dined, we went to the New York Motor Show – it was all very high profile stuff. Then the Plus 8 came along and the rest is history so far as America goes . . .'

Still, twenty years on when Charles came to the company, Morgan had weathered that storm and looked quite secure for the long haul. 'We were profitable at the time, but mainly because my father is a good businessman who watches the bottom line like a hawk. In that sense I respect him wholeheartedly, but having said that, I think the problem was that by then he didn't have the energy to have a long-term plan for the company any more. That perhaps meant that he couldn't see the point of saying, maybe we'll dip our profits this year to increase profitability in the future. He was very risk averse, and wanted a fairly easy life. By that time he just didn't want the pressure. I suppose what he has accepted now is that I'm prepared to take the pressure myself. I hope I'll be the same as he is long-term, because ultimately I want the same things for the company.'

By the time Charles joined on a day-to-day basis, he already knew the workings of the company well. 'When I was working with ITN I used to go to meetings as often as I could as a non-executive director, which wasn't too difficult because I used to work four days off and four days on. I kept up with news at the company – so long as it wasn't one of the times when I'd gone to Iran for six months. When I was in England it wasn't difficult for me to get to a directors' meeting. At the time, of course, the directors were very much my father's team. He'd mainly promoted people from within, with the exception of Maurice who'd come in from outside, and to very good effect – and these guys were Morgan men through and through. They would die for Morgan, they had Morgan printed on their hearts.

'Having said that, an outsider might think, God, this board has absolutely no go at all. So if you like, I was the radical new boy who came in and said things like "why don't we paint the cars orange; why don't we do this or why don't we do that?" They said "good idea, let's try it". But when I went to work there permanently it was different. Then, I either had to toe the line, or take my ideas a lot further – and for a while I couldn't do that. I simply didn't have the experience. And, anyway, it is difficult to do that with your own father in charge; you can't walk in and say, "I can do it dad, I'll take over now ..." any more than he did with his father.

'When my father arrived, in many ways he had exactly the same situation I had. He took on a lot of responsibility with engine negotiations and so on but he worked alongside my grandfather, not taking over from him. But he felt confident, because he'd already done something different. I'd been an ITN cameraman, then set up a video business, with money from the City and employing twenty people; in the Army he'd been responsible for maybe five hundred vehicles and managing two hundred people. Then he has to come here and say, "yes dad, no dad" and wait until 1957 to do what he wants. But from 1957 to 1975, he's the tour de force. We have the Plus 8, we have the Plus 4 Plus, we have waiting lists, we have him as the saviour of the American market, we have the development of the worldwide market for Morgans, in Germany, France, Italy and Spain. Then I arrived in 1985 – and from 1985 to 1995 he's coasting, at least by his earlier standards. Then Harvey-Jones came along.'

Charles admits that, given the family history, the motoring world was already watching him closely. 'Harvey-Jones catapulted both my father and I into a rather dubious sort of celebrity. Even in the late 1970s, *Car* magazine had said Morgan was fossilised, with LJK Setright saying something like, "well, you know, the sliding pillar was a good idea but quite frankly they ought to be on to something new by now ..." and so on. What's interesting is that when Harvey-Jones came along it was exactly the right time for change, and I give him credit for drumming that message in.

'He realised that, given the way the market was at the time, the company had to go somewhere. He thought, obviously, "Peter's old – not that old but a bit old for this business – and Charles is quite clearly full of ideas but hasn't been here that long. The workforce don't know where they're going and they're drifting a bit. They're having a very easy life, probably not working very hard, pushing cars around, looking busy, but not actually doing very much".'

A decade on from the programme, Charles is more philosophical. 'If you read Harvey-Jones's book it's much more balanced than the TV programme, and what he actually says is, "if Charles is given his head and if Peter supports him it will be OK. But if the two of them end up having a row and falling out, it will be the typical family business story – where the third generation is the one that fails".'

It quite obviously put a lot of strain on the working relationship between Charles and Peter, but the personal relationship was strong enough to stand the pressure. 'My father was mortified that the company was criticised in any way at all, which was quite right. But don't forget that the other thing he latched on to was the support we got from Morgan owners, which was massive. It wasn't just Morgan owners either. We took more orders after that programme than at any other time in our history – very few of which came good, but it was nice support. And I think that in a way that actually goes to prove the point that the kind of orders that were around at the time were the kind of notional orders that were floating around at that time for a lot of people in the industry.

'What Harvey-Jones didn't do was predict the recession, which happened only around a year later. The British recession was very big; our German market couldn't have carried us through it, nor could our American market – not if we'd doubled production as he'd suggested.' So was the recession the toughest thing that has happened since Charles has been at Morgan? He is slightly embarrassed by his answer: 'No. It sounds awful to say it but we were buffered so much by the existing orders that we really didn't feel it at all. Having said that, we didn't predict it either, so in a sense there was nothing very clever about it.'

Back on Harvey-Jones, he adds, 'The other thing, I think, was that he completely misunderstood coachbuilding, and still fails to understand it. In fact, even I have to interrogate our coachbuilding methods all the time and think, look, what is it about this that really is the key to its customer value? What is it the customer really wants? I hope I'm going to get this right, because I still believe that people want a car that's built by skilled people specifically for them, using technology that actually deals with raw materials that are tactile and feel valuable. That includes things like hard woods, and aluminium, materials that you might even want on your dining-room table, things that you really want to touch and feel.'

Part of this love of materials probably goes back to Charles's early arts background, but nowadays he sees it as a core part of the Morgan philosophy, both structurally and aesthetically. He looks at the way other designers, and not only car designers, use the same materials structurally and for appearance, and ponders what they are missing. 'When you look at some of these materials structurally as well as aesthetically, you think how much more interesting they are, and how satisfying to make them work in practice.

'The wood industry is currently undergoing a major revival. But to use wood cost effectively you mustn't waste it. In the car industry people have thought, "I can't use it structurally, it's only good as a veneer." But I'm not talking about wood veneer for the dashboard. At Morgan we use wood for three reasons: to keep weight down; to make our cars last longer; and to protect the occupants in the event of an accident. Through our testing at MIRA we have found that our wood acts just like a hammer handle and absorbs energy. Therefore our passenger compartment is a more comfortable environment and can also take shocks. The incidental aesthetic consideration is that if you cut a piece of hardwood through the grain you can see how old it is, how individual it is, and how intrinsically valuable it is. It's wonderful stuff.

The process of coachbuilding still relies on people but, nowadays, those people have to be wood technologists, not chippies. I think Morgan is the first coachbuilder to think like this; if you went to, say, Park Ward they'd say "I'm sorry, we're traditional chippies, we can't do that." That's not our way. At Morgan we have taken coachbuilding one stage further.'

Charles is aware, too, even though it happened long before his time, that the one time Morgan tried to change its methods purely out of fashion, with the glass fibre-bodied Plus 4 Plus, it was a disaster. 'It was, but at least we tried. In truth, it was a disaster because nobody had thought the project through sufficiently to realise that the people in the factory when confronted by a plastic-bodied car would think, my God, that's the end of my job. So it was done rather ineptly in that respect.

He admits, too, that had Morgan stuck with the Plus 4 Plus, whether for better or worse, the whole story of Morgan thereafter might have been very different. If Morgan had carried on down that path, the Morgan might just have become everybody else's car, and then the company might not have survived at all. Charles is pleased that the company never went down that road. 'I think the problem with glass fibre is that it still isn't a very stable material, long term, unless it's very heavy. It's fine for a prototype, and for a car you want to use for five years it's probably OK, but a twenty-year-old glass fibre car? Look at the panel gaps, the ripples and cracks . . .' What he really means is, it is fine for other people, but best not for Morgan.

Considering that he does not think of himself as an engineer, Charles Morgan has made considerable efforts to understand not only the materials that are important to Morgan, but also the methods. In the aftermath of the *Troubleshooter* programme (stung, as he admits, by some of the criticisms in it), he enrolled part-time at Coventry Polytechnic and from 1990 to 1993 spent three years learning about engineering management, first for a Diploma in Modern Manufacturing, then a Master of Business Administration.

'My father thinks training on the job is invaluable and I agree, but we agree, too, that formal training is also important. Some of the people on the DMM course with me worked for Peugeot, and one of the guys I really got on well with ran the Peugeot paint shop, which was more or less a microcosm of the Morgan Motor Company. They have around two hundred people and their responsibility is to paint every Peugeot. A lot of his problems were just the same as mine.

'Coventry was a fine place for sharing ideas, because the people on the course weren't just students, they were working in the industry, on a management level. The basis of the course wasn't just thinking about your own company; you were also put into that blue-sky situation – the "what-if you did run a particular kind of company". Then you'd spend the weekend working out how to do it. It was a marvellous course – and, of course, definitely not only automotive, which made it even better.'

Charles used what he learned at Coventry to initiate the changes in the production process that would gradually increase production, and bring down waiting times, while also improving quality beyond all recognition. He started by adding new paint shop capacity, and continued by improving the flow of cars through the build process, but by far the biggest thing in Charles's CV to date is the Aero 8.

In the first instance, the project, growing out of the racing programme as described in Chapter 6, was only possible because of the support of the shareholders and the board. The shareholders, as ever, were entirely family, including Charles's two sisters and another incarnation of the Trust for future generations. 'My sisters don't really play an executive role, but they are invited to directors' meetings, as much as anything to get information. They're more than observers but I think they both agree their contribution has to be non-professional. What's nice is they can be there and see what's going on, so it's all completely transparent. Even if they want to query, say, the telephone bill they can. And they can bring their ideas. It's more than a family board, but why it's the way it is at the moment is that clearly the company is making a large investment in its future. In order to get the benefit of the shareholders' support you have to be open about it. You have to be able to say we're not spending it all on ornamental fountains, or whatever.'

The board includes Matthew Parkin, Tim Whitworth, Mark Aston and non-executive director Alan Garnett, who built the

Webasto company into a major original equipment supplier of sunroofs, and who contributes invaluable knowledge about the wider industry. Charles thinks the board gives the best of all worlds, the power to make decisions with the perspective to be answerable.

The Aero 8 was only possible with their support, and the support of Peter, and the people who ultimately have to build the car. 'All the shareholders, and all the company, are 160 per cent behind the new car, and to get that level of support before you've even launched a car to the public is fantastic.'

Amazingly, as ever, even given the vastly greater costs of developing any serious car in the modern world, the money to develop the Aero 8 came from the company, not the bank. As Charles says, 'the project started three years ago, but we've continued making a profit. Because we've gradually increased production, development has been financed out of cash flow, and, while that has reduced the profit levels we'd normally expect on turnover, to continue making a profit at all while supporting such a major development programme, is an achievement.

'We've been very lucky with the level of support we had from the other people involved. What BMW did that Rover have never done and Ford have never done, is they said "we must have a proper official agreement, we must plan this to the nth degree, we must go through all the stages. We must have quarterly meetings to discuss whether targets have been met, and to release payments."

'The sums involved are bigger than they have been for any previous Morgan development, but the beauty of this level of detailed planning is that you can show the board exactly where the money is going. I'm the first to admit that the way we developed cars with Land Rover and Rover mainly involved waiting for them to do things: "We'd really rather like to do this radio suppression test, so can we give you a cheque and can we do it next week?", then next week it's "We're a bit busy this week, we'll do it next week", and so on until, six months later, you're saying, "Are we going to have an American spec or not?" and wondering if you're ever going to get this car approved. With the BMW arrangement, everything was done to a date, with milestones and specific targets.'

Charles suspects his father was surprised by how the programme worked. 'He wasn't involved on a day-to-day basis, and I think he still thinks we've gone over the top in certain areas, but that's the difference between being a sort of kit-car manufacturer and a proper manufacturer. Put it that way and I think my father would agree. He'd also say, no, of course we're not a kit-car manufacturer, we have to do it the way we have to do it . . .'

This time with BMW there was never any suggestion that there should be a takeover rather than just an engine agreement. 'I think to a large degree it's down to the reputation we have in Germany as an independent manufacturer doing our own thing. I think that, and the reputation of our cars for reliability in Germany, has stood us in good stead with the people at BMW, and to an extent too with Audi and Mercedes as well, where we also know people pretty well.'

Charles says that with the Aero 8 project, BMW were thoroughly supportive. 'They supported the engineering at the top level. We dealt with Dr Gerhardt Schmidt and that was fantastic. That's how it used to be when father dealt with John Black. Back then it used to be "Peter, let's have a word about the engine you want". Now we're back to that, but sadly for the British industry, it's with a German company. But the whole industry has changed. When I joined Morgan, our contact at Rover was a commercial salesman, middle management. He would take you to lunch or whatever, as you used to back in the 1980s, and talk cars. But what could he really do? Well, not very much in reality. And at the time, of course, Rover had more than enough problems of their own.

'The Aero 8 project was a series of talented engineers banging their heads together, the team led by me and Chris Lawrence. Chris is a great doer. Together we're a good team; the ideas flow but I'm completely useless without either Chris or the rest of the team to execute them. Chris loves the idea of someone coming along and saying "OK let's try this or let's try that".

'The programme for the aluminium chassis started with me searching for materials which could provide a stiff chassis that could also be light. I went to a number of race car manufacturers and ended up at CIBA-Geigy, talking to

Professor Woodley about aluminium honeycomb. They had just provided the material for the chassis of the Ford RS200 rally car, and I believed that a chassis that was almost as stiff as that car's could be produced more economically.

'Together we designed and built a simple honeycomb tub which I brought back to Morgan for appraisal. There were still some problems to be confronted: we found that it was difficult to attach components to the basic tub, because the loads had to be spread across the honeycomb to avoid crushing it in a localised area.

'This led me to Alcan and then Banbury Research Laboratory, where Peter Schiesby showed me the research they had been doing on bonded aluminium structures. At the same time I received a letter from Jim Randle at Birmingham University, asking if they could borrow a Plus 8 to demonstrate an open car on their four-poster rig. Following on from that, Jim helped me design the rear section of the chassis to fit a Morgan ash frame and he introduced me to a company that would manufacture it for our racing programme. In 1977 we went our separate ways because there were some things we wanted to do differently. He wanted to use steel carriers for the mechanical active suspension he'd designed, where Alcan and I wanted to make an all-aluminium car – and for it to be genuinely a Morgan. Jim Randle developed his ideas in his Lea Francis project.

'We paid Jim a fee for his initial input but brought our chassis project in-house, where Chris Lawrence improved the design and we developed other important design features like the detachable front and rear sections. Those make repairs possible after a 10 to 25mph frontal impact without having to replace the main chassis, and that's a very important advantage over a design like the Lotus Elise, say.'

Charles is very serious about the new aluminium technology. 'I did a lot of research into aluminium chassis and actually joined a committee, the EPSRC – Engineering and Physical Science Research Council. There are some good people on it, including [industry analyst] Garel Rhys and Nick Stevenson of Rover. We're a think-tank. We give our opinions on the research the government funds through the universities into transport, according to three categories – telematics, lightweight cars and supply-chain improvements. Telematics aims for safer cars; lightweight vehicles means more environmentally friendly cars, through using less fuel and less materials; and better supply chain means more affordable cars. In the area of lightweight vehicles, aluminium technology is huge. But the big question has always been, "we can easily design the cars, but how do you make them repairable?" Traditionally if you had a ding in an aluminium car it would cost you a fortune; our design is planned to avoid that problem.

'The wood plays a big part in this. It has brilliant properties, including its flexibility and its ability to spring back into shape. It has a memory. Wood as a forming device behind the aluminium gives the ability for the car to regain its shape, which not many materials can do. Wood is also sustainable, replaceable, and it doesn't take a lot of energy to manufacture with it; it's a wonderful material.'

Charles's other passion nowadays is manufacturing methods, and – something that might come as a surprise to some people – production efficiency. It is not as alien a concept to Morgan as many people think. Charles's father and even his grandfather were not unaware of contemporary manufacturing methods in the 1930s. They even visited Ford at Dagenham not long before the Second World War, but did not think the majority of what they saw was appropriate to what they built. Charles is sure that being different was as important in the early days as it is today. 'There was a band of enthusiasts with people like Archie Frazer-Nash, HRG, GWK, Kimber of MG, Bentley of course, and my grandfather – who all disliked the commercialisation of the motor industry. They saw the car for the masses as being a very mundane thing. It wasn't a coachbuilt or custombuilt Phantom V, it wasn't exactly an MG or even a Morgan, it was a jalopy. For years and years, even up to my day, I told people that the Morgan actually handles, when you really drive it, it rewards you. It's a real car, not some jelly mould that you're desperately trying to get round a corner. That was even more of a contrast in the days of the three-wheeler and the Austin Seven – at least until they got the Austin Specials working.'

Charles insists the older generations were not anti-change, but it has taken mass production a long time to catch up. He also knows the Aero 8 chassis and suspension are a giant leap into the present. 'The ride over the Cotswolds to my son's school in Oxford is a marvellous test track, and it was interesting going to pick him up in the prototype Aero 8, then taking him back in my old yellow Plus 8. It's chalk and cheese. Just driving normally, journey times are roughly the same but with the Aero 8 you could probably do 20 per cent quicker, and the comfort and the relaxation at the end of the journey ... well there's really no comparison at all.' But he does not think that he has betrayed any untouchable icon by making the changes that he has. 'My grandfather would have changed the suspension if he'd seen a reason. He changed things all the time when he had to, but not when he didn't need to. The problem with car development is you can get obsessed with development for the sake of development – you need to stand back and say, "What's the point of doing this, why are we changing it?"

'I think I'm the same. If I'm honest, we'd still be fitting sliding-pillar suspension if I was completely convinced that it was the quickest way to go round a corner. Sadly, in 1978 I could win the Production Sports Car championship against the 911, against the V12 E-type, against the Lotus Europa. I could beat them, even with sliding pillars, but that was the last time that was possible. Having said that, in club racing a Morgan driver recently beat the GT2 cars, but I know that that's a freak result, ultimately nowadays the Morgan against the GT2 car doesn't have a chance ...

'But Morgan as a company has constantly regenerated, and if it hadn't we'd have been dead. Park Ward didn't; Alvis didn't. It's awful to say that, but it's true. People think we didn't change but we did – and we do, all the time. What were we doing getting back into America? What were we doing building the Plus 8? What were we doing building the Plus 4 Plus? All the time we were actually changing things.'

In the late 1990s, Charles made the biggest changes to the Morgan production process since the introduction of the four-wheeler in the late 1930s, maybe even since the Z-framed F-type three-wheeler before that. 'Eliminating the buffer stocks and reducing the batches of cars in a particular process,' he says, 'came after being at Coventry and realising that Morgan actually wasn't unique; there was a lot of Japanese and other current manufacturing philosophy that the company could well take on board. Morgan's problems in production are really no different from any other manufacturer's problems. So, although we can design things entirely differently, and offer an entirely different level of customer service; although we can actually produce cars for love as well as for money; the fact is that the factory itself, in terms of its organisation, can learn anything it likes from the latest technology in terms of manufacturing.

'The more we know about the way other people do things, including furniture and boat makers, including the latest superforming technology for aluminiuming, the better we are at making Morgans affordable. I think we're in a strong position at the moment. We can be selective, whereas the problem with the big manufacturers is that they are driven by tenths of pennies on units. But look at the German manufacturers: why are they so successful? Quality. Porsche, only very recently, thought, "let's get a Japanese team in" – and suddenly they dramatically cut their manufacturing costs. Until then that hadn't been their driving force; that had been to make Porsches the best sports cars in the world, and it still is and should be – because if they're only into Kanbans and manufacturing technology from Japan, they'll be just like, say, Nissan, or anyone else.

'The production side of manufacturing is also an interest, but so is quality. My goal is to keep coachbuilding affordable for a reasonably large number of people, I'm besotted with coachbuilding technology. I've seen so many Morgan crash tests at MIRA, and the people there say, "My God, it works, it's the best result we've seen since I don't know when".

'In the specialist car industry people have always known a lot about the subject. The number of times I've had to listen to Morgan owners tell me what to do next. I think the big car industry is only just catching up with a lot of things the specialists have been doing for years – listening to customers, building cars the customer wants to buy. What I'm learning from the big manufacturers, especially the Japanese, is how to build cars cheaply, but what they're learning from us is how to build a car the customer wants, and I'm not sure they can ever do that, because to an extent they've got to be homogenised. They have to satisfy the lowest common denominator; we don't do that.'

Another vital part of the Morgan philosophy is people, and Charles continues the tradition. 'I need people working for Morgan who have focus. All the great cars have been developed by people who have been completely committed. It's getting that commitment that's really difficult. How do you get all those different departments, hundreds of people, all working together in a big company scenario? You need a maximum of thirty people in the team, more than that and you've lost it. And you need somebody with the vision to lead them. I want to create a model of how to develop cars. I think it's about linking design with production, so my model for developing cars wouldn't work for the Ford Focus, but it works for us.

'More and more, the mainstream industry is looking at the specialists. In some ways we're seeing a turnaround. In the 1930s you had the specialists leading the field for anybody who was actually interested in cars; now there is a belief in some circles that the Volkswagen Golf is all the car you'll ever need. That's not true. Maybe it's time for the specialists to show the big manufacturers a few new directions. Certainly the Lotus Elise has done that. The Elise is a seminal design, using very similar chassis technology to the Aero 8's, and I admit we let Lotus get there first. That's another Morgan philosophy if you like – don't stick your neck out too far, because sure as hell that would have been fatal, if we'd designed an aluminium chassis first and it had flown apart.

'Still, you have to be bold. A fascinating thing about the Aero 8 is there are 20 per cent of people who hate it. But that means 80 per cent of people would die for it – and nobody's on the fence, which is great.'

He is sure it would not work without the personal approach. 'The people angle is something the small firm has right in its grasp. We employ one hundred and fifty people. They span the superbike champion, who's one of our painters; a guy who won a kart racing championship, who's foreman of the trimmers; a guy who drives a Ford Escort in classic rallies. In other words, in those one hundred and fifty people there's a whole spectrum of society, and if you listen to all of them there's this huge wealth of experience and knowledge. Listening to one hundred and fifty people is hard but it's a lot easier than listening to three thousand, who will inevitably include some who aren't particularly interested in cars, who aren't interested in anything very much, and you'll have your political agitators.

'As a think-tank, Morgan is an interesting one, just as Ferrari is on a bigger scale, and a company like Porsche is, obviously. Ferrari has lost a bit under Fiat but it's still charismatic. I love the way they build the engine and the car, but having said that it wouldn't interest me in the least to build an engine. I love the technology; I love an engine that works; but to me it's almost like a battery. I just want a perfect battery that I can plug in; I don't want to know what to do when it goes wrong. I just don't want it to go wrong. Gerhardt Schmidt would be obsessed with that flow of fuel through the engine, but leave that to him – in a hundred years I couldn't hope to match his experience, or Paul Rosche's knowledge.'

Charles obviously agrees with his father that his grand-father's decision in the 1930s not to build his own engine was a life saver. 'Personally I don't think my grandfather ever really wanted to make an engine; he realised there were enough people like JAP and Matchless and Blackburne and Anzani in the early days, and Standard or Coventry-Climax later, who could do engines for him. I don't know why he went through the motions of having an engine designed when he did. Maybe John Black said he was going to charge him another fiver or something, and he had a look to see whether he could do it cheaper, then realised that he couldn't. It's such a huge risk.'

With the BMW supply deal for the Aero 8, the four-cylinder cars cruising along quite comfortably, and the on-going availability, at least in the short term, of the old Rover V8 for the Plus 8, engine supply is not Charles's biggest concern. Increasing production capacity is. But how far can Morgan go without losing what makes Morgan what it is?

'The directors decided that we ought to be producing about one and a half thousand cars in three or four years' time. There's no lack of will or investment. The only bit that limits us is if the technology isn't up to it, and I don't think that that will be the case; I think it is undoubtedly up to it.'

To build 1,500 cars a year would be a big leap, but Charles believes they can do it. 'At the moment we're making just under 600. We're moving to 12 cars a week from 1 June 2000, then 14 a week in March 2001 In March we also get to the point where we ask, "The Aero 8 is quicker to build than the old car, therefore can we ramp it up to 15 cars a week?", that's 750 cars a year. Then there's the three- to four-year plan: if the Aero 8 really is that good as production technology, let's raft it across and do a little 2-litre Aero-type car. We've got the football pitch to expand on to. We have to think about the paint shop, but I don't see it as a huge problem; obviously we need more paint capacity, but either we could double shift, which we've never done, or build another paint shop. Double shifting on paint would make a lot of sense . . .'

This is the way current thinking at Morgan goes – considered, and they hope sustainable, expansion. But increasing production is only the beginning of the problem. Whatever cars Morgan build, Matthew Parkin, the Sales and Marketing manager as well as the company's PR man, is charged with making the system work efficiently. Not least, he has had to confront the infamous Morgan waiting list. He knows that production and demand are now tied together in a way that previously they never properly were. 'We have a complicated situation where commercially we have to retain markets. One of the reasons we're still here is that we're not reliant on the UK market alone, and if you look back into the late 1960s you'll find something like 85 per cent of production went to the States. We were far too over-reliant on that market, but had it not been for them we would have been in big trouble at that time. Now, as a company strategy, we aim always to have open access to as many markets as possible. That, again, is why we've spent so much time, effort and money getting European whole-vehicle type-approval for all the cars, because we believe we have to sell them in all markets.

'What we're trying to do is to spread the risk, and what we have to manage is quite difficult as markets ebb and flow. For instance, we might have a dealer in one country who goes quiet, or nowadays we have exchange rates as an issue, which has made huge inroads into our prices. During all the debate about UK car prices, our prices in Germany have gone up 30 per cent because of the exchange rate. We simply can't avoid passing it on to the customer. We charge all our dealers pounds sterling for everything, at point of delivery (in reality we invoice them when the car goes into the paint shop). The price is fixed when the car goes into production, partly because the waiting list is so long, partly because we don't know what legislation is around the corner – you could suddenly find airbags are mandatory or whatever. Because the dealer pays in sterling, they absorb some of the changes, while the customer absorbs the rest. So we have a waiting list in, say, Germany, of seven years that shrinks to one and a half years because the price of the cars has gone up 30 per cent. The reality of it is that those people from the seven-year list are still on the waiting list, they just don't want the car at current exchange rates . . .'

This is far from being the only anomaly which Matthew Parkin has had to face in the Morgan sales system. 'The length of the waiting list in different countries depends on the number of dealers and the number of cars being sold there. We're aiming to get to a point where we have just one list world wide – but we're not there yet.

'Then there are the legislative problems. For example, we got the Plus 8 back into America in September 1998, having had the engines certified for emissions and all the other things you have to do. So we go to the customers and say "We've got the cars right and we can sell them to you; we'll see you in a year's time, or two years, or three, depending on how many orders come in". But by the time we get there the regulations will have changed again. All that time we've had a hundred engines that we've had to commit to, to fulfil the orders in hand. Commercially you just can't do that. On the other hand, once you've opened up the market, you can't ignore it, so we try to keep all our markets afloat as much as possible, while knowing that we're subject to the exchange rate and to legislation – and that affects the waiting list.'

Managing the waiting lists is potentially a political mine-field as well as a commercial one, and the only answer to that, as Matthew acknowledges, is for the system to be transparent, and the same for everyone. 'When I first came, we had dealers who ran their own lists and we just juggled the allocation depending on how long people had waited at individual dealers. At the moment we have twenty-four UK dealers; when I arrived we had everything from quite substantial solus dealers to the ones who just had Morgan bolted on to someone else and wouldn't know a Plus 4 from a Plus 8, right down to the little village garage with an old-fashioned black telephone.'

But managing, and understanding, the waiting list is also the key to planning production, and to commiting to future expansion if and when it is appropriate. 'It became so apparent that something needed to be done very quickly to both the dealer network and the way we processed the orders. Specifically, I had to find a way of telling Charles how many cars we needed to make and how to have a way of understanding the waiting list. Now, we've got an absolutely clear understanding of how the waiting list works and one of the reasons for that is that at the beginning of 1998 I instigated a system where we held all the lists centrally.

'We've always known who our customers are, but we've never necessarily contacted them sequentially. I could never say to a customer, wherever you are in the country, wherever you put your order in, you will pay the same deposit and will get your car in exactly the same time. There were cases where dealers thought they could get cars quicker, and that wasn't always the case. In any event, by the very nature of the way things happen here, with customers visiting the factory to see their cars being built, they talk to each other. The last thing we want is them comparing [as they did] when they placed their orders and finding out it wasn't at the same time; that was highly unsatisfactory, for both them and us. We've got that under control now, and for all the dealers with pre-1998 orders already in place, I can now tell them – very accurately – in what month and what year they should be writing to those customers, after which I tell them in the same way who they should be contacting under the new system.'

At the same time, Parkin has to sell Morgans, and a large part of that is not so much selling an actual Morgan as selling the idea of a Morgan. In the last full year for which figures are available, to May 1999, Morgan made a gross profit of £3 million and after-tax profits of £903,000 on sales of £12.3 million. In spite of an investment in the new Aero 8 of perhaps £3 million over the past couple of years, plus on-going investments into the production process, the company still had no debts; things clearly are not too bad, but at the same time, a company is only as good as next year's orders. 'People think it must be the easiest job in the world selling Morgans,' says Parkin, 'but it's far from it, because you don't have anything tangible to sell. You can't take a potential customer to an actual car and say, look, that can be yours.'

Yet there is always the dilemma of selling enough cars to stay in business but not so many that you cannot manage the production. We don't advertise at the moment but we do chase orders pretty strongly. We've only advertised sporadically in recent years, but I think things are changing around anyway with the worldwide web, so I think if we do anything in the near future it will probably be to advertise the access via that, or the used-car side of the web. On the Morgan website we have a used-car locator, where you can log on, type in what you want, and it will come up with the closest matches. That's from within the dealer network, but it's very recent; I've only just set it up.

'We do spend a lot of money on shows; the UK Motor Show is absolutely fantastic; people turn up and order cars, big time. We go to Frankfurt, we did Geneva this year with the Aero 8 and may well do it again in the future, but the UK is obviously the one where we focus most of our efforts. We don't do American shows at the moment although I'd like to – but only when we've got something that is easily physically produceable and that we can actually feed into the market. So many times we've shown things that people are going to want and then made it difficult for them to get it. The current status is that I'm trying to make it as easy as possible to order a Morgan, and in the past we've made it difficult, which was absolutely stupid.'

Matthew Parkin also believes that this is a fundamental Morgan problem, that people who might order cars simply do not, because they do not know how easy the process actually is. 'You go into a showroom while everybody walks past, saying "oh, aren't they lovely", and "I've always wanted a Morgan". You ask them if they've ever thought of ordering one and they say "oh, no, it's £10,000 deposit and you have to wait ten years". You tell them it isn't; it's only £250 deposit and three to four years' wait. Then they say, "250 quid, is that all?" They see the price of a day at Disneyworld with the family, and it's a completely different proposition. The numbers of people who go through with an order just because they know something that they didn't know before is extraordinary, so we have this massive awareness problem, believe it or not.'

Once the customer is on the list, there is still the not inconsiderable problem of keeping him or her there. 'Now, we obviously know how many cars we're making, and I've done a lot of analysis on the drop-out percentages, so we are much clearer now on how many people on the list are going to take their orders up, and on why people fall off. That might be because they just got bored and bought something else, or they may have moved house, married, had kids, died even. People's lives do change so much more now. So we've instituted a marketing plan that looks at the two areas, trying to keep the people we've already got on the waiting list, while generating new orders.'

In the past, Morgan has not been good about talking to people once they were on the list, but doing that has been another of Parkin's initiatives. 'Because they're not actually on a waiting list for a car as such but only on a list for the start of the build process, we haven't had anything to show by way of work in progress. Recently, however, we've had a lot happening, with things like the improvements in quality, in the build process and so on, so now as soon as a customer goes on the waiting list they also go on a mailing list. We've launched a magazine, the *Malvern Link*, which goes out two or three times a year, and we send letters saying, for instance, did you know that the 4/4 engine has been improved in either this way or that. Customers now have regular contact and regular information, which gives them added value from being on the list, where before all they were doing was waiting for the one call at the end of the process. The first letter they had was the one saying "your name's come to the top of the list, you need to let us know your specification within the next two weeks otherwise we'll cancel your order". That was so intimidating and so impersonal for somebody who might have been waiting for nine years that we wanted to do something more friendly.'

There are areas where Morgan could possibly make it easier still to be a Morgan owner, but Parkin admits some things have not worked out yet. For instance, there is still no 'pay while you wait' system. He wanted to set that up when he arrived at Morgan but it was something slightly at odds with their wanting to reduce the waiting list. 'What we have done is set up a finance company arrangement to make it easier to buy the car once it comes to the point. At the moment the next payment due after the original £250 deposit is £2,000 at the point of specification, with the balance on collection. We would have set up a savings scheme but various people have tried it; it seems you're better off paying into a personal scheme and doing it that way.'

So what the customer is actually waiting for on the famous list is not for the car to roll out of the factory door, but for the opportunity to specify the exact model and the precise specification, at which point the production process starts and the car should finally be less than three weeks from delivery. Parkin also implemented new systems to fit the wildly diverse orders into the production schedule, with minimum time wasted and maximum profitability. 'The time from start of production to delivery still depends to a degree on which model has been ordered, but it's now an average of twenty working days, where it used to be several times that.

'I've also set up a simple computer programme which lets us plan production to suit the balance of orders, which we couldn't always do in the past. Now, I know how many production slots I have, because we have a fairly fixed production schedule. So if someone says "I want a 4/4, when can I have it?", I look for a gap – and in this case the next 4/4 production slot I have is in December 2000 [we are talking in the first week of July], so no one can now order a Morgan 4/4 and be driving it before February next year.

'They've been waiting for four years and for a 4/4 they've got to wait that bit longer because these are the production slots I've got. At the time of the first deposit they didn't even have to specify which model they wanted, although they will now have to specify if it's an Aero 8 or a traditional model, but that's only because it's a completely different build process. We have space for one four-seater a week, where we were doing two a week for a while – but we weren't getting enough orders to do that, so in Week 14 or Week 15, for example, I had a problem filling the allocated slots. Going down to one a week is an example of how we can adjust the mix to keep the volume up – while still keeping an eye on profitability. What we really want to see is full columns of build slots, but we don't necessarily get that, because at the moment you could get a Plus 8 scheduled for October, say, and a 4/4 for November.' That is perhaps not so bad for the customer who has already waited a long time.

The new computer-based control systems extend to stock control and costing. 'We now have a system where we know every single nut and bolt that goes into the car and exactly what they cost us to make; that's been running for around four weeks, so although we've done it sporadically in the past it's taken ninety years to do it properly. We also have a system where when we put an order into the system to build a car to a particular spec it comes up and allocates all the right parts, checks the stock off, so we know whether we can build it or not. In the old days it was all done by paper and pencil. Since 1997 we haven't really started any car that we've known we didn't have the bits for. Now it's all properly planned, which is even more important with a car like the Aero 8 where we have double the numbers of components involved.'

The ultimate aim, every time, is to balance sustainable, long-term demand with sustainable, long-term production capacity, and not be embarrassed when the market takes a major turn. So the waiting list, as much as being a thorn in the side can also be a real comfort zone – so long as it is a reasonable size. 'We'd like ideally to see the list down to two years. Once we get it to two years we could probably sustain that worldwide, rather than it be different from one country to the next. In America at the moment, because of the engine situation, it's probably twelve months and they think that's appallingly long. So we have some education to do there – but we think that when we get down to two years in the UK we can sustain it.

'The problem is that as you get down towards two years, orders keep going up, because the car becomes more available. When I first came here we weren't getting sufficient new orders in to meet the production we were doing, although at the time it wasn't something to panic about, because it meant we were catching up on the backlog of orders, which we desperately needed to do. You wouldn't want to do it for too long, though. The other thing that's been quite fortuitous is that with the strong state of the pound, the overseas orders have diminished slightly, and that's actually good – because we've been oversupplying quite significantly to the UK market.

'But it's still a very comfortable position, and a lot more helpful than it is worrying. We also now know that with future product and the way that we have the Federal emissions standards covered for the future we're happy that very shortly we'll be able to take advantage and the American market can open up again if that's how we want it to be. In fact we could send everything we make to America.'

This brings strange echoes of Morgan's past. The strongest markets have changed dramatically over the years, and there was a time when America was taking a big majority of Morgan production, but nowadays the market for Morgans is largely centred in its British roots. 'In the UK we sell around 250 to 300 cars a year, the German market is around 70 cars. America currently takes about 50 to 60 cars a year, and we'd obviously like to expand the network again, but at the moment we have a situation where the two dealers still have to do a lot of preparatory work to get the cars past the regulations, and that can't go on.

'We're shortly due to get full Federal low-volume approval for fully factory-finished cars and that will make the situation a lot easier. We don't want to appoint another five dealers who have to work the way somebody like Bill Fink [the San Francisco agent whose Isis Imports largely kept the Morgan name alive in the USA with his propane-fuelled conversions on the Plus 8] once had. In those days he was doing such a huge amount of modification on the car, and that's too risky. What we do want is to get ourselves back into a situation where we just send the cars out ready to go.'

The new Aero 8 was central to all these suppositions, and while the fact that the Aero 8 would take up most of the twelve available build slots a week from November 2000 meant another production planning challenge, the reception the new car enjoyed gave Morgan a brighter outlook on the future than it could have had in many years. That reception was remarkable, but again, with a production system like Morgan's, which cannot simply add another line, it created problems of its own.

'The Aero 8 took orders away from the Plus 8, but we wrote to every single customer on the waiting list at the time of the unveiling in February and said, "thank you for waiting; we've introduced this new car and if you'd like to swap let us know before the end of March and we'll put your name into the sequence, and in the order in which the original orders were placed". If you were a customer who was just about to get a car, you would be one of the first to receive an Aero 8. Up to late June, two hundred and sixty-six had converted. That told us two things. First that the cars really weren't that price sensitive, because with the Aero 8 we were asking customers to pay a big chunk extra. People have a lot more disposable income today and they're prepared to pay for something different. Secondly, it probably increased the take-up rate (or reduced the drop-out rate) because without the Aero 8 a proportion of those two hundred and sixty-six converters certainly wouldn't have taken up their orders. As ever, they would have pulled out either because they'd got bored with waiting, or because there's so much competition out there now. And people do say, "I would have had the Morgan but look at the new Boxster or the new BMW"; or whatever has come on to the scene since they originally placed their order.'

The obvious enthusiasm for the Aero 8 did not directly threaten the future of the Plus 8, but engine supply ultimately will. The interest in the Aero 8 from America was phenomenal, but Morgan refused to take any orders immediately because they could not guarantee when they would be able to fulfil them. 'Dealers had expressed interest in fifty or sixty cars, with customers wanting them now.' This inevitably coloured the future of the long-serving Plus 8. From November 2000 Morgan would rationalise the Plus 8 engine choice to the 4-litre V8 only, which would be the engine specified for the USA as well as the one to meet the new Euro 3 emissions regulations. As Matthew Parkin explained, 'Plus 8 production will come down from five, sometimes six a week, to three a week. But bear in mind that a lot of that difference is due to people swapping from Plus 8s to Aero 8s anyway. That will probably push the time between spec and delivery for the Plus 8 out a little bit, until it falls back in with the 4/4 and it all balances out again in the end. All the current cars take approximately the same time to build – a bit longer for the four-seaters because they have a more complex hood as well as the extra seats.' They hope, too, that the Aero 8 will be a substantially quicker car to build.

Parkin is just as aware as Charles Morgan that the Aero 8, and what might eventually become an Aero type family, is the real key to Morgan's future. He says the dealers' response to the car was amazing. 'They were very sceptical when we first discussed it and totally divided when they saw the black prototype, because frankly it wasn't very nicely finished and they're all looking so hard for production quality fits and finishes even in the prototypes. So you say, for God's sake stand a hundred feet away and open your eyes and that's basically what you'll get. Subsequently they've seen the reaction from the public, and we're already up to where we are before anyone outside of the factory has so much as driven it yet, so that's enormously encouraging.

'We spread all the Aero 8 transfers through the existing schedule; any new orders for Aero 8 after March slotted in after that. If you ordered an Aero 8 now, you would get it quicker than if you ordered a traditional car. We had around three Plus 8 people who were between specification and build, so we accommodated them, because we wouldn't want to force somebody to have a car they didn't actually want. There were enough people with specs in for Plus 8s who wanted them as soon as possible so we were able to move everybody forward to fill those production spots. The first dealer demonstrator Aero 8s are due to be built in October 2000, the first customer cars from November, for delivery in January – right on schedule. If you'd ordered in June 2000, as some people did, you'd be looking at a production start in June 2002.'

Parkin is comfortable with two years as an acceptable waiting list, given that in addition, customers could wait up to two years for a Mercedes SLK or a Porsche Boxster when they first came out; the length of the list would give Morgan an opportunity to increase sales dramatically, simply because of availability. The Aero 8 will also be a world car for Morgan. 'It will eventually have everything to US Federal standards, and Europe is now accepting a lot of Federal standards as read across. There's more work to do but we know exactly what it is and basically it has all been designed in to start with. We've got a dealer network that's getting there, but we've got huge tracts even of this country that aren't serviced by dealers actively promoting the product; and that's only the UK. Normally a manufacturer sells the most cars where there's the most money, but we sell the most cars where the dealer gets out and does something. That suggests that if we had dealers who did that everywhere, we'd again have the potential for hugely increasing the market. Everywhere we look there's commercial potential. We get 7,000 visitors [not hits, visitors] to the Morgan website every day. Someone did a survey recently for a college in America and found 80 per cent recognition for the Morgan car.'

In itself, increasing production presents Morgan with a problem that in a way is typical of the way outsiders see the company – romantically rather than realistically. 'People say we have to be very careful about increasing production and we say, well when did you last see a Morgan driving around? "Oh, I haven't seen one for quite a while now". And of course you won't, because the market isn't exactly flooded with them. Two hundred and fifty cars a year into the UK isn't a lot, and even if we did five hundred a year here, doubled the numbers sold, you'd still never see them as being an everyday car.

'People say we have to have the long waiting list to support residual values, but in reality even a two-year list would be a hell of a long time by anyone else's standards, so I don't think that's a big issue. And Morgan residuals by all normal standards are ridiculous. I think they're too high; they're preventing people coming in at a sensible entry point to enjoy Morgan driving.'

Everything is driven by the production regime. 'The old way of thinking here was, this is how many cars we make, this is how many orders we've got; the waiting list is therefore one divided by the other, eleven years or five years or three years, whatever. Now we're saying that's no good; what we have to do now, especially with the Aero 8, is to say this is how many orders we have, the acceptable waiting list is two years, how many cars does that mean we have to make? Which comes back to the original question which Charles wanted to ask of how many cars does the factory need to build. I've told him that from March 2001 we need fourteen cars, including six Aero 8s.

'Charles has always believed in doing it this way around; Peter is starting to agree now he can see that we have the orders and we are starting to create a dealer network capable of supplying us with sufficient new orders to maintain that. We also now know that we will be able to meet the appropriate Federal standards, so we can really begin to open up that market again; and in the European market we have only two dealers in a market the size of Germany, we only have one dealer in Spain, we have three outlets in France – it isn't enough. There are lots of challenges ahead.'

These are times of substantial philosophical changes for the company, but some things do not change. Even with the planned level of expansion, there is still the familiar element of caution in expanding the opportunities without unnecessarily extending the risk. Matthew Parkin echoes Charles Morgan's thoughts. 'The beauty of the situation we're in at the moment is that we have a factory which is only utilised for a third of the day, we've got plenty of space, with the football pitch and loads of car park space, we've already changed the method out of all recognition and we could change it more, and we now understand, far better than we ever have before, the processes needed to increase production. We've said let's not miss an opportunity with the Aero 8. If we have to make fifteen a week, or whatever the number might be, let's do our damnest to meet the demand so that we don't throw the orders away. But if it dips down to six a week, or four a week, we can still say we've had a great success with the car and made a lot of money, but we haven't been pushed into making investments we didn't want to make or changes we didn't want to make to the basic philosophy. It's based on the way you make your cars and the investments you need to make. If you're Vauxhall or Volvo you have to build a new factory that will cost you £50 million or whatever, you've got frightening numbers of employees that can end up sitting twiddling their thumbs, whereas with the way we make cars here you simply have a lot more flexibility. That has always been the Morgan way.'

That particular phrase, 'the Morgan way', has reverberated throughout most of the past century and continues to do so into the present with renewed vigour. At Morgan they understand, just as successive generations always have, what it is that people like about their cars; that understanding, and the way they act upon it, is central to the company's philosophy. The Morgan way indeed.

Index